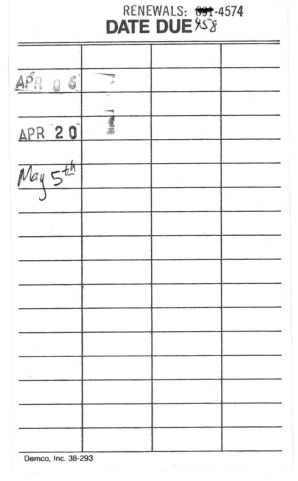

GEORGE S. BROWN

GEORGE S. BROWN
General, U.S. Air Force

DESTINED FOR STARS

Edgar F. Puryear, Jr.

★
PRESIDIO

Copyright © 1983 by Presidio Press
Published by Presidio Press, 31 Pamaron Way, Novato, CA 94947

Library of Congress Cataloging in Publication Data

Puryear, Edgar F., 1930–
    George S. Brown, General, U.S. Air Force.

    Includes bibliographical references and index.
    1. Brown, George S., 1918–   . 2. Generals—
United States—Biography. 3. United States. Air Force
—Biography. I. Title.
UG262.2.B75P87   1983   358.4'0092'4 [B]   83-2998
ISBN 0-89141-169-0

Jacket design by Kathleen A. Jaeger
Composition by Helen Epperson
Production by Lynn Dwyer

Printed in the United States of America

This book is dedicated to
MRS. GEORGE S. 'SKIP' BROWN,
because Gen. George S. Brown would
have wanted it that way.

CONTENTS

ACKNOWLEDGMENTS

The inspiration for this book, as it was for *Nineteen Stars: A Study in Military Character and Leadership* and *Stars in Flight: A Study in Air Force Character and Leadership*, came from the desire to answer the following questions: How does one get to the top of the military profession? How does one lead on the way to the top? What is the leadership role after achieving a high position of great responsibility? The most important factor in the success of the leaders in these studies has been their character. There is a vital need for the leaders of tomorrow to study the character of these great men in order that it might serve as an example of the role of dedicated service to God and country, of service before self.

In researching this book, I have been aided by so many people they are really too numerous to mention, but I am particularly indebted to the hundreds of officers I interviewed and with whom I have corresponded over the years. They gave of their time and of the enlightenment born of the wisdom gained through many years of experience as leaders. I wish to specifically thank Gen. David C. Jones, USAF (Ret.), former Air Force Chief of Staff and Chairman of the Joint Chiefs of Staff; Gen. Bruce K. Holloway, USAF (Ret.); Gen. Robert J. Dixon, USAF (Ret.); Gen. John W. Roberts, USAF (Ret.); Gen. William V. McBride, USAF (Ret.); and very special thanks to Gen. W. L. Creech, Commander in Chief, Tactical Air Command. These men read and commented on the manuscript as it progressed, and I am most grateful for their assistance.

For putting together this book, I have many people to thank: the extensive editing by Robert V. Kane, whose insight and counsel were of immense value. The comments and assistance of Adele Horwitz were also extremely worthwhile. Jinnie B. Mason read through the manuscript with a keen editorial eye, catching errors and offering thoughts; her ideas on the title were especially helpful. Janet W. DeRubbo was involved in typing final drafts of the manuscript and transcribing interviews, and also provided valuable editorial suggestions. My son Chip was most helpful in doing some of the research for this book. Maj. W. Earl Walker, USA, and his wife Suzan provided invaluable aid in researching the archives at West Point on Brown's cadet years. Eugene White also was of assistance in some of the early editing.

The book has been very much a team effort. Annette E. Hilgeman was remarkably dedicated in transcribing the tapes of numerous interviews, typing hundreds of letters and the early drafts of the manuscript, and in other administrative responsibilities; Marie Dene followed up and finished these duties. I also want to thank Ann Fletcher, Donna DiToto, Debbie K. Simpson, Carolyn L. Whittaker, and Kathleen M. Hurley for their secretarial and administrative assistance.

I appreciate the patience of my law partners, L. B. Chandler, Jr., and Daniel R. Bouton, during the research and writing, and the secretarial assistance of Helen M. Slaven.

I owe a special debt of gratitude to my wife Agnes for her remarkable patience during the extensive traveling and the many, many hours of research and writing, and to my sons, Beverly Spotswood Parrish Puryear (Chug); Lt. Edgar F. Puryear III, USA/R (Chip); Lt. Scott Braxton Puryear, USA (Colt); and Alfred Anderson Puryear (Cotton).

FOREWORD

George Brown's military career spanned two eras: He was a genuine hero in World War II, and in the 1970s he reached very top positions in his profession as a military officer. In the latter role, he was an outstanding example of the senior military officers of today, who must combine military leadership with managerial ability. They must carry out military operations under civilian direction which, especially because of the dangers of the nuclear age, constrains military options with international political factors.

That George Brown was able to perform superbly in both roles was a consequence of his human qualities, his intellectual abilities, but above all his character and integrity. That combination enabled him to perform well as a combat commander, as a director of materiel development and testing, as a staff assistant to senior military commanders, as military assistant to two Secretaries of Defense, as Chief of Staff of the Air Force, and finally as Chairman of the Joint Chiefs of Staff.

I knew George Brown for seventeen years. Our paths repeatedly diverged and then met again. During every part of that association, what most impressed me was George's absolute honesty, his willingness to give professional advice and personal views straight—to military and civilian superiors, to members of Congress, and to subordinates. Sometimes this frankness got him into trouble; but to those who sought honesty and professional competence, it made George an invaluable associate, leader, and friend. His courage, whether during the bombing attack on the Ploesti oil fields, the traumatic military operations and political-military policy disputes of the 1960s and 1970s, or in facing his own terminal illness, inspired those around him.

In reading Mr. Puryear's book it is instructive to see how a product of a military family, with a lifetime of military service, was able to work so well in the civilian-military team arrangement that constitutionally and by statute places military commanders subordinate to civilian authority. George Brown understood and worked effectively under a taxing but necessary rule: Senior military officers argue their professional case to civilian superiors and, if overruled, must either support and carry out the decisions, or, if they think them so mistaken that they are not able to support such decisions, retire from the service in order to speak out against them. At congressional hearings, George Brown would be asked repeatedly to speak about issues on which it was known he had been overruled by civilian authority. He handled this delicate problem of civilian-military relations superbly, always speaking honestly and at the same time loyally.

I was proud to have been able to call him my friend. The reader of this book will see why.

—Harold Brown
Secretary of Defense 1976–80

PROLOGUE

Throughout the history of our great country, we have been blessed with the right military leaders at the right times. When a crisis has occurred we have had leaders ready, willing, and able to serve us, men who have devoted their lives to preparing for such times. Gen. George S. Brown was such a man, one of the exceptional leaders in United States history. After spending a year as a second lieutenant while going through pilot training, he was promoted from first lieutenant to colonel in a little over two years, at the age of twenty-six. He went on to become Chief of Staff of his service, then was selected for and served in our country's highest military position, Chairman of the Joint Chiefs of Staff. Why did he rise so quickly in rank? Why was he selected for these positions? Largely because of his capacity for leadership.

I asked those who served with him, under him, and over him throughout his entire military career, "Why was George S. Brown so successful?" The purpose of this book is to present answers to this question. There is a pattern to successful leadership, and George Brown is the epitome of that pattern. His life provides an image and a model worthy of study by all who aspire to leadership or desire to grow more rapidly in their own leadership roles and responsibilities.

On June 18, 1940, after the announcement that Brown had been selected as adjutant of the Corps of Cadets at the United States Military Academy, he received a letter from his maternal grandfather, H. P. Scratchley. "He showed me this letter very early after we were married," reflected his wife, Skip Brown. "I found it later in his desk drawer. Throughout his career it was always with him where he could refer to it, usually in a small box in his desk that contained his important papers. It meant so much to him that I had it framed with glass on the front and back, and he put it in his den. He kept it as a personal guide."

My dear George:

Your Bonne and I wish to congratulate you on your promotion: It is a great honor but every honor carries with it a duty and responsibility. It is in the faithful performance of these that one is to be judged.

I often wonder whether you young people realize what a glorious thing it is to be young, strong, with your life before you. God has given you will to act and talents to act with and opportunities to act in. The greatest and most dangerous gift God has given us is our freedom of will. Because we have this, we are all our lives molding and making ourselves, our characters, and by doing this, our nation. God aids us but we make ourselves.

Today as never before the world is calling for strong, clear thinking, right acting men—men with vision. We Americans have dreamed of a nation of free men, free to live, free to act without too great restraint from others, free to speak out our thoughts, free to worship God as we think . . . , equal before the Law. Against this there has arisen peoples who dream only of domination of the strong, who deny freedom of action to all, who do not hesitate to use force to gain it. You may shortly have to fight against this heresy—to give yourself and your body to combat it. The existence of what America stands for is in the hands of your generation. May God give of his power to do your duty rightly in this darkening world. He has put in this world those things needful for clear thinking and right acting—only we do not use them as He wills.

I know that the young do not like to be preached to however much the old like to preach. But there is no higher type of man in this mad world than the Christian gentleman who does his duty in the sight of God without fear. May you be this.

With love from all of us,

Affectionately yours,
H. P. Scratchley

This letter offers an insight and perspective into Brown's leadership and character, and living by its call for "strong, clear thinking, right acting men —men with vision," to do his duty rightly, Brown was—*Destined for Stars.*

PART ONE
YOUTH THROUGH WORLD WAR II

CHAPTER 1

THE EARLY YEARS

On June 28, 1914, the Archduke of Austria, Francis Ferdinand, heir to the Hapsburg throne, was assassinated at Sarajevo in Bosnia by a group of young radicals whose crime was inspired by Pan-Serbian nationalism. It was an event that precipitated World War I and involved all the great powers of Europe, aligning Germany and Austria-Hungary against Great Britain, France, Italy, and Russia.

Relations were significantly strained between the United States and Germany throughout 1915 and 1916, particularly over the sinking of unarmed merchant ships. When on March 18, 1917, three United States merchant ships were sunk by German submarines, the result was a declaration of war on Germany by the United States in early April 1917.

George Scratchley Brown was born during this first global conflict on August 17, 1918, in Montclair, New Jersey. Born in a time of United States military ascendancy, Brown was destined to become one of the most brilliant air leaders in history. His father, Thoburn Kaye Brown, was a graduate of the Class of 1913 from the United States Military Academy. His mother, nee Frances Katherine Scratchley, came from New York City. Thoburn Brown, cavalryman and career Army officer, served at various Army posts throughout the United States. The year George was born, the elder Brown was stationed at West Point on a four-year tour followed by a year at the

Cavalry School, Fort Riley, Kansas, and another year at the Command and General Staff School, Fort Leavenworth, Kansas. He returned to the Cavalry School as an instructor in 1924 and after four years was posted again to West Point for a second four-year tour.

George Brown grew up on these small posts where personal relationships were strong. One of Brown's contemporaries, Harrington W. Cochran, Jr., said of those days: "Pride in service was unmatched, and the well-disciplined influence of fathers' careers and lifestyles upon their sons and daughters was great. Army brats of that time were exposed to the rigors and rewards of the soldier's life and to the organized discipline which pervaded every activity within the military community. Their fathers were the leaders, heroes, and models upon whose careers many young members of this close society formed their goals."[1]

George Brown went through the usual amusing incidents and growing pains of childhood. While the Browns were stationed at Fort Riley, George, his younger brother, Tim, and the son of the post commander embarked upon a joint business venture selling books to earn spending money. The books were not theirs to sell, however, but were the hymnals from the post chapel. On a subsequent occasion the brothers again needed spending money, so they decided to make face powder from brick dust and sell it. They sold it to a Mrs. Newman for a quarter, went to a movie, and had a nickel left over for popcorn.[2]

But not all of the childhood incidents were amusing. George had one near-fatal mishap. He stepped on a horseshoe nail and ran it far into his foot, a wound resulting in a bad infection which induced lockjaw. Good care from the Army post doctor and the family cured George of this dangerous affliction, but it was several weeks before he fully recovered.[3]

Having survived that, George tempted fate again, this time tree climbing. He climbed up around twenty or twenty-five feet of a pretty good-sized cottonwood; a branch broke under him and he fell and landed on his back. He received a bad concussion but it did not slow him down long.[4]

Tim remembers his brother's reaction to emergencies. "When George was about thirteen and I was twelve, we had gone riding on the levee in Brownsville, Texas. I was not aware of it, but the ground was extremely soft, and my horse proceeded to sink in the mud halfway to his belly, scaring me badly. George calmly dismounted, took the bridle of my horse, and led him out before he could sink any further. I've never forgotten the presence of mind George displayed, even at that early age.

"He also seemed very early to have a sense of order and purpose in life. When George joined the Boy Scouts, he decided then that he was going to be an Eagle Scout. He set up a program for himself and selected those merit badges he wanted to earn. He then proceeded to earn them, one by one. He was an achiever, applying himself to everything he did."[5]

Though the hymnal incident received no official attention, active youngsters on a military installation could hardly grow up without running afoul of the authorities at some point. On one occasion George, with about six or seven other boys, managed to turn over a tub of water just as the general came riding by on his horse. Everybody ran off except George. The general demanded of him, "What's this all about?" Displeased with George's simple reply that the tub had been turned over for the fun of it, he bore in on George. "Who are those other boys who were with you?" George politely refused to name his accomplices, whereupon the general ordered him to appear with his father in the general's office at four that afternoon. Tim's brief explanation of that meeting gives a hint of where George and he had learned their values: "They went over that afternoon to see the general, and my father said George was right not to reveal the names of his friends, and that was the end of that."[6]

As he grew older, it became apparent that George was going to be a very good athlete. When stationed at Fort Brown, he played as a freshman on the varsity football team. Although only fourteen, he weighed nearly 180 pounds. At Fort Leavenworth he played fullback and later was all-league in the Catholic high school interstate league. Also, during his high school years he caught a lifelong bug for tennis. He became good enough to reach the state finals in doubles.

Moreover, these were the years when he acquired basic skills in horsemanship and polo, which he was later to display with amazing prowess at West Point. As Tim recalls it, "George and I did a lot of general riding, a great deal of jumping, but very little organized polo. We started to fool around with it separately as we grew up. In fact, in the beginning we played polo on bicycles, using regular polo mallets. It was just a natural thing to do as kids."[7]

During those days, the youngsters had riding classes on post, just as today they are involved in Little League baseball. The Saturday riding lessons were the only organized activity for most children. George and Tim used to offer their services just to exercise polo ponies for their owners, and George got seriously interested in polo.

Brown's father's last tour at West Point was from 1928 to 1932, from George's tenth to fourteenth year. "They were pretty formative years," says Tim. "We were around cadets all the time, and we just knew that's what we wanted to do—be West Point cadets."[8]

Since his father was assigned to Washington, D.C., in the spring of 1933, George attended Western High School for the ninth grade. A year later his father was sent to Brownsville, Texas, and he went through the tenth grade there. His junior and senior years were spent at Immaculata High School, Leavenworth, Kansas, during his father's tour of instructor duty at Fort Leavenworth; the academic standards were high, and most of the boys wanted to go to West Point.

George's decision to go to West Point was very much his own. Although his father was a West Pointer, both his father and his mother were determined that their sons would make their own career decisions. Mrs. Brown remembers the parents' approach: "We tried to make them be aware that there were other things in the world besides West Point. I was afraid that they just didn't know anything else, and so was their father. We didn't want them to go there simply because their father had."9

But no other school had the attraction for the boys that West Point did. Daly Williams, who attended high school with George, says of those days, "He knew exactly what he wanted to do: with no question in his mind he wanted to go to West Point and make a career of the military. He had more sense of direction than anyone I'd ever known before."10

Another boyhood friend, Maurice G. Miller, has this to say about George's ability to do well without arousing resentment: "George, as a teenager, had solid personality traits which attracted people to him; everyone liked him even though he wasn't a super athlete or an intellectual. He was way above average in the number of friends he had, but he didn't make enemies."11

Although Thoburn Brown refused to influence his sons toward West Point, once they had decided on that objective he had definite ideas about the best way of reaching it. "Dad felt," said Tim, "that if George and I were going to West Point, we should go to college for a year before entering the Academy. He thought it was good for George to get away from home before he went to West Point, to get over the homesickness and everything. It was hard enough at West Point without being homesick."12

Accordingly, George entered the University of Missouri in 1936. There he studied engineering, played on the polo team, and joined Sigma Alpha Epsilon fraternity. He also enlisted in the 128th Field Artillery Battalion of the Missouri National Guard, quickly receiving a promotion to corporal. In the meantime, his father set out to obtain the coveted West Point appointment for him. The competition for appointments to the service academies during those depression years was especially fierce, particularly for the sons of military personnel who carried little weight with congressmen.

However, though few in the regular military establishment had good political contacts, fortunately the Browns did have close social ties to some influential members of the community of Leavenworth. One of their friends in the town owned the newspaper, another was a bank president, and a third owned a flour mill. They all assisted in getting George the Academy appointment from the First District of Kansas he so badly wanted, and on July 1, 1937, he entered the Class of 1941 of the United States Military Academy.

NOTES

1. Letter from Col. Harrington W. Cochran, Jr., USA (Ret.), to Edgar F. Puryear, Jr. (hereafter EFP), October 14, 1977.
2. Personal interview with Brig. Gen. Thomas W. Brown, USA (Ret.), August 8, 1979.
3. Ibid.
4. Ibid.
5. Ibid.
6. Ibid.
7. Ibid.
8. Ibid.
9. Mrs. Thoburn K. Brown interview.
10. Personal interview with Daly Williams, August 6, 1979.
11. Letter from Col. Maurice G. Miller USA (Ret.), to EFP, December 3, 1979.
12. Thomas Brown interview.

CHAPTER 2

WEST POINT CADET

"Every story must begin at the beginning," wrote a classmate of Cadet George S. Brown, describing their first year. "For the West Point Class of 1941 the beginning was July 1, 1937. That morning we were five hundred and forty-eight more or less callow youths, gathered from all the states and possessions, from farm, town, army post, and city. That night found us 'new cadets,' apprentices in the profession of arms and the service of the nation. More than that, it found us already cognizant of the fact that we were members of a class, that the words 'class' and 'classmate' at West Point had a new meaning, a clearer and closer significance than the same words had possessed in previous schooling. And on that first day we had learned another clear lesson. We stripped off our coats and ties, rolled up trousers, dropped and retrieved our suitcases many times, moved our chins and shoulders back, and in the confusion of doing so we learned the fundamental lesson in the schooling of the soldier, prompt and unquestioning obedience. From confusion we learned as well the meaning of rapid action. We began to run: we ran to the first sergeant, we ran to one room and then to another, we ran to an alleged barber shop to be trimmed, we ran to the cadet store times unnumbered. West Point seemed to have been visited with the true spirit of the prophet Daniel, 'Many shall run to and fro, and knowledge shall be increased.'

"For four weeks we ran and we learned," he continued. "Drill, calisthenics, weapons, marksmanship, guard instruction, and athletics were our daily lot. We learned how to conduct ourselves in the mess hall and how to hack a roast. We memorized our Plebe Bibles [a book that contains information to give the new cadet a complete though brief picture of West Point traditions and customs] or wished that we had. We learned a new language, West Point slang. At last came Presentation Parade, and we were 'Mister' instead of 'New Cadet.' Beast barracks over, we felt as veteran as Caesar's *triarii*. But it was only the beginning.

"With September came our introduction to the academic system at West Point, vastly different from high school or college. Algebra and solid geometry, French and English did not seem too formidable a curriculum; yet each Saturday showed many of us deficient. Academic travail had its compensation, however; football games and trips were welcome diversions. We nearly beat Notre Dame; and we thoroughly sank the Navy."[1]

George Brown's first roommate that September offers this description of what awaited them there. "At West Point, competition is the driving force which produces leadership. It exists in several fields: in academics; in military science and tactics; in athletics; in the social, cultural, political, and recreational aspects of cadet life; and in discipline and conduct. All-pervasive is the cadet honor code, from which a potential leader derives the strength of his essential honesty and moral integrity.

"In the case of George Brown, his background gave him a head start in military science and tactics. He had been exposed to it all his life. He was at ease and self-confident with it. He was among the top of his class in this field."[2]

Another classmate felt that the cavalry background had a lot to do with George's development: "Of all the officers on duty at the Academy, and of all the 'Army brats,' those officers who served in—and those 'brats' who had been reared in—the horse cavalry were head and shoulders above the rest. From his beginnings as a cadet, George was already knowledgeable in the ways of the Army, already a fine horseman and good polo player while most of his classmates were still falling off their mounts three days per week. But there's far more to a cavalry upbringing and the traditions of cavalry leadership than playing polo. Somehow, it molded character and molded men. It gave them a particular 'set.' "[3]

Although he derived certain advantages from having been raised in the military, Brown's brother believes that his plebe roommate was also a big help to him: "George's first roommate, Cochran, had previously been at Virginia Military Institute and was initially better adjusted to the rigors and routines of cadet life. It was a big help to George that he had somebody living with him who knew how to keep the room neat, the brass and boots shined. I think the first year at West Point was pretty tough for George. His study habits were not that good, and it was pretty tough going from college to plebe year at the Academy. I know that his math course at the University of Missouri devoted a whole year to a textbook which was covered at West Point between September and Christmas."

December 1937 brought the first series of written examinations, and one of the class members reminisced in the yearbook that "January 14, 1938, brought the saddest day of our class history, the first Foundation Day [meaning flunking out]. Many left us, good friends and good classmates, but we knew that the inexorable standard must be met."

Meeting that standard was not always easy for Brown, who was "turned out" (forced to take and pass a make-up exam or be flunked out) in both math and French. "I can remember Dad saying," commented his brother, "when he heard that, 'Well, he'll be home; there's no way he's going to pass both of those.' "[4]

Many cadets in Brown's class found themselves turned out for a final exam in one subject, and it was a formidable task to take a comprehensive exam to catch up on a half year's work. The success ratio of those who had two subjects to contend with was extremely low, but Brown showed the dedication and determination at this time that were the hallmarks of his later years. He shunned all vacation activities, secluded himself, and devoted full effort to the task at hand.

Brown's experience with academics played a large part in his character development and probably brushed him with just the right degree of humility. Being turned out in mathematics and French was a frightening threat to his planned life's career. Nevertheless, he launched himself into a solid week of cramming, night and day, with the result that he passed the turnout examinations and was retained. For the next three years his resolve was to avoid any recurrence of such a near disaster.[5]

Classmate Ben I. Mayo commented about George: "He had an abundance of good common sense, but he was, as a cadet, far from brilliant academically. As a matter of fact, such things as calculus and solid geometry threw him for a loss to the extent that at one time he was close to flunking out. To those of us who were close to him, this was unthinkable. Some of us (and I am proud to be numbered among them) tutored George for long hours, both before and after taps. And, with his usual grit and determination, he made it. We all rejoiced, for even at that time it seemed obvious that George was going places in the service."[6]

Brown's experience with academic subjects during his plebe (freshman) year helped to shape his character and future path of leadership, by strengthening his resolve. It also heightened his sense of humility and compassion, developing in him a greater willingness to listen, weigh decisions as opposed to making snap judgments, and respect differing viewpoints. With such academic hurdles behind him in his plebe year, he never again had any problem with his studies. When the "make list" came out for yearling (sophomore) corporals, he and roommate Cochran were ranked respectively numbers one and two.

While Brown's studies were certainly important to him at West Point, it was in other areas that he excelled. "I think George's pursuit of academics," recalls a later roommate, John Norton, "was sort of a necessary function with him, one that he had to pursue. He eventually did well enough, but it was in military tactics that George Brown really found himself and stood near the top of the class."[7]

"George and I were, at this early stage, in friendly competition for the highest military rank in our company," related Ben Mayo, "and for a while I was on top. Over the course of four years, this changed and he wound up as a regimental cadet captain. I never resented or regretted this result at all. All of us wanted George to do well. He was one of the most affable men I have ever known, but there was, below the surface, a toughness and drive that one could detect and admire. When George gave an order, he never said, 'Do this,' or 'Do that'; he would say, 'Let's do this,' or 'Don't you think we should do that?' He always gave consideration to the views of others, and in the long run, everyone really wanted to do it George's way."[8]

During Brown's tenure at West Point, war clouds were becoming a storm. On March 15, 1939, as he neared the end of his second year, Germany invaded Czechoslovakia and occupied Prague. At the beginning of his third year, on September 1, 1939, Germany began its attack against Poland. Two days later, Great Britain and France declared war on Germany. It was inevitable that the cadets watched these events with anxiety and curious expectation about the impact upon their futures.

At the beginning of his "cow" (junior) year, Brown was given the task of working with the new plebes. "I first encountered General Brown during the summer of 1939 during my plebe year at West Point," recalls Edward McGough of the Class of 1943. "For eight weeks he was one of my Beast Barracks cadet officers. His leadership ability was instantly evident to all of us. He was a tough disciplinarian, but for some unexplainable reason none of us resented or felt abused by his tough demands. He seemed to instill in all of us a real desire to cope successfully with the hardships and humiliations of plebe year. Perhaps the even tone and relaxed voice he possessed and the ever-present twinkle in his eyes convinced us that he would always treat us fairly, yet would not tolerate disobedience. He just plain commanded our respect from the start.

"After my plebe year I encountered him occasionally during military drill period. He was in charge for sure, yet he had the knack of introducing a bit of humor into otherwise dull situations. This trait, mixed with firmness when required, gave him an easygoing style of command. He just matter-of-factly issued commands and instructions and assumed they would be followed. They always were, as we all felt that we were not going to be the ones to let him down. You became very loyal to him quickly."[9]

The black clouds of war continued to form while George was completing his education at West Point. It was written in the 1941 cadet yearbook, the *Howitzer,* that the passage of the Selective Service Act and the consequent rapid expansion of the Army renewed the possibility for an early graduation. "November found us purchasing uniforms and equipment. . . . We were preparing for a premature debut as bewildered new junior officers. Our brother class at the Naval Academy was to graduate in February. . . . We entered the new year; the uncertainty persisted. When instructors were ordered away for duty . . . twenty of our classmates were selected to fill the academic breach."[10]

At the beginning of that senior, or First Class year, George Brown was appointed cadet captain and regimental adjutant. This placed him among the top five cadet officers in the corps. With his usual humility he made light of it to his parents: "When George was made adjutant he said to us, 'Oh, that's nothing. All you have to be is good-looking and have a loud mouth to be adjutant at West Point.' "[11] His positions, however, carried a great deal of responsibility. In addition to playing the key role at routine parades and other regimental formations on post, he had to handle the intricate problems of arranging and directing military ceremonies elsewhere, such as the pregame march-ons at Yankee Stadium. "It took a lot of head work," recalls Cadet First Captain John Norton. "Somebody had to plan all of this. The tactical officers did a lot of it, but a great deal fell on the cadets. George, without any particular urging from the officers in charge, or myself, saw the job had to be done, and he just moved out and did it. He was very good at assigning people duties. He could be as tough as nails when he had to be, even with his own classmates, in trying to lay out the procedures for conducting a special ceremony. There was never any crisis within the corps. He always had it under control."[12]

His duties, however, revolved around more than ceremonies. He also had to make sure all cadet details were properly handled by rosters, that they met a certain standard of performance. Just posting the orders sounds like a routine thing, but something could easily go wrong. With some eighteen hundred cadets, with twelve companies and three battalions, and each part of the corps housed in different ways, he had to check that all cadets were in at night and lights were off, and he had to make sure certain inspections were made and cadets serving disciplinary tours were doing so. Various cadet officers made these checks, with Brown handling the schedule. Also, there were visitors coming and going in different parts of the Academy and quite often cadets on duty to handle the visitors.

Another challenge for George Brown as adjutant was the responsibility for making announcements at all of the meals. The written material for these announcements would come in to him in various forms, such as notes from the Superintendent, the Commandant, the dean of the faculty, members of the Tactical Department, members of the Academic Departments, the officer of the day, or the members of the Corps itself. "This was a strain on a young man," continued Norton, "but George had a great presence. He had a stentorian voice and was the sort of person to whom people would listen. He articulated probably better than anyone else that I knew in the corps, and he put his whole heart and soul into it and everybody knew it. He would make his announcements and in the next breath might have to introduce a senior head of state. He had perfect timing and selected his words well. There were many opportunities to really blow it, but he just always kept his cool. He thrived on that sort of challenge, and that's a very special form of leadership."[13]

The effect of these responsibilities was well summed up by roommate Harrington Cochran: "Pretty inconsequential stuff? Not at all, for here is where George Brown became conditioned to stand 'out front' of a large body of men, with ease and confidence in himself and in the fact that he had earned it through a competitive process in which he had excelled. It was important in the building of his pride and character as a leader, later to be proven so convincingly in combat."[14]

"My first meeting with George," said Alice Colhoun Brown, called Skip by her friends, whom Brown married after graduation, "was more or less prearranged, but very reluctantly so on my part. I had been dating at West Point several classes before George's class and thought that I really knew the ropes up there. I had all my special friends picked out. One particular June Week when I was dating a cadet in the Class of '39, my father asked me if I would please attend a party that a classmate of his, who was stationed at West Point, was hosting for the sons of the Class of '13 who were presently cadets in the Academy.

"I didn't want any part of this. I thought it was going to interfere with the good times that I was going to have at June Week. But having been brought up to do as I was told, I said I would do it. So I excused myself from my date on this particular afternoon and went to the party.

"Anyway, I got there, and in the group here was this divinely handsome cadet. I found myself finding him interesting enough to stick around and talk to for a while. He was nice, but we didn't make any overtures about having a date at that point at all, though I did think he was pretty cute. So I left the party and went on through June Week with my other date. The next fall I received a letter from Cadet George Brown, who was now a first class-man, saying maybe you don't remember me but we met at the party last June Week. Would you like to come up for a football game weekend? And, of course, I was tickled because I had hoped I had caught his eye. I accepted and went and had a ball. I dated him through the next year and also dated some of the others and some classmates of his. I really thought George was by far the nicest guy up there."[15]

George Brown was certainly not all business. One weekend Norton's girl and Skip had been at West Point for a date. Weekends terminated at Sunday dinner, and the corps had just entered the mess hall. As usual, First Captain Norton and his staff, which included Brown, had stood by the door as they entered. Normally, they entered last and took their seats on the "poop deck." But that night George and Norton wanted to go back and see their dates off. Thayer Monument was nearby. "George and Skip," recalled Norton, "went behind the monument, which was across the street from where they formed up. It was dark, and Brown went around behind the monument to kiss Skip goodnight. If the mess hall doors were closed before they got in, they had to report themselves. Well, as George and Skip were behind the monument, one of the tac officers was coming down to that area. It just happened to be one of the really tough guys. They could hear the clinking and clacking of his boots, but the tac did not know they were behind the monument. They kept the monument between them and him, so if he advanced in one direction, they advanced in another. George wondered if they would ever get into the mess hall before the doors closed. Fortunate-ly, there must have been slow motion on the part of the fellow who had to close the doors that night because he got through the doors just before they closed. Had he been caught, he would have been confined to quarters every weekend for a month."[16]

A point may be made that George Brown was selected for high cadet rank *because* of his demonstrated potential for leadership, and that the very exercise of cadet rank served, in turn, to further develop his leadership potential. Due consideration should likewise be given to the role played by polo and horsemanship.

In the outside world, polo, by its nature, has been the sport of the social elite. At West Point it was, in Brown's time, still a holdover, a part of the ancient martial act of military equitation. Intercollegiate competition was limited by the nature of the sport to schools like Harvard and Yale, and a couple of military colleges. In addition, the Army polo team was often invited to play against such socially prestigious groups as Squadron A of New York, probably the best polo team in the country, and at certain private estates on Long Island. In the eyes of their fellow cadets, the polo players had achieved an enviable social status. As captain of the Army polo team and a nationally ranked player, George Brown stood out. Although his development as an outstanding polo player contributed little to his education as an officer, it did add an important element to his character.[17]

Said classmate Burton Andrus: "The Ivy League players had been involved in competitive polo from a very early age. Despite this, West Point won the national polo championship in 1939. During our First Class [senior] year, we were in the finals, losing to Princeton in that last game, the blackest day of our lives."[18]

In the solemnly measured phrases of the 1941 West Point Yearbook, the *Howitzer,* "The finals brought Princeton who squeezed out a victory. . . . In this tournament as throughout the season, Brown led the team with great distinction and his calm manner served to redeem many situations."

Andrus went on, "Polo was one of the minor sports at West Point at that time. It certainly did not have the standing that football did, but because it represented a sport that was very close to the profession, the cavalry, it was highly respected. We were well regarded because of our very successful win-loss record."[19]

But polo was not all fun. It was a rough, aggressive sport and further developed in George Brown those qualities that would stand him in such good stead in his later years as a leader. When two horses hit each other there is quite an impact, and the objective is to knock the other man off the line of the ball so that you can get control of it. George played very aggressively but was never regarded as being a dirty player in any way. "You knew when he hit you that you were really going to be belted," said Andrus, "but there was never an elbow or anything that was not part of the gentleman's way of playing the game. That was the way he was perceived by us, and I believe by our opponents as well."[20]

According to John Norton, "The real understanding of George Brown's leadership as a cadet would probably be from his polo. Here, he had a natural role of leader on a fast-moving athletic field. Those were bone-crunching days. You talk about riding horses with reckless abandon; they did some miraculous things with the horses. I used to go back to West Point just to watch them play. They were an inspiring group."[21]

Burton Andrus expresses it this way: "If we had had all-Americans in those days, George clearly would have been on the all-American team. On the polo field he was not the kind of leader who would ever raise his voice or say to you, 'You pulled a dumb stunt.' He led largely by example. He had a steadying influence. He played back, which was the critical point on the team, defending the goal, turning the play back from a defensive posture to an aggressive posture. George simply had ability, and I believe it would be described in modern terms as 'cool.' "[22]

"As with all the cadets on the polo squad," recalls George's old polo coach, Harry Johnson, "I feel that I knew George quite well because I played with them, played against them, but mostly I just watched and helped them all I could. George was quiet, easy to coach, and quick to catch on. He was a wide open player, had a beautiful stroke and was an excellent horseman. Why, hell, he even looked good when missing a ball. He would just shrug his shoulders and go on with the game."[23]

Polo also played a role in Brown's development as a leader because it had more to offer than just the athletic aspect. After games, they might have a tea, where they would balance a cup, eat a cake, and chat with the wives of the West Point officers or, if it were an out-of-town match, with the people involved in that game. It was like rugby in Britain, where they sit around and have beer afterward. When they played at Yale, the game usually was on Derby Day, the same day as Yale's boat race with Harvard, a big weekend. After the game, they would go back to a fraternity house and mix with the people there—the girls from Radcliffe and Vassar and other schools around. It was a much different environment from West Point.

The best perspective on the value of polo in George's development is offered by Harrington Cochran: "George Brown found himself in a select group which let him excel and lead. As an impressionable youth growing up in the days of a waning world of the U.S. Army horse cavalry and artillery, he became an excellent horseman, playing polo as the Army brats on active 'horse posts' were able to do. With such a background it was natural that he and a few others with similar backgrounds made up the West Point polo team."[24]

In concluding this examination of Brown's character and personality as perceived by his West Point contemporaries, it remains only to address the question of what George Brown's own insight was into the development of military character and leadership. That perception is developed by his analogy between horsemanship and leadership of combat troops: "Horsemanship inculcates habits and attitudes that are directly applicable in leading troops," George Brown once said. "To be a competent horseman you must take a large, muscular animal many times more powerful than yourself— with a mind of its own, a survival instinct for panicky flight, and the capability to kill or maim you—and dominate it and train it to perform useful functions for you reliably, when and as desired, within the limits of its capabilities. To do this you must recognize the hazards involved and develop the self-discipline to accept them and to carry yourself at all times with calm assurance in your dealings with your horse (or men). You must study your animal until you know its physical and mental capacities and its fears and motivations; you must learn how to communicate with it effectively and how to establish effective discipline by rewards and punishments—and to apply these fairly and never emotionally. Then you must devote long hours to training, to discipline, and to building the animal's trust and confidence in you. In so doing you establish patterns of conduct in yourself until you always think first of the welfare of your animal (or troops) no matter what your own state of fatigue or ill health. When you have trained your horse (or unit) and built mutual confidence, then you have an effective element with which to carry out your mission. Concurrently, you have done much to improve your leadership skills. Leadership isn't just jumping out in front and yelling, 'Follow me!' It lies largely in building up a highly trained, physically fit, well-equipped, well-disciplined organization that not only can, but will, carry out your mission when the time comes.''

As graduation approached, the first classmen began their decision making on branch of service. When classmate Bill Seawell was asked why Brown selected pilot training, he responded, "We had opportunities to talk about branch of service at polo practice and on our polo trips. We'd talk about the Air Corps, particularly as the selection came about. I don't re- member any formal sessions on the pros and cons of all the branches of the service. Very early that year I had made up my mind that I would probably choose the Corps of Engineers as a base branch, but I wanted eventually to go into the Air Corps. George Brown decided he also wanted to go into the Air Corps."[25]

In the previous year, a smaller percentage of cadets than usual elected to enter Air Corps training, and it was probably Gen. Henry H. Arnold who exerted the strongest influence on the decisions by Brown and many of the Class of 1941 to go into the Air Corps. Theodore ("Ross") Milton, from the Class of 1940, who had entered the Air Corps immediately after gradu- ation, made this comment regarding his early contact with General Arnold: "I knew him when I was a boy, as a friend of my family; in fact, he gave me my first airplane ride when I was about twelve years old. But I didn't really know him; after all, I was only a lieutenant when he became Chief of the Air Corps. After my graduation from West Point, he ordered me to report to him, demanding to know why more of my class had not chosen Air Corps. Our class was slightly below the norm that year in selecting the Air Corps, and he wanted to know why. He decided that his best source of information would be the newly graduated cadets.

"I answered that we had had a very bad time on the Air Corps trip during our First Class year. They had not treated us like grown-ups. They had been overly rigid on discipline. Mitchel Field was a disaster. The indoctrination was dull, with lectures all day long on the most stupid ground-school subjects, and then they flew us around in B-18's, which wasn't satisfying. We wanted to get into pursuit planes and transports, where the instructors would give you a hand in flying. I told General Arnold all this, and he made notes and looked fierce. He then made the comment, 'This is the last time that will ever happen.' "[26]

The results of General Arnold's resolve to improve the cadets' exposure to air training were reflected by Bill Seawell, a classmate of George Brown, who, when asked about his own Air Corps exposure, replied, "I was favorably impressed by our Air Corps trip in 1941. I didn't have the same reaction as Ross Milton had had the previous year. It was properly organized and went off well. Everything that they said they were going to do, they did. The officers took an interest in us, and we had a good experience. That probably reinforced our decision to go Air Corps."[27]

Similarly, the *Howitzer* wrote of the Air Corps experience: "The first highlight of the summer was the Air Corps trip; one-third of the class at a time, we took off from Stewart Field in Douglas transports for the first leg of the journey. At Langley we saw G.H.Q. Air Force in action at bombing and gunnery practice, we took over the controls of Flying Fortress. . . . The next leg took us to Dayton and Wright Field, home of the Materiel Division, where we enjoyed a glimpse of the experimental and research laboratories. . . . Home again two days later, many of us were convinced that wings were what we wanted."[28]

"Near graduation," recalls classmate Cochran, "assignment of commissions within allocated vacancies was according to choice in order of class standing. Vacancies in the cavalry having run out ahead of George Brown, the only remaining options open to him were the infantry and the Quartermaster Corps. He elected the former, together with an application for flight training which, if passed successfully, would permit a subsequent transfer to the Air Corps."[29]

After George made the decision he wanted to fly, he selected the primary flying school in Pine Bluff, Arkansas, for his flight training. With the rest of his class, he was commissioned a second lieutenant on June 11, 1941.

Having made their decisions, Brown and his fellow cadets left West Point to begin their military careers. "May brought academics' end," wrote a classmate, "and our June Week arrived. The old, familiar scene was re-enacted, we, the principal actors. The course was run and won; we of the Class of Nineteen Hundred Forty-one proudly took our place in the Long Gray Line."[30]

NOTES

1. *Howitzer,* 1907.
2. Letter from Col. Harrington W. Cochran, Jr., USA (Ret.), to EFP, October 14, 1977.
3. Letter from Col. Gregg L. McKee, to EFP, December 6, 1979.
4. Personal interview with Brig. Gen. Thomas W. Brown, USA (Ret.), August 8, 1979.
5. Cochran correspondence.
6. Letter from Col. Ben I. Mayo, Jr., USAF (Ret.), to EFP, October 31, 1979.
7. Personal interview with Lt. Gen. John Norton, USA (Ret.), May 24, 1979.
8. Mayo correspondence.
9. Letter from Maj. Gen. Edward A. McGough, III, USAF (Ret.), to EFP, August 27, 1979.
10. *Howitzer,* 1941, pp. 374–76.
11. Personal interview with Mrs. Thoburn K. Brown, August 8, 1979.
12. Norton interview.
13. Ibid.
14. Cochran correspondence.
15. Personal interview with Mrs. George S. Brown.
16. Norton interview.
17. Cochran correspondence.
18. Personal interview with Col. Burton C. Andrus, USAF (Ret.), June 28, 1979.
19. Ibid.
20. Ibid.
21. Norton interview.
22. Andrus interview.
23. Letter from Maj. Gen. Harry Johnson to EFP.
24. Cochran correspondence.
25. Personal interview with Brig. Gen. William T. Seawell, USAF (Ret.), January 18, 1980.
26. Personal interview with Gen. Theodore R. Milton, USAF (Ret.), June 28, 1979.
27. Seawell interview.
28. *Howitzer,* 1941, pp. 363–66.
29. Cochran correspondence.
30. *Howitzer,* 1941, p. 377.

CHAPTER 3

PREPARATION FOR WAR

Second Lieutenant George S. Brown arrived for pilot training at the Pine Bluff, Arkansas, primary contract training school on August 20, 1941. There were to be three phases of training, each lasting two-and-one-half months. "I was either first or second to solo," recalled Bill Seawell; "George was among the very first to solo. We were the only two student officers in the crowd, so we had a special assignment; along with being students, we had the responsibility of drilling our classmates. It was a good experience and we enjoyed it.

"Our class at Pine Bluff numbered forty or more—a fairly sizable class," recalled Seawell. "The largest single group in the class came out of Princeton University. Maj. Preston M. Spicer was the commander and ran a good school. He was the one who ordered George and me to drill our classmates. We were flying Fairchild PT–19s, with no difficulty."[1]

At Pine Bluff, Brown received 24 hours, 38 minutes of dual flying time and 35 hours, 26 minutes solo. He had 34 hours of airplane engineering, with a grade of 79 percent; 22 hours of air navigation with a grade of 86 percent; 32 hours of flight characteristics with a grade of 84 percent; 30 hours of meteorology with a grade of 82 percent; and an overall average in grade subjects of 83 percent.

From Pine Bluff, George and his class went to Randolph Field, Texas, for the second phase of their training. Burt Andrus recalls the experiences there: "It was called basic pilot training, and George and I were roommates.

I remember I had a little bit of trouble, making dumb mistakes, and George was instrumental in keeping me motivated and confident that I could make it. He never had a bit of trouble."

Brown's "cool" was demonstrated early at Randolph. "On our arrival at Randolph Field," continues Andrus, "we ran into a first lieutenant who had been designated assistant commandant of student officers. He and George were only two classes apart, and they knew each other quite well. When we reported in, we naturally observed the correct military procedure. When George reported, the first lieutenant apparently didn't think George's salute had quite enough snap to it. George had sort of a friendly smile on his face, and the first lieutenant said, 'Lieutenant, go outside and do it again.' This shocked everybody, because to us rank among first lieutenants was about as obscure as virtue among ladies of the street. George good-naturedly went out, and this time banged on the door, and came in with a red-hot salute. The first lieutenant then said, 'George, I want you to know that while you're here, I am a first lieutenant and you are Second Lieutenant Brown.' That, of course, got the first lieutenant off to a very uncomfortable start among the twenty-five or thirty members of our class. The thing that I was impressed with was how well George took the rebuff. I was upset personally, but not George."[2]

Bill Seawell, Ben Mayo, Burt Andrus, and George Brown were together at Randolph when the Japanese bombed Pearl Harbor. "My calendar says December 7, Pearl Harbor Day," reflected Ben Mayo, "and the memories of that day come back vividly. I was in bed (Sunday morning, with a hangover) when my beautiful bride of a month came running in with the news that Pearl Harbor had been attacked, and that we would soon be at war. I told her the hell with it and to get back in bed. But word soon came that all personnel should immediately report back to base. We all checked in, expecting anything. The mood was of high spirits; I suppose subconsciously we had all been expecting something like this and were glad that the issue had been joined—all confident we would win, and quickly. Of course we won, but not quickly or easily. And, we paid the price.

"You will never imagine how we spent the remainder of that day. We were ordered to taxi our PT-9s and PT-14s to the air base perimeter, disperse them, and camouflage them by covering them with mesquite bushes. I suppose the base commander figured that if Pearl Harbor was the number one priority target, certainly Randolph must be next on the enemy's list. Seems sort of silly now; we didn't have a machine gun or a bomb, and there was no way that the Japanese (or the Germans) were going to invade Texas. But I do not fault the base commander; out of utter frustration he had to do *something.*"[3]

On January 10, 1942, Brown completed his training at Randolph Field. It was then necessary to choose between fighters and bombers, but because George was 6 feet tall and the height limit for fighter pilots was 5 feet 10 inches, he went to bombers. The final phase of pilot training was at Kelly Field, San Antonio, Texas, and George completed it on March 7, 1942. Having been awarded his wings, he then was transferred from the infantry to the Army Air Corps.

Brown selected his preference for assignment in the United States in order of priority: Westover, Langley, and MacDill. He received none of these choices, being posted instead to Barksdale Field, Louisiana, for transition training in the B-24 heavy bomber.

Brown was a member of 344th Bomb Squadron, 93rd Bombardment Group. His West Point classmate Tom Corbin joined him there. "There were very few experienced pilots around," said Corbin, "so right out of our own training, we became instructor pilots. It was unbelievable at that time for anyone who flew to think that a man with less than a hundred hours' flying time would be an instructor pilot. But we were the most knowledgeable and experienced people around."[4]

In mid-May of 1942, the 93rd Group was moved to Fort Myers Army Air Base, Florida, to practice antisubmarine patrol, and George formed his first aircrew. The navigator, then 2d Lt. Carl Barthel, remembers, "As soon as I arrived, I was assigned to George Brown's crew, and I stayed with it almost two years. Our crew had ten men: pilot, copilot, navigator, bombardier, flight engineer, radio operator, and four gunners. As soon as we were ready, we went on submarine patrol up and down the Florida coast."[5]

In selecting his first crew, Brown exhibited the same perception and thoroughness that was to help him throughout his career. "I learned later that I was chosen because I had gotten the highest marks in my class in navigation school," continued Barthel, "and George made the effort to investigate our records; he did not leave things to chance. As a result, only one member out of the original crew proved unable to stand the pressure and had to be transferred to ground duty.

"George was every inch a commander; he knew what he was doing, with completely natural leadership. His approach to crew training was simple: when things didn't go exactly right, he had us keep on doing them until they did go right. By the time the crew was molded together and had gained some experience, we were all extremely good at our jobs, worked together like clockwork. We saw other crews that never got that way because they didn't have the leadership we did."[6]

One reason Brown was able to lead others so effectively was that he knew their jobs almost as well as his own. According to Barthel, "George learned as much as possible about each of his crew members' duties. He could fire the guns and strip them down as well as the gunners. Frequently we discussed together what my duties were as navigator. Back then we had the old A-10 sextant—which was a good device but a 'dog' to use. I explained to him that you need a stable platform to operate it from and gave him the opportunity to actually shoot some sextant shots. I particularly emphasized that you can't be in a turn or can't be climbing or diving, because the acceleration would give a poor shot. Thereafter, when I was making a shot, I would tell him and the aircraft would fly steady as a rock. There wasn't a system on the aircraft that he didn't understand, and he made sure the rest of the crew was ready, too, rotating bombardier and navigator through the cockpit, so that if both the pilot and copilot were killed or wounded, one of the survivors could possibly get the aircraft down.

"And he was a gifted pilot. When I gave him a new course direction, he knew exactly how long it was going to take for him to turn it. I could compute that into my figures and know that he would hold that heading to within a half degree."[7]

The group commander of the 93rd was Lt. Col. Edward J. Timberlake. He had been in the Air Corps for something more than ten years, which at that time was a great deal of seniority. "He recognized George Brown very early," said Barthel, "and really gave him the opportunity to develop."[8]

Reflecting on those formative months at Barksdale and Fort Myers, General Timberlake comments specifically on why George Brown stood out so early in his career: "First, he was presentable and articulate. He was one hell of a good pilot. He was, in fact, one of the finest officers I have ever known.

"As it turned out, there were three particularly outstanding officers in the 93rd Bomb Group—George Brown, Keith Compton, and Ramsey Potts," continued Timberlake. "You could look at them and you knew they were going to climb to the top. We moved from Barksdale down to Fort Myers and began their training and then flew to England. All three were promoted to captain during that period. They were natural competitors; they didn't see it that way, but I felt it. Keith Compton and our group eventually moved to North Africa to support the landing down there, where Compton caught the eye of the head of the 9th Bomber Command in Cairo. He was subsequently 'stolen' from me and made a group commander there. He was a colonel within a year. George Brown made colonel about a month later, within a year after our group's arrival in Europe. Ramsey Potts followed the same pattern, and thus all three ended up as group commanders."[9]

Brown's crew departed Fort Myers on August 1, 1942, for Grenier Field,

New Hampshire. There they flew another 50 hours before leaving for the European theater on September 1, 1942. "When we left Fort Myers," recalls General Timberlake, "Brown had as an additional duty that of being squadron operations officer. The squadron commander was not the strongest guy in the world, and Brown was pretty much running the squadron. Brown subsequently led a flight of several bombers to England."[10]

Carl Barthel remembers, "During the flight, we were flying due south of Iceland because we had been briefed to fly a rhumb line rather than a great circle route, due to bad weather up north. The rhumb line carried us south of the great circle course until we reached our point of destination. We were flying in formation, and our wing man called George and commented to him that we were two hundred miles south of our course. George called me and asked, 'What about it?' I said, 'Allowing for reasonable error, we are within five miles of course.' Then he asked me, 'What do you think this guy is talking about?' I responded, 'I don't know, but *you* know there can only be one of us leading this outfit.' The problem was that the other pilot had not heard that we were going to fly a rhumb line rather than a great circle. The thing I appreciated was the fact that George backed me up completely."[11]

Reminiscences of those who served with him in England indicate that Brown's mature, responsible outlook set him apart as a leader even at this early stage in his career. "There were four of us who were squadron operations officers during our early period in England," recalls Ramsey Potts, "Joe Tate, Kenny Dessert, George Brown, and I. The others were West Pointers, but I was not, and when Colonel Timberlake would hold meetings with the squadron commanders and squadron operations officers, he seemed quite solicitous about the fact that I didn't know a lot about military administration, and so he was very kind to me. The three other squadron operations officers were all very professional, but they never gave me the feeling that they 'had the drop on me' because they were West Pointers. Without any question, George Brown was the most mature and steady of all the officers I knew who were in the age bracket twenty-two to twenty-seven.

"Our group commander regarded George as the most mature of the four of us in terms of his composure and demeanor. In observing and getting to know him during that period, I was impressed with the fact that he never lost his composure. He seemed to have an understanding of everything going on in administrative and operational matters and was by far the most mature of the younger officers that I knew during the entire war. He didn't conduct himself like a man in his mid-twenties, but rather as if he were thirty-four or thirty-five.

"When problems would be brought to the attention of the squadron commanders by Colonel Timberlake, George always seemed to have a better appreciation of the correct military solution than anyone else. He had a great sense of duty, was courageous, and yet never flaunted his courage. And, he never tried to give the impression that he was doing something unusual, something extraordinary. He was just businesslike and professional, and he was respected by all of us."[12]

In England, the 329th Bomb Squadron became part of the 93rd Bomb Group. "Very early, before lead crews were officially designated, Brown's crew was accepted as the lead crew of the squadron," recalls Barthel. "The concept of lead crews was just coming in. When we formed up, we were always put in the lead slot. There were a few times when we even flew as group leader or deputy group leader."[13]

Regarding the lead crew concept, General Timberlake has this to say: "I think we arrived at the same conclusion at about the same time as General LeMay did with the B-17s. I called in the key people and told them about my plan to designate certain crews to be lead. I didn't want the squadron commanders to do it because they didn't fly enough. They were running their squadrons. I wanted in each case a professional crew that worked together. I remember that I called in Brown, Potts, and Compton to talk over the idea, and they all bought it."[14]

Ramsey Potts comments that "all of us began to feel that the most competent flying combination would be a crew that practiced, worked, and gained experience together. Then, if they showed the right proficiency, they would be the crew to lead. The commander, who would by definition command the formation instead of flying as pilot and 'bumping' the airplane commander out of his seat, would instead occupy a jump seat or perhaps take the copilot's seat. In this way crew integrity would be maintained. Coordination and cooperation, especially between pilot, navigator, and bombardier, were quite essential to the success of any mission. General Timberlake's concept was a good one."[15]

There were certainly good reasons to make the best crews as useful as possible. "When we got to England," recollects Barthel, "we had some real problems, particularly with the weather. It seemed to be cloudy much of the time; it was all instrument flying, and we had to get some very intensive training for the whole crew.

"We did not have the instruments then that we have today. The only radio navigation we had was the low-frequency compass. Everything else was up to the crew. We would go out, climb through the clouds, top out at 22,000 feet, and then practice our mission. Then when we would come back in over a beacon, we would have to let down in a pattern and hope that when we finished that pattern there was an airport in front of us, because we normally did not break out until we were at 500 feet."[16]

As difficult as conditions were, George Brown was ready to meet the challenge, and soon his crew was tuned to a fine edge, ready for combat.

NOTES

1. Personal interview with Brig. Gen. William T. Seawell, USAF (Ret.), January 18, 1980.
2. Personal interview with Col. Burton C. Andrus, USAF (Ret.), June 28, 1979.
3. Letter from Col. Ben I. Mayo, Jr., USAF (Ret.), to EFP, October 31, 1979.
4. Personal interview with Maj. Gen. Thomas C. Corbin, USAF (Ret.), June 29, 1979.
5. Personal interview with Col. Carl Barthel, USAF (Ret.), May 17, 1979.
6. Ibid.
7. Ibid.
8. Ibid.
9. Personal interview with Lt. Gen. Edward J. Timberlake, USAF (Ret.), July 18, 1979.
10. Ibid.
11. Barthel interview.
12. Personal interview with Ramsey Potts, April 15, 1980.
13. Barthel interview.
14. Timberlake interview.
15. Potts interview.
16. Barthel interview.

CHAPTER 4
COMBAT IN WORLD WAR II

George Brown and his crew's first combat mission was to bomb a railroad yard near Lyons, in France. Barthel's description of it is a masterpiece of brevity: "The weather was clear, it was a nice day, but we didn't do too well. We did hit the railroad yard, but we didn't accomplish as much as we might have. We were pretty damned green. Dropping bombs from 24,000 feet, unpressurized, when they're shooting at you, was quite an experience. We had no fighter cover, and that certainly did not make things any easier."[1]

Despite the less than totally successful outcome of the mission, Brown fared well as a leader under pressure. "George as a combat leader," recalls his navigator, "was really cool. There was never any excitement or panic in the cockpit, no matter how heavy the flak or the enemy fighter attack. Everything went exactly as it was supposed to. I got a little excited after we had just completed a scrap with some enemy fighters and mistakenly told him to turn 90 degrees to the right rather than to the left, and he came right back to me on the intercom and said, 'Don't you mean 270?' That was the way he operated."[2]

It was during this period in his career that Brown received his only battle scar. "George once told me about one of his more unusual missions over Europe," recalls his brother, Tim. "They were flying over Le Havre, bombing a concentration of submarines, and the flak was heavy. George just happened to place his flak jacket underneath the seat. It was probably standard procedure; anybody with any sense would have done that. He took a big wallop in his bottom when some flak hit underneath the seat. He thought his whole back end was shot off, but he was in the middle of a combat mission and still able to function, so he just pressed on. After they got out of the flak area and were on the way back to base, he started to feel around to see if he was still in one piece. The whole cockpit was full of goose feathers from the disintegrating cushion, and a piece of flak had cut him on the thigh.

"That was his twenty-fifth mission, and after they had thrown him into the water tank (following the tradition of the times), he went to the dispensary to get the gash in his leg taken care of. He said to the doctor, 'I guess that gets me a Purple Heart?' The doctor replied, 'Nothing doing; I'm not going to write you up for a Purple Heart for this little scratch!' And that is as close as George ever got to a Purple Heart."[3]

The completion of twenty-five missions marked a milestone in Brown's career, and his response to it was indicative of his tenacity in seeing a job through to successful completion despite the fact that there was an easier way out. Barthel explains that "when crews finished their twenty-fifth mission, there would be a big celebration and then they could go in and ask for reassignment, saying, 'I'm finished.' But Brown's crew didn't stop flying after the twenty-fifth mission. It just never occurred to any of us to stop. We felt that our job was very, very interesting; I think probably more so because we were always leading. Our responsibility was to go and get the job done, so we never said anything about reassignment."[4]

General Timberlake's rating of Brown's performance for the period from January 1, 1943, to June 30, 1943, when Brown served as a combat flight leader for two months, a squadron commander for four months, and an S–3 (Operations Officer) in Headquarters, 93rd Bomb Group, for two months, consisted of a few succinct sentences: "A well-mannered and alert officer. He has a distinguished and attractive presence. He is extremely serious and tends to be hypercritical, although he is adaptable. He seeks responsibility and is loyal to his subordinates. He is a formalist in his thinking and slightly biased. He is well read, very conversant. A tireless and energetic worker who attains successful results."

"After Brown had gotten his twenty-five missions," relates General Timberlake, "General Hodges very much wanted him up at his headquarters in the 2d Air Division to run operations. So you see, I wasn't the only one who was impressed by George Brown."[5]

Hodges valued Brown both as pilot and leader, calling on his crew for innovation and new approaches. "For example," says Barthel, "they were having trouble with guns freezing up at higher altitudes. So our crew took our aircraft up to 32,000 feet to see what would work and what would not.

We finally developed a technique using low-temperature oil which solved the problem."[6]

George Brown had been promoted to major in mid-February, 1943; seven months later he went to lieutenant colonel. He was then only a quarter of the way into his third year of active service. Much of Brown's rapid rise in rank was undoubtedly due to attrition—to the fact that so many crews were being lost during this early period of the war. As more and more senior people—of whom there were comparatively few—were killed or disabled or completed their missions, promotions became almost inevitable for those who had the ability and luck to survive. Clearly, however, there was more than luck involved in staying alive in combat. Brown had trained his crew well, and they performed their combat missions safely under his cool, steady leadership.

The December 30, 1943, entry in Brown's personal diary provides further insight into the effectiveness of his crew: "We went to Ludwigshafen just across the river from Mannheim. Pulled out of bed at 0400 this AM and briefed at 0530. We took off at 0830 and I was commander of the 20 C.W. leading the 93rd, 446th, and 448th Bomb Groups. We were to join the B–17s at 13,000 and go on in with fighter cover all the way in and out. Everything went fine until we got to 15,000, then we got a gas leak from the P-heater line so I had to turn back, and Boylan, my deputy, took over. We did a beautiful job and they went on in without loss and bombed on PFF works. I was heartbroken because I hated to turn back at that point, I get to go so seldom. Well, we got back here about 1230 and had lunch, then I worked until about 1800 and came back to the hut just sick because I had read up on the heater system and found that if I had thought, and if the pilot or engineer had been on the ball, they could have turned a switch and cut off the line; head up and locked. Went to the show with Robert and then back here to find that I had to go back to the office to work up the problem for tomorrow."[7]

The crew's fine performance also came from the personal loyalty they felt for their leader, a loyalty engendered by his feelings toward them as people as well as battle comrades. Brown's consideration for others, particularly his crew, was demonstrated in many everyday, yet significant, ways. During a period in which his unit was temporarily based in North Africa, he was invited to spend a weekend with one of his father's classmates, a cavalry general named Cheeves. At the end of it, the general placed a case of beer in the car for George to take back with him, with instructions that he was to drink it all. Brown remonstrated, "I can't take it, if that's the rule." Cheeves relented, and Brown made sure that the men in his crew shared the beer with him.[8]

Brown had a great sensitivity for the people he led. One of his crew members, Sergeant Treadway from Montana, was deeply depressed. Brown counseled with him, and then Treadway left him and went back to his tent. A little later, the sergeant emerged from his tent fully outfitted in cowboy boots, broad-brimmed hat, and everything else that went with traditional western gear worn in Montana. He then proceeded to parade around the base for an hour or so. This, of course, was against all uniform regulations, but after his hour was up, he returned to his tent and put his uniform back on, a new man. Brown had told him to do this, and it turned out to be very effective therapy.[9]

During the Sicilian campaign in the late summer of 1943, the Army Air Forces staged the famous raid on the oil fields and refineries in Ploesti, Rumania. This was then the most heavily protected target in Europe, for good reason. The Ploesti fields at that time supplied two-thirds of Germany's gasoline, so their destruction would provide needed help for Russian forces on the eastern front and would assist the Allied invasion of Europe by drastically reducing the fuel supplies available for the Germans. It was such an important mission, in fact, that as one crew member put it, "They told us before takeoff that if none of us were to return, the mission would be well worth it—provided we hit the target!"[10]

To be sure they would not miss the mission, Brown and his crew had to do much overtime work. Damaged on a previous raid over Rome, they landed on Malta to patch up their aircraft before returning to base. "All of us," says Barthel, "worked on changing the four engines on our aircraft the day before the Ploesti raid. We worked night and day so that our aircraft would be ready."[11]

The great attack was launched on Sunday, August 1, 1943. A total of 1,763 Americans took off from Bengazi, Libya, in 178 B–24 bombers to fly some twelve hundred miles. Maj. George Brown was deputy lead for the 93rd Bomb Group, which had about forty aircraft flying. The lead aircraft of the 93rd was piloted by Col. Addison E. Baker. The target-finding crew, piloted by Brian W. Flavelle, mysteriously went down on the flight en route.

Without their target-finding team, the lead group turned twenty miles short of the initial point that was to guide them to Ploesti. Many of the crews detected the error and broke radio silence to try to prevent the consequences. "We're turning too soon!" screamed Walter T. Stewart. Norman Appold agreed, "Not here! Not here! This isn't it!" Ramsey Potts called out, "Mistake! Mistake!" Other aircraft joined in the calls, but they all had to turn together to avoid collisions. As a result, the first wave of aircraft was heading toward Bucharest. Colonel Baker, leading the 93rd, followed the mission leader through the turn, but then, explains Russell Longnecker, "there was no doubt about his decision. He maneuvered our group more eloquently than if he had had radio contact with each of us. He turned left 90 degrees, and we all turned with him. Ploesti was off to the left and we were going straight into it and we were going fast."[12]

James Dugan and Carrol Stewart in their study, *Ploesti,* describe the ensuing action:

> Brown, in his aircraft *Queenie,* followed Baker in the improvised turn and proceeded to fly, with his own followers, a course parallel to that of Baker's. As Baker's aircraft approached Ploesti, it struck a balloon cable. The aircraft continued on. It then received a direct hit on the nose and dropped its bombload. . . .[13]
>
> Brown reached Colombia Aquila and bombed it. Now came a peril few Americans had anticipated. Buttoned around the refineries were the tank farms, actually strategic trivia. The mission was not concerned with destroying a few days' product awaiting shipment, but the gunners could not avoid lacing into the storage tanks. The airmen, as ordered, were throwing out armloads of incendiary bombs on them.
>
> The tanks began exploding in flames. A plane skimmed one just as it went off. The bomber was tossed up like a flaming brand. Brown's following echelons flew out of the flak beds into red-hot tank tops spinning like coins and girders blowing in the air like straws.[14]

Brown's crew dropped their bombs and hit the target that they were assigned. "We dropped four 2,000-pound bombs," said navigator Carl Barthel, "and were so low to the ground that the bombs didn't have time to straighten out. When dropped, they bounced up and went in. They had brick walls around the refinery, and the bombs went through them like mush. Our gunners also set a lot of fires by shooting armor-piercing incendiaries."[15]

James Dugan and Carrol Stewart describe the ensuing action:

> Colonel Brown, now in command of the circus after Addison Baker's death, picked up more of his ships on the outskirts of Ploesti and led them on a southwest withdrawal heading. Brown saw that one of his wingtips was crumpled. "It doesn't look like it hit a balloon cable," he said. Top turret gunner Lloyd Treadway said, ". . . you hit a church steeple, remember?" Brown wondered where the circus was (meaning the rest of their group).

That morning 39 planes had taken off, and 34 reached the target area. Now he had 15 in a scratch formation. Only five were relatively undamaged. Others carried dead or wounded. A feathered prop was their cockade and the marching tune of air whistling through broken glass. The circus formed a flying hedgehog to save itself. And the shifting fortunes of battle had seen that Brown was getting lucky. There were no fighters in sight. It looked as though the riddled circus might slip through between the Rumanians at Bucharest and Gamecock Hahn on the north [that is, the fighter aircraft].[16]

The originator of the idea of the Ploesti raid, Col. Jacob Smart, says of Brown's role, "Even though he was only a few years out of the Military Academy, he was older than most of his contemporaries in judgment, powers of concentration, intensity, and scope of interest. His perspective was larger than the primary objective, that of destroying a specific target. The primary objective, however, never suffered because of his larger view. When Brown's group commander was shot down on the low-level attack over Ploesti, he assumed command of the group and took them over the targets, bringing home those remnants of the group he could muster, under fire by antiaircraft artillery, light machine guns, rifles, and everything else the Germans could throw at them. He did a superb job on that raid, and it was my privilege and honor to recommend him for the Distinguished Service Cross, which was, indeed, awarded to him."[17]

The Distinguished Service Cross is our nation's second highest military decoration, only the Medal of Honor taking precedence over it. Here is the text of George Brown's citation:

GEORGE S. BROWN, 0–24021, Major, Headquarters, 93rd Bombardment Group (H), for distinguished service, extraordinary heroism, and gallantry in action while participating in operations against the Ploesti Oil Refineries on 1 August 1943. Major Brown was deputy force leader of a formation of heavy bombardment aircraft detailed to attack one of the Ploesti Oil Refineries in a mass low-level assault. Just as the target was reached, the force leader's plane went down in flames, and it became Major Brown's task to take over the command at this perilous moment. Under his leadership the force swept over the target in waves, inflicting devastating damage upon it. Then Major Brown reassembled his force, and led it back over the long and perilous journey to its home base. His coolness, good judgment, and magnificent leadership were of paramount value in the accomplishment of this dangerous and important mission; his service was such as to reflect great credit upon himself and upon the forces of which he is a member.

Why did George Brown and his crew survive the Ploesti raid? Luck played a part, certainly, and he also attributed much of their success to his crew's gunnery skill. But Brown's clearheaded leadership was an important factor in his survival of this decisive mission.

Brown's performance report for the period read as follows: "A well-grounded, thorough, serious-minded, dignified officer with plenty of initiative. He performs duties excellently in an unassuming manner and obtains positive results. Can be relied upon to carry out any task assigned to him."

Although George handled the tragedy of war with remarkable maturity, one incident moved him more deeply, perhaps, than any other. His West Point and pilot training classmate, Joe Tate, was with him in Europe during World War II. They had been extremely close friends for many years. On December 22, 1943, Brown wrote to his wife:

Today Joe Tate and Col. "Pop" Hayden are missing along with 5 of our finest crews. It should have been an easy mission to Osnabruck but everything went wrong. Cloud forced them to 26,000 ft. and the fighter support was nil. The German fighters did their job well. But to start at the beginning. I went to briefing, slapped Joe on the back and told him to be careful as he had done to me just two days ago, and then went to hold a court. We had one case that took all morning. After lunch I drove to Norwich with Ray Walker to have a jacket altered and cabled you and mother some flowers. Then back to the field in time to see them land at 1600 and to almost cry like a child when Joe did not come back. There was not much dope on it. He was seen to reach the enemy coast on the way out. He flew with Dick Mays. It was Dick's last mission. Joe should not have gone, for he had done 32 which is 7 more than is required. The bird was seen to drop out of formation and blow up. No word on Ford and Pop Hayden, also Hunt and Daywalt. I dread writing to Boo and Honie and Danny, and Joe would want me to do that, although I think and believe he is OK and I will hear from him sooner or later. I pray I will. Good night, darling, I love you and need you tonight. . . .

I was called from a very restless sleep about 0530 and went to the line where I studied long enough to brief the crews for a practice mission. I had not really missed Joe until then, but it had become my habit to sit at briefings and critiques with Joe and some of the old gang. Today I was all alone. . . .

Then to a critique on yesterday's mission. It was all very tied up and we did not learn any more about anyone, but I must admit I am glad no one had anything definite on Joe. I pray he had a fighting chance to bail out and will walk back to us in a few months or is a P.W. and we'll hear from him in a few weeks. After the critique I went to Joe's room with his adj. Williams and went thru his stuff. I gathered everything such as money, decorations, photos, etc., which I'll send home to Boo. It was no fun but I could not help but think how things would certainly be in a helluva mess if he came home in a few weeks. I'll kick him in the seat of the pants for upsetting me so completely. I have never been so upset over anything in my life before. I certainly hope I never hear of a C.O. ordering a man to go on a mission after they completed their tour and have been relieved. I never agreed that Tate should go on a mission. In fact, I fought like hell to get him taken off. He was too flak happy, not seriously but he was beginning to "sweat 'em out" too much.[18]

Joe Tate had grown up in the Army just as Brown had. He had completed his twenty-five missions but elected to stay overseas longer. Thus, instead of going home after his first tour, he "upped" for a second, and it was during this second tour that he went down. "As I remember it," says Burton Andrus, "he was flying in the tail-gunner's position, which was a concept that they were experimenting with at the time. They thought that if you're in command when you're in the cockpit, there was a problem in that you couldn't see the formation behind you. Therefore, they put Joe in back in the tail to better observe what was happening with the formation astern of the pilot. The theory was that when you're not worrying about flying your own airplane, you can better control operations there from the tail-gunner's position. I'm quite sure that's what Joe was doing when he went down. It was a blow to all of us because he was a very selfless man and quite unlike the average guy, who when he finishes his tour, figures he's paid his dues and goes home and has a little R and R."[19]

But the war stopped for no man. Brown had to put aside his emotions and get on with his responsibilities. He was eventually moved from the 93rd to higher headquarters but continued to keep his hand in combat flying. "If a mission was what appeared to be a milk run," says Barthel, "George would let the new people handle it. But if it were going to be a rough one, he'd say, 'We're going to lead it.' That's the way he was."[20]

Brown's brother, Tim, offers this interpretation of events that led to his next promotion: "After George had flown his missions, he was moved to division level, where they had some real problems. The division commander had to publish the orders each night, but it usually fell to George to do it. Before long, George was doing most of the commander's work. He was staying up every night, getting orders out, assuming responsibility for the daily briefings. The general knew what an outstanding job George was doing, well aware of the load taken off his own shoulders. Meanwhile, George became concerned that he was never going to get promoted to full colonel there. So George told his boss that if he were ever going to make full colonel, he would have to go back to his group. By that time, the general was so dependent on George to do his work he said, 'Now George, don't you do that. I'll get you promoted to colonel here,' and he did."[21]

At division level Brown didn't forget what it was like to be a squadron commander. George S. Boylan, Jr., relates the following incident: "I was a squadron commander when George was at division and led the 93rd Bomb Group on a mission to Emden, a German port on the River Ems, tucked in behind the Frisian Islands along the North Sea coast. The mission required the 93rd to join two other B-24 groups over The Wash, a deep indentation in the east coast of England, between East Anglia and Lincolnshire. We had a nondirectional radio beacon there, and I was supposed to meet two B-24 groups at a specified time. Our wing would then join a B-17 task force on its way to bomb Emden. We were to fly in trail behind the B-17s.

"I got there on time with all of my airplanes, but there weren't any other B-24s in sight. Meanwhile, the B-17s were departing. So I joined the B-17s as a single B-24 group. We stayed behind the B-17s and had no radio contact with them, since none was expected. We approached the initial point over which we were to make a right turn to begin our bomb run into Emden. The B-17 commander overflew it, continued to the northeast, and as I came up, I was faced with a decision whether to follow the B-17s or turn into the target. With a little more experience, the decision would have been easier: stay with the formation regardless. But not this young commander. I turned and went into Emden alone. The B-17s started on their turns shortly after that, but we got over the target first and were met with about thirty fighters. We fortunately sustained no losses and very little battle damage, but I had violated air discipline. If we had lost an airplane, I'm sure the results would have been much different.

"We recovered and proceeded back to England and landed. Shortly, I went to 2d Air Division to explain my actions. George met me and was in the room when General Hodges carefully but forcefully gave me my first lesson from a general in air discipline. I well remember George's presence. I knew he was there as a friend, and I knew he had prepared the way for me. The lecture was positive and the alternatives carefully drawn. I had been guilty of a flagrant violation of air discipline.

"After it was over, George assured me what General Hodges had said was in my, the group's, and the Air Force's best interests."[22]

His rating officer made the following evaluation of Brown's performance as executive officer, operations, Headquarters, 93rd Bomb Group, and as assistant A-3 for operations, Headquarters, 20th Bomb Division:

"A conscientious, capable young outstanding officer, honest and alert in all duties assigned or assumed by him. . . . In my opinion this officer has capabilities, both mental and physical, to develop into an outstanding commander and/or staff officer. For his age and service he has carried out his responsibilities of command and leadership in combat in an outstanding manner."

On October 1, 1944, George Brown, only three years and four months out of West Point, was promoted to colonel. Tom Corbin, who had also risen rapidly, reflected, "I believe there were only three of us in the Class of 1941 who were promoted to colonel before the end of World War II. I simply outlived everybody, but in George's case it was skill."[23]

His final rating officer in Europe, Col. Robert H. Terrill, in covering Brown's service from July 1, 1944, until December 31, 1944, was brief but laudatory: "An exceptionally intelligent, capable, and forceful young officer whose qualities of leadership, judgment, and common sense have been developed far beyond his years."

On November 9, 1944, George Brown left the European theater of operations and returned to the United States. Although he did not realize it at that time, his work with the Eighth Air Force was finished.

NOTES

1. Personal interview with Col. Carl Barthel, USAF (Ret.), May 17, 1979.
2. Ibid.
3. Personal interview with Brig. Gen. Thomas W. Brown, USA (Ret.), August 8, 1979.
4. Barthel interview.
5. Personal interview with Lt. Gen. Edward J. Timberlake, USAF (Ret.), July 18, 1979.
6. Barthel interview.
7. Gen. George S. Brown's diary, December 30, 1943.

8. Paraphrased from a personal interview with Mrs. Thoburn K. Brown, August 8, 1979.
9. Barthel interview.
10. Ibid.
11. Ibid.
12. Dugan, James and Carrol Stewart, *Ploesti* (New York: Random House, 1961), p. 93.
13. Ibid, p. 117.
14. Ibid.
15. Barthel interview.
16. Dugan and Stewart, *Ploesti,* pp. 128–29.
17. Personal interview with Gen. Jacob Smart, USAF (Ret.), July 17, 1979.
18. Brown's diary.
19. Personal interview with Col. Burton C. Andrus, USAF (Ret.), June 28, 1979.
20. Barthel interview.
21. Thomas Brown interview.
22. Personal interview with Lt. Gen. George S. Boylan, Jr., USAF (Ret.), April 27, 1980.
23. Personal interview with Maj. Gen. Thomas C. Corbin, USAF (Ret.), June 29, 1979.

PART TWO
BETWEEN WARS AND THE KOREAN CONFLICT

CHAPTER 5

FORT WORTH, TEXAS, AND BARKSDALE FIELD, LOUISIANA: MAY 1945–NOVEMBER 1946

Col. George Brown arrived in the United States on November 10, 1944, and was sent directly to Atlantic City, New Jersey, the nearest rest and rehabilitation point. Skip joined him there, and she recalls that their stay lasted far longer than they expected: "We went thinking we were going to be there for two weeks," said Mrs. Brown. "As it turned out, time dragged on and on and on, and we were there through Christmas. There wasn't much to do except eat and drink and sleep and walk on the frozen Boardwalk. We got thoroughly tired of it. I learned to play shuffleboard and beat George for about three weeks. Finally he got mad at that, so he started beating me religiously. He was like that. He would let himself be beaten for just so long and then would start to win. He was a fierce competitor, and that spirit of competition was displayed in fishing, tennis, everything. And he enjoyed it even more if there was a bet on, or if the competition was really good."[1]

His departure from Atlantic City was delayed due to uncertainties caused by the initial success of the Ardennes offensive launched by the Germans in mid-December. "George was instrumental in keeping morale reasonably high," recalled classmate Ed McGough. "He acted not only as an unofficial 'master of ceremonies,' but also as leader of our singing sessions.

His seemingly unlimited repertoire of songs and jokes did much to keep the spirits of both the men and their wives from slumping. The fact that he was a colonel and a war hero, and still was willing to be one of the group, was not lost on most of those present. I believe his lack of aloofness was a trait which enhanced his leadership throughout his career." [2]

Mrs. Brown tells the final story about that rest and rehabilitation period: "In the hotel one day, someone asked him, 'George, did you get your assignment back to England?' I thought, 'What in the world is that man talking about? George isn't going back to England. He's home. He's just done two-and-a-half years.'

" 'What did that man mean?' I asked him later. It turned out that guy of mine had in fact requested another overseas assignment. He was so gung-ho that he had come home, checked on me, and without my knowing it, put in to go back for another tour. Well, I guess we had a few words, but since he didn't get that assignment, he was 'saved by the bell.' " [3]

After his leave in Atlantic City, Brown was assigned to Headquarters, Army Air Force Training Command, Fort Worth, Texas, on January 1, 1945. Initially, he was Assistant Chief of Staff A–3 (Operations) and Chief of the Pilot Training Section. Then in February of 1946, he was assigned to Barksdale Field, where he served in Operations Division.

Lt. Gen. Albert P. Clark describes the impression that Brown made at Barksdale: "George Brown at that time was what everybody would call a 'young' colonel who had come up really fast during the war as a result of his outstanding performance. He was very circumspect and quiet, a dignified guy who was not at all pushy. He was personable, articulate, and fine-looking and had a wonderful family. Even back then, you could see he 'had all the tickets.' " [4]

Clark had graduated from West Point five years ahead of George Brown and was one of the senior officers at Barksdale. He had had the great misfortune of spending World War II as a prisoner of war. When he was asked if there had been any jealousy toward Brown because of his rapid rise in rank, he remarked, "George Brown was entitled to all the rank and prestige he could get for his performance in the war. He was a very young officer who had performed brilliantly in several leadership roles. He had a fine personality, and there wasn't anything shifty or difficult about his relationships with others. He was always warm, friendly, and comfortable with people. No one ever felt ill at ease with him, and his rapid rise in rank certainly didn't bother me at all." [5]

It had, however, bothered others. As it happened, Col. Thoburn Brown, George's father, was also stationed in North Africa at the time George was there with the 93rd Bomb Group. "I remember the old man giving him hell," said Barthel. "He told George, 'What's a young whippersnapper like you doing as a colonel?' His father just could not understand a man being a colonel before he was thirty."[6]

Indeed, Brown's rapid rise in rank sometimes caused him some discomfort. "I can remember going to a West Point football game in Yankee Stadium," said Tim Brown. "At halftime, I happened to run into George and Skip. It was interesting: we were down where the faculty had their seats, many contemporaries of my father, all colonels, professors at West Point, and there was George, also a full colonel. I think George was embarrassed."[7]

Whatever his own feelings about his position, however, it is clear that his superiors found him entirely deserving of his rank. While assigned to Headquarters, Army Air Force Training Command, following his return to the United States, Col. E. W. Suarez, his rating officer for the first six months of 1945, wrote: "An outstanding young officer who readily adapts himself to newly assigned duties. He is enthusiastic, well-mannered, conscientious, and extremely capable. His intelligence and initiative enable him to carry out assigned duties in a superior manner. . . . With additional experience, he should develop into a well-rounded staff officer."

A similar evaluation was given by Col. Clifford H. Rees, who summed up his performance from July 1, 1945, to December 31, 1945, by stating, "Colonel Brown has proven in combat to be outstanding. He has a clever and ingenious mind. Colonel Brown's judgment is not backed by sufficient experience. He is, however, eager, conscientious, and loyal and will develop into one of the outstanding officers of the Army."

The developmental road that Brown traveled during this period was not an entirely smooth one. Some of the problems he encountered are described by Maj. Gen. Thomas C. Corbin, who was stationed at Barksdale with Brown. "When I arrived at Barksdale, I was assigned to the Inspector General's office. George was already there, working in Operations under Tom Darcy. It was a hell of an operation, and when I think over all of George's assignments, I consider that this was probably one of the most difficult. Darcy was a most difficult man to work for, unreasonable at times, and quick-tempered. He was a brigadier general at the time, and George and I were colonels. We were the new boys on the street, and there were a lot of old-timers who had been around for quite some time whom we had equal rank with, or outranked, because of our combat promotions and experience. There was quite a bit of resentment toward us 'young bucks,' full colonels at twenty-five or twenty-six.

"George performed a very difficult task and did it amazingly well. Merely working for Tom Darcy was difficult enough; but in addition,

George had a big job in its own right—Operations of the Training Command, which at that time was the Air Corps' largest command. As Deputy Chief of Operations, he was responsible for supervising both the Technical Training Command and the Flying Training Command. It covered a broad scope, and it took a very capable man to handle it."[8]

While at Barksdale, Corbin and Brown served under Maj. Gen. Alvin C. Kincaid. "He was the meanest man in the world," said Corbin. "He was chief of staff and used to love to chew George and me out; he chewed us out at every available opportunity. Kincaid was under General Cannon, who was an excellent general, but Kincaid was scared to death of Cannon. George and I both managed to get along with Kincaid, but by then we had learned to get along with all sorts of people."[9]

Further insight into some of the problems Brown encountered with his senior officers is provided by Col. Burt Andrus. "Barksdale Field in 1946 and 1947 was not an easy billet," he recalled. "George was working for one of the most paranoid brigadier generals in the Air Force. Our commander, Joe Cannon, was a highly respected commander, with a brilliant war record. With the war over, there really wasn't a tremendous amount of pressure, unless it was induced internally. But General Cannon brought with him, as his chief of staff, a man who was as difficult as anyone I've ever known. In addition, the other key staff officer under Cannon was a brigadier general who, in my opinion, was almost paranoid. Cannon was running the command as a commanding general should, but one problem was his chief of staff, Tom Darcy. Darcy was a hyperactive guy, hard to live with. Of course, George, one of the key men under Darcy, was perceived as 'little boy colonel.' He handled the situation extremely well, because that's the kind of officer he was. George would not transmit pressure put on him to those below him. He played the buffer, and it takes a real man to do that. He was highly regarded by his contemporaries. I knew the kind of men who were up there above him. George was always a calming influence in the face of two very difficult general officers who were trying to do things but could not get them done."[10]

Darcy was not kind to George in his efficiency report for the period from January 1, 1946, to June 30, 1946. Darcy said of his performance: "This officer appears to be inherently capable and qualified to do an assigned task. As a staff officer, he seems hesitant to take an aggressive attitude for fear of acting contrary to popular opinion or accepted routine. Better qualified to follow than to lead."

This effectiveness report was quite a blow to George. "I was back from Japan in Tucson," recalled his brother, Tim, "and George flew over from Barksdale to visit me. During our visit he told me about the bad efficiency report. 'I don't know what I'm going to do about it,' he said. 'I guess there's nothing I can do about it. It's sure not very good.' Five was as good as General Darcy gave any of his officers. It may have been good in his opinion, but it certainly wasn't good in George's eyes. As far as I know, it was the only time he ever had any difficulty with an efficiency report."[11]

Despite his problems with Darcy, however, Brown was recognized by others. Charles W. Richards, for example, wrote a one-sentence word picture: "A creative officer with ability to express himself clearly and to see the necessity for corrective or other action."

There was clearly a need for corrective action at Barksdale then. "George and I had a difficult management problem at Barksdale," said Burt Andrus. "We were in Training Command with the wartime draft still going on, with recruiters still recruiting the way they had during hostilities. We had people coming into the service who had been given great, grandiose promises by the recruiters; if you enlisted you could go anywhere you wanted; you could go to Europe, see the ruins, all that good stuff. Yet the budget was being cut back, with personnel reductions going on, and we couldn't deliver on these promises. We were getting letters from congressmen to General Cannon, and General Cannon was passing these letters on to General Kincaid. Kincaid was constantly on the phone, shrieking at people because some guy who had enlisted in Timbuktu was promised he would be trained as an aircraft mechanic and that he would be in downtown Paris tomorrow. Our military structure was being compressed too rapidly, and nearly all experienced people were being separated from the service. At the same time, the pipeline was feeding draftees in, and we had no way to accommodate them.

"Let me give you a good example. I flew up to Scott Field on a staff visit and saw two hundred men on their hands and knees on the parade ground cutting grass with hand sickles just to keep them busy. Failing that, the men would go AWOL, get into fights. Black troops and white troops were still segregated in those days, but there were problems between blacks and whites anyway. So George was trying to structure an almost impossible thing. How could we keep moving these people through the Training Command pipeline? The Air Force desperately needed them because so many of the experienced people were getting out. Commanders were screaming for people, yet our training facilities were in such a compression state that the manpower input could not flow through the pipeline. We found that on some bases, the pipeline had become so constricted that there was over a year's supply of recruits and draftees waiting to get into training.

"This was the kind of problem George had to solve. He had the responsibility of trying to manage the people through various training programs, quite an array of training requirements: telephone operators, firemen, cooks, bakers, mechanics—the whole gamut, probably over a hundred different training categories in all.

"Another example is, let us say, aircraft mechanics. The course would have normally entered two hundred men a week, but between the time they'd been screened down at the base and you started them in training, a span of four or five weeks, we would be told suddenly to reduce the input from two hundred men to only one hundred because of budget cuts. These men comprising the one hundred surplus became very disgruntled. They had been told they were going to do something specific and instead were pulled out of the program just before entering technical school. Unfortunately, the people above us thought you could solve the problems by screaming at colonels."[12]

Burt Andrus was lucky enough to have been extricated from this rather dismal situation by his transfer to Hickam. Brown, however, remained at Barksdale. Yet because of his motivation to constantly improve himself, he managed to create situations that would lend value to what could otherwise have been an almost completely unproductive period.

While at Barksdale, George did a great deal of flying. "Quite often we would go out on weekends," said Tom Corbin, "just for the hell of it but, of course, what we were looking to do was to stay proficient. We would fly anything we could get: PT–13s, C–47s, A–26s, B–24s, or anything else that was available."[13]

A good perspective on Brown's career during this period is provided by Maj. Gen. Thomas C. Darcy. "I do not feel any comment on the 1946–47 period is complete," said General Darcy, "without some reference to the mood of the Air Force in those days.

> There are probably as many interpretations of that mood as there are pseudo-analysts but, for my book and at the risk of oversimplification, one might divide our Air Force Officer Corps of those days into three (3) basic categories somewhat along the following lines:
>
> A. The Washington Inner Circle—those concerned primarily, if not exclusively, with the transition of the Air Force to a position of legal equality, separate and distinct from the Army and Navy.
>
> B. The Happy-It's-Over Group—those Air Force officers who felt that the task of winning the war was accomplished, and that there wasn't much reason to worry about anything else for the moment.

C. The Back-to-the-Drawing Board Group—those few officers who recognized the problems ahead and realized the need for rebuilding.

In the framework, I believe that category B was far in the majority, and I feel that George Brown had adapted himself well to the majority. He was young, had a fine war record, was very personable in his associations, and was obviously very anxious to "get along." He didn't make waves. He fit into the picture naturally and easily.

General Darcy went on to place George Brown in further perspective by saying: "To me, there is a very pronounced parallel between the careers of General Brown and Gen. Earle Wheeler of the Army. They seem to have been cut from the same cloth. Although the thought that either or both would ever become Chairman of the Joint Chiefs was not a matter for my consideration in the late 1940s, it is highly unlikely that I would have made predictions in that direction in either case. In retrospect, however, both were naturals for the job. Both were very much in tune with the times, and both (still in retrospect) were possessed of those characteristics which American political authorities look for in their 'leaders' in time of peace."[14]

NOTES

1. Personal interview with Mrs. George S. Brown, August 7, 1979.
2. Letter from Maj. Gen. Edward A. McGough, III, USAF (Ret.), to EFP, August 27, 1979.
3. Mrs. George S. Brown interview.
4. Personal interview with Lt. Gen. Albert P. Clark, USAF (Ret.), June 29, 1979.
5. Ibid.
6. Personal interview with Col. Carl Barthel, USAF (Ret.), May 17, 1979.
7. Personal interview with Brig. Gen. Thomas W. Brown, USA (Ret.), August 8, 1979.
8. Personal interview with Maj. Gen. Thomas C. Corbin, USAF (Ret.), June 29, 1979.
9. Ibid.
10. Personal interview with Col. Burton C. Andrus, USAF (Ret.), June 28, 1979.
11. Thomas W. Brown interview.
12. Andrus interview.
13. Corbin interview.
14. Letter from Maj. Gen. Thomas C. Darcy, USAF (Ret.), to EFP, March 11, 1980.

CHAPTER 6
MITCHEL FIELD, NEW YORK: DECEMBER 1946–JUNE 1950

In December of 1946, Col. George Brown was assigned to Mitchel Field, New York. First he was assistant to the chief of staff for Air, and then was made chief of the ROTC Branch. On July 1, 1947, he became assistant chief of staff for Operations for Air Defense Command Headquarters. He assisted the chief of staff in carrying out the mission of the Operations Division, which consisted of establishing requirements for, and implementing the air defense of, the continental United States; the training and the administrative supervision of units assigned to Air Defense Command; Air Force components, the organization and manning of Air Defense units; tactical air cooperation with surface forces; and the organization and training of reserve forces.

His rating officer during this period of time was Col. Bruce K. Holloway, an Air Force officer with a brilliant combat record in the Pacific during World War II. He wrote of George Brown: "This officer possesses the tempered judgment of a normal man of twice his service and experience. He is a natural leader, capable of a large quantity of efficient and completed work, and possessed with an unusual degree of initiative, intelligence, and quiet force."

Others also recognized Brown's capabilities. "In 1948, I was on the staff of Gen. George Stratemeyer," said then Col. Jacob E. Smart, "as his deputy for Operations at Mitchel Field. I had the option, of course, of choosing my own assistants, so I chose as my assistant George Brown, even though he was much junior to every other colonel that worked for me. There were some twenty officers in my office, and perhaps fifteen of them were full colonels. I made it very clear to all of them who were senior to George that I had selected him because of the quality of his thinking, and that seniority had no bearing on it. It soon became clear to them that he was a superior thinker and doer. So he earned his position on his own personal merit and had the respect of those much senior to him."[1]

Brown and his fellow officers had their work cut out for them during this period. "We were in the throes of reorganization," recalled Lt. Gen. Herbert A. Thatcher, "trying to assemble bits and pieces of the Tactical Air Command and getting the Air Defense Command started. I think we had four groups scattered throughout the United States. The reserve forces— the Fourteenth Air Force, the Fourth Air Force, and the Tenth Air Force— were better organized than the regular forces at that time, although their manning was poor. There was a surplus of retired and reserve officers, and we had to set up the principles for them of what was active reserve, flying reserve, and inactive reserve. The Air Defense Command took most of our time, and George and I spent many hours in Washington, first at the Pentagon getting the plans approved, and then going to Congress to get the money."[2]

During his association with General Thatcher, George got his first exposure to the workings of Congress. "It seemed as though we were before fifty-two congressional committees in one year," continued Thatcher. "George was always with me, handing me notes, prompting me, correcting me, and occasionally speaking in response to questions and queries—my right-hand man. Our job was to sell the concept of an adequate air defense for the United States. We sold the concept of three air forces throughout the country, of the northern tier, and of the Dew Line, which became an enormous radar complex throughout the country. George also put my position reports together, after which we worked out the principles. He did much of the preliminary work on these papers in organizing our posture.

"As a staff officer, you don't have much opportunity to exercise military leadership as it is normally thought of. Leadership in a staff context is mostly derived from intelligence. George handled the staff extremely well, working smoothly with everybody."

Brown's personal capabilities were also evident at Mitchel Field. "He was absolutely honest," continued General Thatcher. "He abhorred mediocrity, as we all did. This may have been his one fault, if he had a fault. He simply could not stand people who didn't produce, and he wouldn't tolerate them. But he also possessed a great understanding of human nature. He was quick on his feet with a ready answer to most questions. If he didn't know the answer, he would say, 'I don't know.' "[3]

Summing up Brown's performance at this point in his career, Colonel Smart in his rating dated July 8, 1949, wrote: "As Assistant, and as Acting Deputy for Operations, it has been necessary for this officer to assume responsibility for the control, supervision and direction of Directors on the ConAC staff, many senior to him in grade and years. This he has done unflinchingly and in such a manner as has earned for him the admiration and respect of officers both senior and junior to him."

In the latter part of 1949, Gen. Ennis Whitehead took over command of what had been Air Defense Command, now redesignated Continental Air Command. General Whitehead, concluding that there was no adequate war plan existing for the air defense of the United States, promptly put together a group to create one.

"We had a team engaged in developing a new war plan for General Whitehead," recalled then Lieutenant Colonel Yudkin. "It started out with over twenty people but was subsequently reduced. George Brown joined the group and became the key element in it. He was designated to run things, and we knew that, and there was no uncertainty about it. But the fact remained that in the arguments and discussions that took place within the group, he had to defend his ideas and his positions every step of the way. This he did, and in such a manner as to leave no question about his competence and his ability. In our planning group he established his leadership entirely by the quality of the contribution he made to it, without regard to what he wore on his shoulders."

The nature of the group's responsibilities is further developed by Yudkin. "We were forever being trotted around to various locations throughout the country to present our proposed war plan. Once Whitehead took us to SAC Headquarters at Offutt Air Force Base, in Omaha. George was with us and was really the key man among the working level people. The SAC group were briefing Gen. Curtis E. LeMay, Gen. Thomas Power, Gen. Walter Sweeney, Gen. J. B. Montgomery, and several others. Our group had Generals Whitehead and Myers, but the rest of us were colonels. We got into this meeting and the big wheels were sitting up at one end of the room. They were carrying on their conversation, and at some particular point in the thing, George apparently didn't understand what was being said and wanted some clarification. George spoke up, and I can remember to this day how the entire group of SAC generals turned as one person, starting with LeMay, to see who this upstart colonel was who dared to speak up from the other end of the table. Apparently that wasn't done at Omaha. But, George pursued his point and got his answer. He was not one who could be overwhelmed, buffaloed, or intimidated."[4]

Brown's capabilities were clearly recognized by his senior officers at Mitchel. "There was," said Jacob Smart, "a deliberate effort on the part of some senior Air Force people to assist in his development and advancement. One of them was Ennis Whitehead, a superb person with many qualities of leadership, both positive and negative. He once told me that he recognized George Brown as a man of unusual capacity and had encouraged his growth, recommending George's assignment to positions that would further broaden him."[5]

Whitehead himself commented on June 9, 1950, in his endorsement to George's effectiveness report, "Of all colonels of 15 years of service or less, I rate Brown number one. In my judgment, he is the most competent officer of a similar length of service whom I have ever known."

It was during that tour in Headquarters, Continental Air Command, that Brown got his first opportunity to work closely with the air force of another country. Continental Air Command was developing an air defense capability for all of North America. The United States recognized the necessity of our having a common defense system with Canada.

General Smart describes this part of his assignment at Mitchel Field and, in so doing, emphasizes its role in Brown's professional development. "This introduced an interesting aspect of the work I was doing during the period when George Brown was my deputy. The Canadian personnel had a job comparable to ours, and we began working closely together without much pomp and circumstance. For example, a phone call would suffice to set up a visit by one of our people to Canada, or by a Canadian Air Force officer to us. George Brown had a lot to do with these arrangements and with the setting up of the defense plans themselves. This, of course, added to the scope of George's experience and his capacity as an air officer."[6]

Despite the time required for his new responsibilities, Brown kept his flying proficiency well honed during this period. "While George was stationed at Mitchel," said Burton Andrus, "I was at West Point, serving as a tactical officer. George and I would often get together to fly. There were not too many full colonels who would get into an airplane, climb into the left-hand seat, and take the responsibility of flying themselves. The usual method was to have a major fly the airplane with the colonel flying as co-pilot or command pilot or something else, because when you were working the kind of hours that most staff officers had to work, you could not be as proficient and sharp in the cockpit as you might be. But George never let that trouble him. We would sometimes take off in the dirtiest kind of weather, and he would fly the outleg and I the backleg. This was typical of

George; he was not the kind of fellow who would let his flying proficiency escape from him. He was just as sharp a pilot then as he had ever been. He had a lot of natural ability, plus a high degree of mental and physical coordination. He felt that maintaining his fitness and flying proficiency was simply part of his job."[7]

"General Whitehead and Gen. Charlie Myers, who was Vice Commander, leaned on George Brown a lot. He was an awfully fine front man, very articulate, very personable," said Gen. Albert P. Clark. When asked what he meant by "front man," Clark responded, "Well, when somebody would have to make a speech on short notice, George would be asked to do it. They could always count on him to give an outstanding performance and make a good impression for the command wherever he went. I remember when he went up to Connecticut on very short notice to make a speech, representing General Whitehead. It had been an extremely busy day, and he had to leave Headquarters at the end of it, jump into an airplane, and give the speech that night. But that kind of thing never bothered George at all."[8]

Summing up George Brown's years at Mitchel Field, General Smart stated, "George was used to hard work. We kept up an intense pace because the work demanded it. He was not bound by habit, but was a man who responded to whatever the situation was. If the mission required working long hours, he worked long hours. If it didn't, he would get out and play golf or squash, go swimming, or spend time with his family."[9]

Finally this staff assignment came to an end and Col. George S. Brown returned to what he loved most, command, not in bombers, but in a new aircraft and a new mission: transport aircraft and troop carrier duty.

NOTES

1. Personal interview with Gen. Jacob E. Smart, USAF (Ret.), July 17, 1979.
2. Personal interview with Lt. Gen. Herbert A. Thatcher, June 17, 1980.
3. Ibid.
4. Personal interview with Maj. Gen. Richard A. Yudkin, USAF (Ret.), July 30, 1979.
5. Smart interview.
6. Ibid.
7. Personal interview with Col. Burton C. Andrus, USAF (Ret.), June 28, 1979.
8. Personal interview with Lt. Gen. Albert P. Clark, USAF (Ret.), June 29, 1979.
9. Smart interview.

CHAPTER 7

McCHORD AIR FORCE BASE, WASHINGTON: JULY 1950–JULY 1951

On July 17, 1950, Col. George Brown assumed command of the 62nd Troop Carrier Group at McChord Air Force Base, Washington. All personnel of the 62nd had been shifted to McChord on TDY (temporary duty) from its home station, Kelly Air Force Base, Texas, to form one of the elements that came to be known as the Korean airlift. Its mission was twofold: to transport reinforcements to Korea and to bring the wounded back to the United States.

It was an assignment Brown was pleased to receive. One of the officers stationed with him at McChord, Adriel N. Williams, recalls that Brown had remarked that he took this command because he wanted to serve in all parts of the Air Force during his career.[1]

Early in this assignment, Brown had to reorient himself and his personnel to a mission that was not consistent with their training and background. While operating air emergency transportation services to the Orient, they had the added challenge of replacing their C–126 aircraft with C–119s, not a simple task.

Brown's wing commander at McChord, Col. Richard F. Bromily, wrote at the end of Brown's tour, "He does all possible to achieve high morale and safe operation. In spite of difficulties . . . and faced with the problems of leading an organization serving on temporary duty from its home station, which created a multiplicity of personnel problems, this officer continuously maintained his organization in a state of readiness so that it could perform unannounced missions on short notice.''

Brown's "can-do" outlook helped him accomplish the task before him. Courtney Faught, a member of the group at McChord, stated: "Because we were a troop carrier outfit, TDY to McChord and serving temporarily under MATS, we had to combine missions of the organizations in many ways diametrically opposite to their functions. Even though we used some of the same equipment, our missions were quite different. The troop carriers were under Tactical Air Command, yet we were assigned to MATS to fly the Korean airlift. MATS had some operational policies that just did not fit our situation. We voiced our opinion on them, but the MATS people were not listening to us. Our concern was that these discrepancies in policies made it dangerous for the crews. But Colonel Brown took the bull by the horns and went to the MATS commander above us, Maj. Gen. J. S. Stowell. George and the general finally came to an understanding, and the general told the MATS people who were giving us the trouble to 'knock it off.' ''[2]

General Stowell was obviously impressed, and he subsequently characterized Brown's performance at McChord as "outstanding in all respects." For the first time there appeared on one of George Brown's evaluations the comment, "Potential general officer."

Brown's search for improvement included the personal as well as the professional aspects of his men's welfare. Courtney Faught again provided a good example: "When the Korean War broke out, all the men were shipped TDY to McChord Air Force Base and the families remained at Kelly. Instead of living in quarters or in places off the base with our families, we were living in bachelor officers' quarters. They were essentially World War II-type barracks, with big, open bays; not even the bathrooms had any partitions. George didn't care for this, and so he got after the base commander and pestered him until finally he found some money to put in partitions for the latrines and the rooms. George Brown got these rooms for every officer and airman in the group."

Brown's success in accomplishing his ends at McChord came from the full support of his subordinates, instilled by his reciprocal loyalty to them. "We always appreciated the fact that he had short staff meetings," reflected Courtney Faught. "He knew what he wanted, said what he wanted, and our job was to go out and do it. What I particularly appreciated was that he was willing to take a gamble at times on the advice he got from his subordinates. The advice wasn't always right, but he would stand up and defend those people to his superiors even though they had sometimes given him a bad steer. I think a big part of George's leadership was that everybody wanted to do whatever he wanted them to do."[3]

Another reason that Brown instilled such loyalty is that he was willing to listen to their points of view. Adriel N. Williams, an officer assigned to the 62nd Troop Carrier Command, during his career briefed several chiefs of staff. He commented, "There was a similarity between General White's and General Brown's approaches in that they were extremely kind to briefing officers. Generals LeMay and McConnell were often very curt. I remember that George Brown while at McChord, and also as Chief of Staff, would still hear you out even if he had already made up his mind, and never let you know."[4]

Gen. Courtney Faught amplified the comments of General Williams: "One of Brown's great attributes was his ability to listen to a briefing or a conversation. He would be able to get to the crux of the thing really long before you finished your briefing, but I was impressed with the fact that he would always hear you out." I asked why George Brown would do this, since it could often result in waste of time, and General Faught responded, "In some cases he might have saved some time. However, he believed that he might learn something further from the briefing that would be advantageous to him. He realized that it would be devastating to cut short an officer who had worked hard on a briefing."[5]

Concerning time that might be wasted by being patient and listening to the briefing, Brown told Faught that he would simply make up the time later. He said, "If you want to keep your friends, even if you have a stringent schedule, the briefing should be done without cutting people off."[6]

Brown's feeling for the personal aspects of his men's lives was exhibited in many other ways during this period. General Faught recalls one of them. "He would not jeopardize his schedule but managed to make time for his people. The weather at McChord Air Force Base was challenging, with what are called Northern Maritime Fronts, which result in low fog and drizzle most of the time. But once in a while, when the overcast would break and the sun would come out, George would call us in and say, 'Okay, get your sticks; we're going to the golf course!' Then we would play golf while the sun shone and make up the time by working at night. You might think that all commanders would do something like this, but that is not so. It was an unusual experience to run into a commander like George Brown. Instead of working us twenty-four hours a day, seven days a week, he was able to get an outstanding job done with reasonable hours. He was always on top of the job, and was always self-assured—with enough confidence in his abilities to know that he could do this sort of thing without any recrimination from his bosses. He was getting the job done; he knew it, and his bosses knew it."[7]

A strong family man himself, Brown was also concerned with the relationships of his men to their families. "While at McChord Air Force Base," reflected General Faught, "our families remained at Kelly Air Force Base. This created a serious morale problem for our people. George called the maintenance people and explained to them the number of airplanes we needed in commission to fulfill our daily schedule in flying troops over to Japan and bringing back the wounded. He decided that if we could keep the required number of aircraft in commission, we could also operate a shuttle between McChord and Kelly, to enable our people to fly back to see their families occasionally. He set up a roster so that about every two-and-a-half weeks, the lowest airman to the highest ranking officer could take trips to Kelly to visit their families."[8]

Brown was, of course, a full colonel at McChord Air Force Base and commanded a provisional wing which was under another colonel senior to him. "I can't remember his name offhand," said General Faught, "but I believe that he felt some jealousy toward George. Brown did not buck him in the day-to-day routine of carrying out the mission, just did what he was told and delivered more than what was asked of him. So, this colonel tried to take it out on George's subordinate commanders. George had put four of us in for promotion, but that colonel was not going to have any part of us being promoted. He believed that we were simply troop carrier personnel not deserving of promotion. George informed him that he was going to see General Stowell personally about the matter, but before that occurred, the commander gave in and agreed to the recommendations for promotion. None of us ever forgot this effort on George's part."[9] Nor did this go unnoticed with Brown's rating officer, Col. Richard F. Bromily, who wrote, "He is loyal to his people and his organization to a fault."

While at McChord, Brown continued to maintain his flying proficiency. "George," said Courtney Faught, "was a very good pilot as commanders go. By that I mean that that's not the commander's primary job, so he wouldn't get to fly as much as the crews, and certainly not as much as George wanted to fly. Brown was checked out in all aircraft types that we flew, particularly the C-54s and the C-124s."[10]

He also did his best to stay in good physical condition. "Every day after work," remembered General Faught, "we'd change our clothes and go to the gym. George was a great squash player, but at McChord we had no squash courts. They had a handball court, so we made some homemade wooden rackets, about three times the size of a Ping-Pong paddle. We then played on the handball court with squash rules and called it paddle ball. We had a competitive ladder, and George was always at the top. He was a very good athlete, and I still have the scars to show how competitive he was."[11]

General Faught made a comment about him that gets to the heart of his ability as a leader: "When George Brown would walk into a room filled either with subordinates or superiors, he never made any fuss, never made any noise, but he had a certain presence. He exuded self-confidence and self-assurance. I think the thing that impressed me the most was his quiet air of authority."[12]

The thing General Williams remembered best about George Brown was that "he was the world's greatest listener. He would always listen to you, and you felt that you had his undivided attention."[13] But this great listener would speak up for his organization and his people when needed.

After leaving the European theater of operations after World War II, George Brown had been assigned to staff duty, so his tour with the 62nd was his first command responsibility since the war. Brown continued to exhibit his abilities and high standards throughout his tour at McChord, yet this was but a formative stage in his development. Now he was destined for another new challenge, this time in fighter interceptors.

NOTES

1. Personal interview with Brig. Gen. Adriel N. Williams, USAF (Ret.), August 6, 1979.
2. Personal interview with Maj. Gen. Courtney L. Faught, USAF (Ret.), August 6, 1979.
3. Ibid.
4. Williams interview.
5. Faught interview.
6. Ibid.
7. Ibid.
8. Ibid.
9. Ibid.
10. Ibid.
11. Ibid.
12. Ibid.
13. Williams interview.

CHAPTER 8

SELFRIDGE AIR FORCE BASE, MICHIGAN: JULY 1951–APRIL 1952

In July 1951, after one year with troop carriers, George S. Brown was assigned to Selfridge Air Force Base, Michigan, as commander of the 56th Fighter-Interceptor Wing, a part of the Air Defense Command. Selfridge, an air base with one of the finest histories in the United States Air Force, had always been a fighter base. Brown's World War II background was as a bomber pilot, and he had just commanded a troop transport unit. "He'd been a big bird man, four engines," reflected then Col. Ernest J. White, who was a veteran fighter pilot from World War II and Korea stationed at Selfridge when Brown arrived. "In fact, he said to me once that the only thing he didn't like about an aircraft that had four engines was that it would have been better if it had eight."[1]

In addition to commanding the fighter wing at Selfridge, his responsibilities included the support of an air base headquarters, the headquarters of an air division, and a number of outlying facilities. Another fellow officer stationed at Selfridge, Col. Frank Rogers, put Brown's assignment into perspective: "We were at the Indian level, away from the so-called big thinking of national defense planning. When you're a colonel running a fighter wing at a place like Selfridge, with three or four outfits at outlying stations underneath you, you're dealing with the day-to-day problems of needing so many airplanes combat ready, seeing that the guy in the guardhouse gets his meals, making sure that the pilot had enough breakfast when he gets in the airplane so he doesn't pass out at the controls, taking care of the community relationships, and making sure that the chapel functions. It's a different ball game. I think it's important to know that one of the great things that George had going for him was that he understood the little guy operating in the field without much talent, in many cases, to help him. It was an assignment that stood him in good stead in the Air Force in preparing him for the top jobs he later received."[2]

One of Brown's initial problems at Selfridge was his less than cordial welcome by his subordinates. Albert S. Kelly, then a lieutenant colonel, recalled:

> I first met George when he came to Selfridge as the new Wing commander. Most of us looked forward to having a jet fighter pilot as the new C.O. Well, the word leaked out that we were going to get a new C.O. of the Wing that had *never flown fighters,* was currently a troop carrier pilot and, of all things, a *bomber type* prior to that! We were sorely disappointed—to say the least!
>
> As time passed, we began to hear of Colonel Brown's war record—the Ploesti raids, his other actions in combat, his rapid promotion from second lieutenant to full colonel, a West Pointer yet! Well, sure, that answers all the questions! No wonder he got promoted so fast. Anyhow, the setting was not what the fighter jocks had in mind, even at having such a distinguished War Hero in our midst. Our false pride perhaps, our arrogance perhaps, or just our plain selfishness put our attitude beyond our better judgment. We were going to accept him, because we had to, but we were not going to be happy about it.
>
> Little did we know that we were about to witness, and become a part of one of the finest organizations in the Air Force.[3]

Ernest White further reflected, "It's very difficult to understand how a man with his background could take over a fighter wing and do such a terrific job with it in such a short time. He really wasn't there as long as I'm sure he and Skip would like to have been, but it was enough to leave a great impact on his officers and noncoms."[4]

How did he improve the effectiveness of his far-flung command? One thing was to focus as quickly as possible on the core of the problems that arose. "One of the things," said White, "which demonstrated his leadership was to establish a new procedure for staff meetings, which began at eight o'clock in the morning. Before George took over, they would go on for hours. He ordered the meetings be a maximum of half an hour, so at 0830 either the first sergeant or the adjutant would hold up his hand, and Brown would stand up and say, 'Okay, the meeting's over. Anyone that has any additional items that they want to bring up, put them in writing. If you have any comments about the meeting today, send them up to me in writing and I'll read them before I get out of here today.' "

Brown was always attentive to the views and suggestions of others, regardless of rank. "During the course of those meetings," continued White, "I never heard him raise his voice or get excited about someone challenging his views or those of his senior staff officers. In our meetings there would be captains, lieutenants, and sergeants. Everyone was encouraged to speak up. Because some guy was a colonel didn't make any difference. A captain might have a better idea, and George would accept it."[5]

A specific example of Brown's attention to the views of his subordinates was given by Albert Kelly. "George also had weekly meetings of both his wing staff and the fighter squadrons and their support units. I shall never forget my first such meeting as a squadron commander. I sat through the meeting listening with glee as some of the major staff directors were squirming as they tried to answer some of George's penetrating questions. Then he asked if the fighter group commander had anything to say. Col. Francis Gabreski was the group commander then, and Gabby said, 'No, sir.' So George said, 'Well then, since the group commander has no problems perhaps the squadron commanders have a few.' It just so happened that he called on me first. Not being a timid type, and knowing full well that I might be in hot water with the group commander, I nevertheless stated, 'Colonel, I couldn't cover half the problems that the fighter squadrons have in a whole day, let alone the time allotted thus far.' I was serious, for we did have problems that had been neglected. Brown replied, 'Fine, Kelly, I will meet you in the morning at 0800 in my office and I will devote the whole day to you and you can bring me "up to speed" (one of his favorite sayings) on them.' Needless to say, I spent a very busy night, in fact all night, putting together a briefing for him, covering all the details that I thought he would like to know. I was scared to death.

"The next morning I dragged all my paperwork, a flimsy, a briefing chart, and overlays to Brown's office where I found him at 0730. Outside his office were all the wing staff directors. I knew then that I had just signed my death warrant, for I was aiming most of my ammunition at the wing staff. Brown invited all of us in and *served us all coffee*. I then began to see a slight bit of light as to what it took to be a great man. The substance of our meeting is irrelevant to this picture other than the fact that he let me expound for about an hour and a half, when I concluded. Colonel Brown then said, 'Gosh, Al, is that all? I was prepared to go the whole day with you, but since you don't have any more problems than that, why don't you take me down and show me through your squadron area and then you can take me up and give me an aerial view of our operating area in a T-33' (a jet trainer). This was the beginning of one of the greatest friendships that I have ever known and the start of my realization that here was a man who would go down in history as one of our nation's greatest leaders.''[6]

Brown's determination to get to the heart of problems was as evident in his meetings with seniors as it was with subordinates. ''I observed,'' commented White, ''that George was the same way at meetings conducted by senior officers. He was the most honest man I've ever known, honest to a fault at times. It would have been easy at these senior meetings to be quiet, but he never was. He'd speak right up to what the problems were. I've seen him do it in meetings with colonels, which was pretty easy when everyone else was a colonel or lower in rank than that. But, more significantly, I saw him do it when general officers for whom he was working were conducting meetings. Some of them really didn't like to hear the things he had to say. He told me, 'If these are the facts, these are the facts. If they don't like it, they can always fire me.' ''[7]

Brown, after having moved onto the base and acquainted himself with most of the organizations, their functions, their attitudes, and their accomplishments, set about to learn about his people, not just the commanders, but everybody from the bottom to the top. He did it by visiting the barracks, mess halls, and functional areas where they worked. He checked out the Officers', NCOs', and Airmen's Clubs, squadron day rooms, the BX, all recreational facilities. He did all this within a few weeks after his arrival.

These visits resulted in a number of changes. One was a ''first.'' He was annoyed that it used to take about two full days to check into an air base. One had to go everywhere—from the hospital to the finance office, to supply, to the adjutant, to billeting, and to many other places. At each office someone had to initial a piece of paper indicating that you had been there and then record your name proving that you had checked in. At Selfridge, Brown designated a building at the end of the main road where all base departments were represented. An airman could drive up, park his car, walk in, and clear in or out of the base in a matter of twenty-five minutes instead of two days.

One of Brown's difficulties was the problem of the outlying areas under his command and the isolation the commanders in these areas felt. In the late 1940s and early 1950s, the philosophy of Gen. Ennis Whitehead, the senior commander of Continental Command and Air Defense, was to deploy all his squadrons around the country in such a way as to protect both SAC bases and industrial areas. Thus, units were deployed on bases without the kind of logistical support they needed.

"The years 1950–51 were extremely difficult times both for the Air Force itself and for the individuals involved," reflected then Col. Robin Olds, one of these commanders. "My own circumstances attest to that, having arrived at greater Pittsburgh airport as an F–86 squadron commander to find myself also base commander and the innocent inheritor of a $32 million construction program. All responsibility fell on my young and inexperienced shoulders. Frankly, the ever-shifting chain of command dangling over my head was a burden and obstacle, not a help. At the end of my tenure, George Brown assumed command of the wing at Selfridge, and my unit was placed under him. It was like a breath of fresh air and absolutely the first time in that period that the man for whom I worked gave any kind of damn for the circumstances, problems, and needs of my unit."[8]

Brown's solutions to the requirements of his diverse command were realistic. Ideal solutions were not always possible, but he was able to make the best use of the options available. For example, during Brown's Selfridge tour the materiel mission was taken away from the air divisions and given to the bases to support all the AC&W aircraft (control and warning) in division headquarters installations.

"In our case," said Frank Rogers, "we had a lieutenant colonel named Jim Johnson, who became available and was made our A–4, that is director of Materiel for our wing. Jim had a real problem in that he had to establish logistic support for the AC&W sites of the two division headquarters in our area. I recall discussing with George an effectiveness report that he had rendered on Jim. In this discussion he said to me, 'I have put an awful lot of responsibility on Jim to work out these problems. He's been doing it with little or no help.' I then realized Brown recognized that there were some built-in limitations in everyone.

"The system that provided us with our people was such that not everyone could be a Ph.D. or a Napoleon in battle. One had to have a sort of feeling of compassion, or at least understanding, that some people were just busting their butts and really putting out, yet the results weren't always perfect. These kinds of people had a place in the organization and had to be handled accordingly. I had known Jim for a long time and although he was an extremely capable man, I think it's fair to say that there were better qualified directors of materiel in the Air Force. He was, however, our man, and he was doing the best he could do for our commander. George Brown appreciated his effort and wanted to see his career blossom. He took into consideration all of the factors that make up a human being."[9]

Brown, while at Selfridge, and as he progressed up the ladder, had the ability to find the best people, but also to realize there were going to be times when the best people weren't available. A leader has to learn how to get the most out of what he has, to take up the slack where he needs to, to support some people more than he supports others because of differences in ability. Johnson went on to become a colonel and had a fine career.

A further example of this is provided by the case of Col. Ed Heller. There was a rather large guardhouse installation at Selfridge. Because of the Korean conflict there was a denuding of talent, and Selfridge was left with a weakened military police outfit. Because of this and other factors, a small riot occurred in the jail, and the officer in charge simply could not handle the problem. Ed Heller was commander of a P–51 National Guard squadron that had come in from Lansing, Michigan. He had a fine war record in Korea, but had also worked as a Pennsylvania state trooper. It was in his personnel folder, but the personnel officer was not aware of it. "Brown learned of it," recalled Frank Rogers, "and immediately placed Ed in charge of the military police activities on the base. The guardhouse problem was quickly solved. I cite this because it shows George's ability to find the square peg for the square hole as rapidly as possible when a problem came up."

George Brown's rapport with the troops, particularly the noncoms and the enlisted men, certainly came in part from his background in the military. Yet, he also had a broader knowledge of the importance of all people, the civil service employees as well as the military personnel. At Selfridge there was a nine-hole golf course that had been there for years. None of the civil service employees at Selfridge were allowed to play golf on the course. It was reserved strictly for the military. Brown learned about this in the base barbershop soon after he took command. The barber, an avid golfer, said, "I sure would like to get a chance to play the golf course out there once in a while." Brown said nothing then, but decided that civilians could play the golf course during the week, but not on Saturday and Sunday when the military were off duty. A large number of civilians began using the course in the morning before office hours, evenings, and three or four holes on their lunch hours. The fact that they were included as part of the team was extremely important to them. Brown told Colonel White of his decision. "You cannot afford to ignore part of your command and treat them like poor peasants." Colonel White comments, "He treated everybody exactly the same way, officers, enlisted men, or civilians."[10]

Despite his successes in personnel matters at Selfridge, there were still some things that Brown had to learn. One was an early lesson in protocol. Shortly after his arrival at the base, Gen. Benjamin Chidlaw, the Air Defense Commander, came from his headquarters in Colorado Springs for a visit, along with several senior staff members. They were put in the visiting VIP quarters. Unfortunately, the maid had made the mistake of not emptying the wastebasket of the previous occupant in General Chidlaw's room. It was full of papers and orange peels, which displeased Chidlaw. At the critique, which was held after the staff visit was over, most of the time was spent by the general giving his credo about orange peels.

"We never had a VIP come to the base after that that somebody didn't check the wastebaskets," recalled Frank Rogers. "But a lesson was learned by all of us. I note that George was one of the learners. He said to us later, 'Let's develop high standards. Let's remember to do things right, even the smallest of things. If you can do it well, do it that way, whatever it is. As long as you don't cheat the taxpayers, as long as you remember what the real mission is, there is no reason to downgrade ourselves by carelessness or injudicious application of effort, no matter what. Try to do it well with a high standard of performance.' "[11]

Brown's desire for the most effective performance levels can be seen in other areas as well. During his tenure at Selfridge a new universal code of military justice was passed by Congress. Prior to this there was only special court jurisdiction at Selfridge. The base had a number of problems, as did most base-type organizations in those days, one of which was a lack of legal talent to assist the commander.

For many years commanders let the court people know what was expected of them. Under the new system specific rules were established. One was that a commander could not talk to a court after it was constituted. Thus, the problem seemed to be how to get around the possibility that the court might come up with wrong decisions in arriving at rulings and punishments. "Wrong decisions" were those contrary to what the commander thought about handling his disciplinary problems.

Col. Frank Rogers came up with an idea to resolve the courts-martial problem. He suggested that they teach a course in military justice to forty officers. Brown was not only willing to listen to Rogers' solution, but also willing to try it. "Since I was making the court appointments for his approval," Rogers said, "we had a number of special courts set up and I would present him with a list of jury members. He could talk to them and generalize and explain what military justice was in his eyes. We appointed a blue ribbon special court that consisted of me as president, our only lawyer assigned to the base, and some other fairly senior officers. It was an unwritten rule that we were assigned the tougher cases. The legal fellow kept us clean. Everything went according to plan, and we didn't do anything that we shouldn't have done. We all had a pretty good idea by this time of what our responsibilities really were, assuming that the evidence we had heard justified our finding an airman guilty. This resulted in avoiding some of the tragedies that took place at other installations around the country where people simply mishandled their military justice problems."[12]

Brown's desire to make sure that his people were treated fairly was evidenced in other areas. "In my days in the 4th Fighter Wing," recalled Colonel Rogers, "I had picked out several people I thought were quite qualified to do certain types of jobs. One was Joe Johanson, who returned to us as a major from Korea. We made him assistant to the Director of Wing Operations, a lieutenant colonel's space. Joe was qualified and able, and subsequently made a great record for himself in the Air Force.

"A couple of weeks later, my wife and I were at George's house for cocktails, and a long distance call came through from Eastern Air Defense Headquarters at Stewart Air Force Base from the personnel director, no particular buddy of mine. He advised me that he was sending out a lieutenant colonel to become our wing director of operations, Johanson's job. I told him that we had a man in the job with whom Colonel Brown was satisfied, so we didn't need a replacement. I told him I would speak immediately to the colonel since he was standing next to me. I proceeded to do this. George said to me, 'Do you know this guy he's proposing?' I said, 'No, I've never heard of him.' He said, 'Is there anything wrong with leaving Johanson in this job? Isn't he doing all right as far as you can see?' I said, 'As a matter of fact, I think he's doing fine. If you're satisfied, why bother to buy a pig in a poke? Why not just keep what we have?' I then got a nod, 'Yeah, let's go that route.' I notified the colonel on the other end that we didn't want his selection. We got into a little discussion about that, but I had my way with Brown's backing. The point I'm making is that George understood and valued the relationship between command and staff people. He understood loyalty. This I found to be the case all through my associations with him. This was the first instance of it I observed personally, and I never forgot the backing he gave me."[13]

"George Brown was not a fighter pilot," commented Albert Kelly, "but, God, would he have made a great one. One day he called me and said, 'Al, I want you to check me out in the F-86 and the F-94.' I had already checked him out in the T-33, and he was eager to fly our organizational aircraft. We had two squadrons of F-86s and one converted to F-94B (an all-weather fighter-interceptor). He said, 'Now look, boy-san, I ain't no fighter pilot and I don't want you to try to make me one. I just want to fly them at my own speed.' I found that all George needed was procedural instruction, for he was a fine pilot, even for a bomber jock. I checked him in the F-86 and he flew it, completing transition. In the F-94, he insisted that I ride in the backseat where the radar operator normally rides. After completing transition, we flew a lot together. I checked him out on our gunnery range, we did some acrobatics, and he loved it.

"One afternoon," he continued, "after we had completed some aerial gunnery up near Oscoda, Michigan, we were on the way back to Selfridge, and I had relaxed in the backseat and was about half asleep when BAM! I didn't know what happened. The cockpit depressurized and I got thrown up against my seat belt, grabbing for air. George had seen me snoozing in the back, so he had popped the speed brakes, rolled it over in a split S and scared the hell out of me. He was laughing his head off, splitting his sides, and he told me over the radio, 'Never trust a bomber pilot!' He never lost his sense of humor.

"Shortly after our flying together, he called me and said, 'Al, you are going to be my new Director of Wing Operations.' My chin dropped. I objected strenuously because I wanted to stay in the cockpit and run my fighter squadron. I mentioned the fact that I was the most junior lieutenant colonel in the wing and that I would be giving directions to people senior to me. His classic remark was, 'If you can't handle it or the job is too big for you I'll get someone else.' He had a manner that got his point across forcefully, yet in a way that endeared him to you. I wasn't about to turn down the job after that remark." [14]

Brown's support of his people was not only on a professional level but extended to their social lives as well. For example, Brown made it a point to have his officers and wives get together by the base boat house for Sunday night cookouts. Everybody would come, bringing little cook stoves, supplies, and liquor. They had great times at these occasions; many good friendships were being formed during that time.

Colonel and Mrs. Brown also emphasized the spiritual life. "It is difficult to really define what leadership is," reflected Ernest White, "but as we all know, when you have a happy air base it runs more effectively. This occurs if you have people going to church on Sunday. George was in church with his wife every Sunday at Selfridge, which was a fine example to the rest of the troops." [15]

Brown also involved himself and others in civic activities. As White recalls, "Both George and I became Rotarians. It was a nice place to go; meetings were held in a church basement, and the food was wonderful. The members were responsible citizens, and we thoroughly enjoyed the meetings because they were a wonderful bunch of people. I think this is something that too few leaders do: get out in the local community and join a service club like Rotary or Kiwanis and present what the military's all about." [16]

Christmas was made a special time by the Browns. For years Selfridge had some pine trees originally planted by a noncom in the early 1930s in front of wing headquarters. The sergeant's idea was that at Christmas the trees would be decorated with lines of lights up to the flagpole with a crèche atop wing headquarters. "No one paid any attention to this until George Brown showed up there," recalled Ernest White. "I have to give his wife, Skip, primary credit for this. Whenever she thought something was a great idea it usually got done, just like it does with most good Air Force wives. That first Christmas, we had the darnedest traffic jam. People came out from Mount Clemens and Detroit to see the display. It really was beautiful."[17]

There was also an active officers' club, and one of the highlights was when the famous orchestra leader Woody Herman came through. He had a night off in Detroit and was willing to come out and play for a dance on a Tuesday night for six hundred dollars. Colonel White thought of getting him, and Brown got behind him. It was described by one of the officers as a "real wingding." They were faced with a lot of problems at the base, but Brown insisted that the men take time off to relax and enjoy themselves.

Some officers tend sometimes to forget about the enlisted personnel, but not George Brown. The two fighter squadrons had permanent brick barracks, each with its own mess hall. Brown made this comment: "I can't understand why these men on Sunday morning have to get up and walk three blocks to the PX to pick up their newspapers and then come back to the mess hall." The mess hall, unfortunately, had the same hours on Sunday as it had throughout the week, although the base was closed and the men not working. This meant that on Sunday, breakfast was served from 0600 to 0800. Brown said, "None of us living in quarters eat breakfast between six and eight on Sunday. We have a leisurely Sunday morning breakfast and read the papers. Why shouldn't the troops in the barracks have the same thing?" So he changed the mess hours on Sunday for breakfast from 0800 to 1100.

"The troops just loved it," said White. "They could go down to the mess hall anytime between eight and eleven o'clock in the morning in their bathrobes and slippers—they didn't have to put on uniforms. The newspaper people were instructed to deliver the newspapers to the mess hall rather than to the exchange. The men could pick up their various newspapers and walk through the chow line and say to the cook, 'I'd like a couple of eggs over easy and some bacon and pancakes.' Then they could go over and sit down at the table. Since nothing was precooked, they'd read the paper until their food was ready. Some skeptics told Colonel Brown, 'Why,

they won't show up to eat until eleven o'clock, and it will be a big mob.'
That wasn't what happened. In fact, the majority showed up at eight or
eight-thirty and sat in the mess hall eating breakfast, reading newspapers,
and chatting all morning with friends. Colonel Brown used to show up at
the mess halls Sunday morning before church, sit down and have a cup of
coffee, smoke a cigarette, and yak with them a little bit. It was again one of
the great attributes that he had, which of necessity is something that every
commander has to have, to follow through, to check and see if things were
being done the way he wanted them. He asked himself, 'Do the troops really
want this, or something else?' He'd get his answer.''[18]

Another example of Brown's concern for people occurred when a sergeant called him one Sunday morning out of great frustration and said,
"My baby is real sick. I took her to the hospital and I got the nickel-and-
dime treatment from the doctors. What can I do about this?" Colonel
Brown said to him, "Come to my house. I'd like to talk to you." He did,
and Brown was disturbed by what he heard, so we went to the hospital with
the sergeant's family. "I saw him do this," said White, "with the sergeant,
the mother, and the baby. He walked in and, obviously, because he was the
commander, they really gave the baby a complete checkout. It was a little
thing that might seem unimportant when you're thinking about the airplanes: what they do, what the pilots do. What he did for this family spread
immediately from one end of the base to the other. They were saying, 'Hey,
he really cares.' George did this many times. He had a concern for people
and demonstrated it. You can say you're concerned, but you had better
demonstrate it by your actions. As we used to say in Korea, don't slicky
slicky the troops. . . .

"He made a statement to me at Selfridge," White continued, "and I
think it is something that a junior officer particularly ought to know: 'No
one in the military ever gets court-martialed for doing something for the
troops. The only time you really get in trouble is when you try to do something for yourself. The only privileges that a commander has are those that
are given by the people working for him.' ''[19]

Part of the success he achieved as commander at Selfridge was because
of his wife, Alice Colhoun "Skip" Brown. White commented, "At Selfridge, Skip was very important. She saw to it that everyone got with the program, the social aspects, having a nice time among the families. I'm supposed to be reporting primarily on George, but no one is of value in this
man's military or in any other endeavor unless he has the right wife. I've
often thought that we ought to have a book written about what Air Force
wives have to put up with—husbands gone so much, bills to pay, kids they

must rear while their husbands go off to fight in three wars along the way, as George did.''[20]

Colonel Rogers also had some thoughts on the wife's role. "I'd be remiss if I didn't discuss Skip a little. She and George arrived with one son, Dudley, and she immediately made several impressions. First, she was an Army brat, as was George, and fully appreciated the role of an officer's wife. She was attractive physically, outstanding in personality, and a devoted family person. She always knew what her duties were on the official side and was well received by all the other wives, as well as the officers. They were a great couple to fit into the world which George made for himself, highly motivated, and politicized in the sense that they were always interested in the world around them. They had strong convictions as to what the country was all about and what each person owed his country. They were early risers. George told me, 'Skip and I would sit over coffee early in the morning and talk things over under better circumstances than when the family were all running around screaming for their Grape-Nuts. In those early hours of togetherness we formulated ideas that were part of our career together.' ''[21]

"When George left to go to Korea," said Frank Rogers, "he gave me what probably was the best efficiency report I have ever had. It went up to Eastern Air Defense Headquarters whose vice commander came running out to Selfridge with it. He said to George, 'I know Frank pretty well and you can't do this kind of thing. You can't give him that kind of report. He's not that good.' George said, 'I disagree with you. You can change it by your endorsement. That's the way I feel about it and that's the way I'm going to leave it.' Needless to say, that made a very favorable impression on me. It may not have made me a full colonel, but I thought that was a pretty decent thing for him to have done, particularly considering the personalities and rank involved. It's only one of the reasons why I have always had such a high regard for George."[22]

In the 56th Fighter-Interceptor Wing and its successor, the 4708th Air Defense Wing, there were some excellent fighter pilots. Many of them had returned from Korea with the experience of flying F-86s or F-84s against Koreans and Russians. Some units were good, others not very proficient, with problems that time alone would correct. Brown was at Selfridge only a short time before being reassigned to Korea and further combat experience. Not all of the problems at Selfridge were corrected. At the end of his seven-month tour, his rating officer, Maj. Gen. Frederic H. Smith, Jr., wrote that Colonel Brown's command "steadily improved in effectiveness." "There was a period of great improvement," added Frank Rogers. "In a short period of time I watched the progress of all units under his command. It was a long time before anything was in absolute order, but this was a great period of flux, and George's contribution to the 56th and its successor outfit was exceptional."[23]

For Brown, it was back to combat, this time for a key leadership role in the Korean conflict.

NOTES

1. Personal interview with Brig. Gen. Ernest J. White, USAF (Ret.), March 1981.
2. Personal interview with Col. Frank Rogers, USAF (Ret.), July 18, 1980.
3. Letter from Col. Albert S. Kelly, USAF (Ret.), to EFP, April 9, 1981.
4. White interview.
5. Ibid.
6. Kelly correspondence.
7. White interview.
8. Letter from Brig. Gen. Robin Olds, USAF (Ret.), to EFP, January 27, 1981.
9. Rogers interview.
10. White interview.
11. Rogers interview.
12. Ibid.
13. Ibid.
14. Kelly correspondence.
15. White interview.
16. Ibid.
17. Ibid.
18. Ibid.
19. Ibid.
20. Ibid.
21. Rogers interview.
22. Ibid.
23. Ibid.

CHAPTER 9
FIFTH AIR FORCE, KOREA:
MAY 1952–JUNE 1953

The Korean War started in June of 1950, but it was not until January 1, 1952, that George Brown was assigned to the combat theater of operation. His first assignment there was as Assistant Director of Operations for Headquarters, Fifth Air Force (FEAF). His responsibilities were to monitor correspondence for the Director, disseminate policies prescribed by the Director of Operations, receive visitors to the area, interview replacement personnel prior to their assignment to the Office of the Director, and assume the duties of Director in his absence.

"George Brown and I arrived at FEAF and Fifth Air Force HQ at about the same time," recalled Lt. Gen. Glenn Barcus, Commander of Fifth Air Force, "and received our indoctrination briefings together. George initially was Assistant Director of Operations, but became Director shortly. I had never met him before and knew nothing about him except that my boss, Gen. O. P. Weyland, seemed pleased about his assignment. Most of his early experience had been in heavy bombardment, and the Fifth Air Force was, of course, a tactical air force. However, it didn't take long to see that our operations section was in the hands of an outstanding officer."[1]

Barcus described Brown's job in operations as "enough to challenge the ability of any officer. Since this was a United Nations action, we were responsible for all air activity based in Korea, and a great deal of coordination was required. To help accomplish this, Operations, under George, conducted an evening briefing where that day's activities were reviewed and the plans for the next day's activities were presented. In addition to the Fifth Air Force, the Eighth Army, U.S. Naval Air, Marines, and Royal Navy Air Force made reports when appropriate. The Eighth Army Commander attended these briefings. George always gave an impressive presentation. Then, first thing in the morning, Operations conducted a much smaller meeting to review what had happened during the night and any change in our planned activities for the day."[2]

George Brown also planned the combat missions. "He would call the wing commanders commanding the F–84s and F–86s," reflected then Col. Ernest J. White, a wing commander in Korea, "and they'd come in and sit down. He'd say, 'OK, this is the target we want to take out.' Instead of acting like a big dog, that he knew everything, that 'I'm the deputy for Operations,' he'd say to them, 'What's the best way to do this? What do you recommend? What are your thoughts?' As a result, the wing commanders themselves figured out the routes to run to the target and what bombloads they ought to have. If, however, he thought they were off, George would very quietly say, 'You don't mean that. You mean this,' and would talk with them so that they actually were doing exactly what it was he wanted them to do. The important thing was he never made a big issue about the fact that he was running things, which he could very well have done. All he had to do was put out a field order and they obviously would have obeyed. As a result of his approach, they felt that he was a person to whom they always could turn. One might say, 'Wait a minute, instead of me having thirty-two airplanes, I can run this mission with only thirty. What do you think, George?' And George would make the decision at that time."[3]

"In conducting the combat operations planning at Air Force level as Deputy Director to me," wrote Director of Operations Col. Joe L. Mason in his official evaluation, "he left nothing to be desired. Colonel Brown possessed the capacity to get along well with both junior and senior personnel of all services. His natural ability to grasp the current combat situation made it possible for him to step in and carry the major share of the planning load on such air strikes as the North Korean hydroelectric system and the major effort on the target systems in the city of P'yongyang. His leadership was felt by the entire Fifth Air Force . . . and contributed greatly to the success of the air strikes."[4]

On July 15, 1952, George moved up to become Director of Operations for Fifth Air Force, succeeding Colonel Mason. His primary responsibility was for all combat operations that Fifth Air Force performed in Korea. One of the officers who worked under him was Col. Ben I. Mayo, Jr. "I had returned to HQ, Far East Air Force, in Tokyo," reflected Mayo, "after flying another 103 combat missions in Korea with the 48th Fighter Wing. I believe that I was the only officer there who had flown a full combat tour over Korea. Partly as a result of this firsthand experience, Gen. Jake Smart picked me out, along with a Colonel Randolph (an experienced and capable staff officer), to write a staff study on the best methods to exert pressure on the North Koreans through air power. General Smart was obviously frustrated with what we were doing in our target selection."[5]

The deputy commander under the command of Lieutenant General Barcus was then Brig. Gen. E. H. Underhill. "We all worked together," remembered Underhill. "I knew what the commanding general wanted and so did George. General Barcus talked with us each day about what was to be done. The three of us worked very closely together."

Initially, however, there was some estrangement between Underhill and Brown. Underhill's predecessor had taken very little interest in the operations phase and pretty much let George do his own thing, subject, of course, to General Barcus's approval. Underhill, on the other hand, wanted a more active role in planning missions, and his views did not always coincide with Brown's. At one point early in their association, there was a disagreement that caused such friction that General Barcus had to step in to mediate. As a result of this incident, however, Brown was convinced that Underhill truly was interested in combat operations, and their association from then on became a close one.

"I had wanted desperately," said General Underhill, "to be in Korea because I thought as a professional it was my business to be there. I was very much interested in operations. So when I first arrived I would go with the planners into General Barcus's office, but I made no suggestions or did anything at all for a while. I just listened until I knew pretty much how General Barcus liked things done. The planners had been working on one mission for a while and I was observing them as they decided what they intended doing. I suggested that we do something else, and George said, 'No, we're going to do it this way.' I said, 'I don't think the old man would like that.' George said that he was the operations officer and it would be done his way. I said, 'Come with me to the old man; we might as well get things straightened out.' So we walked into the office and I said, 'General Barcus, we're setting up this mission and George thinks we should operate in a certain way, so I'd like to have George explain it to you.' So he did, and Barcus said, 'Well, wouldn't you?' I said, 'No, I feel that under the circumstances we should put in some more aircraft for top cover.' General Barcus thought for a few moments and said, 'I agree with you. George, do it General Underhill's way.' So we left. I went to George's office and said to him, 'Look, I'm not trying to be your operations officer, but as deputy commander I am interested in what's going on. If I have any comment or criticism I expect to make it and to be listened to. I'm sure we'll have no trouble, but,' I said, 'I expect to know what's going on. I am interested in the combat operations. I don't care what the previous vice commander did.'

"George and I liked one another," continued Underhill. "We really got along well. There was no problem after that incident. I don't think he really realized what he was doing on that particular occasion. The previous deputy hadn't been at all interested, but I was. I felt that I had to make it clear that I did have a say and I was going to say it when I thought it was necessary. I used to spend a lot of time down in Operations, going over the things with George and with those who worked for him. I knew many of these officers, particularly some of the junior officers. I'd either been their instructor or they had worked for me somewhere else."[6]

The procedure for mission planning was for Brown to meet with his staff, after first conferring with General Barcus to set guidelines. After the initial approval of the idea, they went back to decide on how to implement the concept, how many units and what type of aircraft would be involved, how bad the flak was, how many bombs should be dropped, and who would drop the bombs.

Operations thus involved much work and many people. Everybody had to know what was going on. Once the mission was planned, the orders would be transmitted. If an operation were sufficiently complicated, Brown would have the group commanders in and go over the mission with them to make sure that everybody understood what he was supposed to do. "It was work, work, work," recalled Ernest White. "I was a subordinate commander; I could expect George to be calling me any time of the day or night, and he would expect me to have the answers.

"In Korea, George had Plans, Operations, and Intelligence all working for him. They all worked together in full coordination. I've seen many times where they just fell apart because of a lack of cooperation. Not under George. The reason they didn't was that George gave each of them an opportunity to run things under his benign guidance. That's what it really was."[7]

The operations section monitored the missions very carefully. "Once a mission started, we never left the office until it was done," said General Underhill. "One of the missions involving the cutting of the bridges was a four-day operation. Neither George nor I left the operations building until that mission was over. We were there night and day to keep current, to read reports as they came in, how heavy the flak was, and so forth. We would get reports direct from the group commanders as they returned and also by radio from the air. We had to keep track of how it was going and how to make changes if and where necessary."[8]

It is important in analyzing Brown's leadership during this period to put the Korean War into perspective. It was a peculiar war, completely different from anything that either George or any other U.S. military leader had ever been involved in. Normally in operations one does something because it will help one's side to advance and go on to achieve victory. In Korea these men knew they weren't going to achieve victory in the conventional sense. But they still had to do their best to support their own forces within the limited war missions given them.

One of the things that disturbed the Air Force more than anything else was that the Army was still operating along the front line with the Koreans and Chinese attacking them. The Army was trying to keep them off and to maintain the status quo, making sure we were holding our lines. When the Army needed assistance for any operation, what they needed was close air support from the Air Force. That meant that they had to assess the cost of any operations in men and in airplanes. They had to consider the cost in relation to the worth of the mission.

"How he ever found the time to do it I can't imagine," recalled General Barcus. "Within his restrictions, George conducted a study to determine the best tactics and the optimum altitude for the dive-bomber and light bomber missions. He then revised the night intruder and tactical bomber programs, achieving better results with sharply decreased losses."[9]

It was a significant achievement. "George," reflected General Underhill, "couldn't see that we should conduct operations in the same way as we would if we were going to win the war in the end. If we were out for a real victory, our aircraft should go down within 200 to 500 feet and take whatever losses were necessary to destroy the target. But we weren't destroying any targets at that particular time. All we were doing was keeping the enemy underground so the Army could move its troops around. They only stuck their necks out whenever they wanted to shoot.

"It was George's idea," said Underhill, "approved by General Barcus, that we limit the altitude at which our fighter bombers would operate for safety reasons. He thought we could accomplish just as much that way at far less cost to us. Brown suggested we do our bombing at about 1,000 feet. Thus, we lost fewer airplanes and fewer pilots."[10]

Brown was responsible for another lifesaving innovation. The Air Force was constantly working against the railroads, one of the principal means by which the Communists supplied their troops. Earlier, they had an almost set procedure where they would hit certain areas all the time, and the enemy had so built up his air defenses that it became dangerous to continue these tactics. Brown changed that. He modified their procedures so that they hit the railroads wherever they could, but ordinarily where it was the least dangerous or where the enemy would least expect it. This caused the enemy to move his air defenses around, thereby increasing American air flexibility.

"Another example of Brown's outstanding ability was his planning and directing operations against the Yong Mi Dong bridges in the fall of 1952. These bridges were used for the movement of supplies by the North Koreans and Red Chinese, and they were heavily defended by antiaircraft guns. It took careful planning," commented General Underhill, "because those bridges were very important to the enemy and we would have to suppress the flak. General Barcus had said, 'I want those bridges cut, and I want to keep them out.' So George went to work on it. The first thing he did was to send out reconnaissance—very carefully photograph the whole place and pick out all of the known antiaircraft defenses. Next, George had to decide how many fighter bombers he needed to cut the bridges and how many for antiaircraft suppression. The problem was getting the aircraft to the flak positions at the right time and suppressing them simultaneously. Then the fighter bombers had to come in to cut the bridges. This huge planning effort was George's responsibility. He performed well, and it turned out to be a real good operation. I think General Barcus was really more than pleased with the operation because we didn't lose a single airplane. Many of the men in our attacking outfits had been in Europe with fighter bombers in World War II. They said there was more flak up there than they'd ever seen in World War II. Yet it was all suppressed and the fighter bombers got in and out and cut the bridges."[11]

In addition to his planning some very tough missions, George's job was not always easy on a day-to-day basis. "General Barcus," said Underhill, "was tough—a difficult, arbitrary man to work for. He'd get very angry easily and walk out of a meeting."[12]

Brown, however, managed to alleviate most situations with Barcus with his unflagging good humor. "George Brown was a dedicated officer and might appear to be all business," reflected General Barcus, "but he also had a delightful sense of humor illustrated by an incident that involved me. At various meetings, I frequently cautioned those present not to try to sell me any wooden nickels. I guess that in my own inimitable way I overdid it. Anyway, at the next conference, the first time I mentioned wooden nickels, George interrupted the proceedings and presented to me on behalf of the commanders and staff a replica of a nickel six inches in diameter and three-quarters inch thick, beautifully carved out of wood, sprayed with chromium, and mounted on an engraved silver base. Needless to say, it is one of my most prized possessions."[13]

General Underhill also recalled the wooden nickel incident: "George got up and made the presentation to the old man. General Barcus thanked him for it, and we all laughed. It was a pretty good indication of George's ability to judge character. What he hoped to accomplish with the presentation of the wooden nickel was to ease the situation, for Barcus to understand that people did have feelings. Everybody was curious, wondering what would happen. Then General Barcus grinned, and he accepted it in the spirit it was offered. It affected not only the giver and the taker, but everybody present. It made for a calmer atmosphere, relaxed the situation."

Brown was receptive to the ideas of others. For example, there were a lot of railroad tunnels in Korea that would be bombed and then quickly fixed up, with the trains running the next day. One of the group commanders came to George and said, "I think we could skip bomb those tunnels as they skip bombed ships in World War II." George said, "Well, it's all right if you can pick the right place, because you've got to come in and can't be too high on a hill in front of you. You've got to be able to get out of the way." "I know where there's a tunnel," said the group commander, "and I think I can do it." So George said, "Okay, go ahead." The pilot reported back and said, "You've never seen anything like it in your life. I dropped one right in the tunnel. More stuff came out the other end than you can imagine. Those tunnels were just loaded with stuff. I blew up a locomotive engine. It was a little short tunnel, but that was what they were doing, hiding themselves and the materials there."[14]

Perhaps the reason that Brown was so willing to listen to and often implement the sometimes risky ideas of others is that he himself had the spirit of adventure. During the time he was in the Korean War, his brother, Tim Brown, went to see him. After the weekend, his brother had to get back. George told Tim, "I'll fly you back up to your post." Tim asked, "What are you going to fly?" George replied, "We've got some L-20s." So they went out and he crawled in the L-20. "I noticed that the crew chief was sticking his head in the window," said Tim, "in the front seat, the backseat. He was pointing out all kinds of things to George. George was nodding okay. I didn't realize it at the time, but George had never flown an L-20 before. Well, he cranked it up and we started flying back to my post. We were having a terrible time with the engines running wide open and it didn't seem like we were getting anywhere. I noticed George looking around and I then proceeded to get on the intercom and ask him, 'What's going on? What's the matter with this thing?' George said to me, 'I don't know. It's not flying very well.' Well, as it turned out, the problem was that the flaps were still down. He finally realized it and got the flaps where they belonged, and it then flew fine. I never let him forget that he flew that L-20 with the flaps down."[15]

Frequently, subordinates know a person better than superiors do. One such staff officer, then Col. Russell A. Berg, gave some insight when he rhetorically asked, "Did George perform his duties better than others? I'd have to believe he did, because he seemed to do everything better than anyone else. I know I certainly valued his judgment and direction. Also, I find it extremely difficult to measure leadership of one in a staff position who reflects the direction and desires of his commander. You may ask, 'Well, how well did he do that?' Once again I would have to give George the highest marks. He understood the subjects under discussion and sorted out all the controversy before they became major issues. Usually a discussion with George was factual, clearly presented, and to the point, with little room left over for disagreement or argument. I liked my associations with him. I never came away from a discussion feeling I was short-changed, even though the conclusions reached were not always exactly as I wished them to be."[16]

Despite the less than successful outcome of the Korean conflict as a whole, Brown demonstrated himself an entirely capable officer during this period. Part of the reason for his success was his capacity to get along with both superiors and subordinates. Insight into this aspect of Brown's success as a leader was provided by Lt. Gen. Glenn O. Barcus, who wrote, "I recall George Brown as having a twinkle in his eyes and a smile always ready to surface. Although he was by no means a 'yes man,' I don't ever recall his engaging in any unpleasantness with anyone. He had a faculty of getting the job done without it. But I don't think anyone was stupid enough to think he was a weak one who could be exploited because of his good nature."[17]

His most immediate boss, General Underhill, in answer to the question, Why was George Brown successful? responded, "George had a good mind, he had an imagination, he had confidence in his own ability, in himself, and his people had confidence in him. He knew what he was talking about, knew how to do things. I don't think he ever asked anybody to do anything that he wouldn't have done himself. He was a man of integrity and trust. If George said this was it, you could believe him, and his people did. He changed procedures from time to time, which would enable him to accomplish what he wanted to do at less cost in lives and aircraft. He was very aware that our combat was a dangerous business, that people could get hurt in it. He didn't want any more people getting hurt than he could help. But he had imagination, and he understood things when people talked and explained things to him. He understood quickly and with ease."[18]

But there were times in Korea when he enjoyed life. General White reflected, "We both believed in the work ethic, but there was another side. There's an awful lot of fun to be had within the United States Air Force and within the military, and I think that most of us thoroughly enjoyed ourselves on occasion. George and I took an R and R from Korea. We spent a week in Hong Kong and had a lot of fun. I think sometimes when we start talking about generals we don't realize, 'Okay, they work like dogs, but often have a good time.' The junior officers, particularly, ought to look forward to the fact that it's a rough row to hoe to get to the top, but there's a lot of fun along the way. And I mean good, clean fun that is something all of us thoroughly enjoy.

"Actually, in a lot of ways George was a rough, tough guy when it came to getting a job done, but away from the job he could enjoy himself as much as anyone. We went from the Peninsula Hotel in Hong Kong to the Parisian Grill where we had an absolutely marvelous meal.

"We then found the ferry going across Hong Kong harbor had stopped running at midnight. So we got in what's called a walla walla. We had been told, 'Don't ever get in a walla walla. You'll either sink out in the middle of Hong Kong harbor or get hit over the head and never be heard from again.' Well, we got in anyway. When we got out in the middle of the harbor, the walla walla stopped running. It had a kind of an in-line engine in front. We were the only passengers and couldn't speak a word of Chinese. They probably spoke fluent English if they wanted to. George said to the crew chief, 'We'll get this damned engine going.' He picked up a hammer and banged on the engine like you see in television commercials when people are kidding about things. There were frantic movements by the crew at the other end, and all of a sudden the engine started running. I told George later that the Chinese were scared to death that he was going to break up their engine completely and that this was why they got it started."[19]

White observed that "Brown had a lot of pressure from his job and worked very long hours. When he returned to Korea, he reverted to his excessive work habits and began to have trouble with his back, so much so he could hardly walk. General Barcus said to him, 'George, you get the hell out of here and go in the hospital in Japan.' When he went to Japan, the doctor who checked him at the hospital looked at him and just made a flat statement. 'Your problem is real simple. You've been working more than you ought to, and you have complete fatigue. Just get in bed.' They kept him in bed for about a week. After he had rested he was brought back to Korea and there was never a problem with fatigue from then on."[20]

In closing his tour in Operations, Col. Joe Mason tied together Col. George Brown's leadership performance by stating in Brown's effectiveness report:

> Colonel Brown is a highly intelligent, sincere and dynamic officer. He has proven himself outstanding in his ability to assimilate a problem and present a sound decision in a minimum

of time. Although he was not previously experienced in tactical air operations, he was able in a very short period of time to thoroughly grasp the fundamentals of this type of operation and to recommend new methods and types of attack which have resulted in an increase of the effectiveness of the Fifth Air Force against the enemy. He has the ability to recognize the pertinent features in a situation and to develop a logical, succinct approach to its solution. His management of the personnel and resources under his supervision is superior. I would fight to get him in my command in any capacity.

A final perceptive leadership perspective was provided by Ernest White, who said, "During this time George established many procedures that he never received the proper amount of recognition for at the time. But he did things that were completely different. There wasn't anything he had to prove to General Barcus, and thank God the general was smart enough to recognize this, that if George came up with an angle, it probably made sense. In most cases it did, and we as subordinates could see it, too."[21]

Thus, in his second war, Brown continued to get exposure. It was another opportunity for growth and combat experience from which both he and the Air Force benefited. He was now to move on to an entirely new challenge, that of training pilots.

NOTES

1. Letter from Lt. Gen. Glenn O. Barcus, USAF (Ret.), to EFP, March 14, 1980.
2. Ibid.
3. Personal interview with Brig. Gen. Ernest J. White, USAF (Ret.), March 15, 1981.
4. Officer Effectiveness Report on Col. George S. Brown written by Col. Joe L. Mason.
5. Letter from Col. Ben I. Mayo, USAF (Ret.), to EFP, October 31, 1979.
6. Personal interview with Lt. Gen. E. H. Underhill, USAF (Ret.), April 4, 1980.
7. White interview.
8. Underhill interview.
9. Barcus correspondence.
10. Underhill interview.
11. Ibid.
12. Ibid.
13. Barcus correspondence.
14. Underhill interview.
15. Personal interview with Brig. Gen. Thomas W. Brown, USA (Ret.), August 8, 1979.

16. Letter from Brig. Gen. Russell A. Berg, USAF (Ret.), to EFP, May 10, 1979.
17. Barcus correspondence.
18. Underhill interview.
19. White interview.
20. Ibid.
21. Ibid.

PART THREE
THE STAR BEGINS TO RISE

CHAPTER 10

WILLIAMS AIR FORCE BASE, ARIZONA: JULY 1953–JULY 1956

On June 6, 1953, George Brown was posted to Williams Air Force Base, Arizona, as Commander of the 3525th Pilot Training Wing. It was an assignment with broad and sometimes awesome responsibilities, involving not only the direction and supervision of the pilot training program, but also the operation and management of the base and its activities: security, supply, sanitation, transportation, housing, construction, maintenance, morale, and the well-being of personnel. For the next three years he was to exercise these responsibilities with great distinction, but at the outset of his command he faced inherited problems of a serious nature, not all of which could be dealt with overnight.

One of them, however, proved capable of immediate solution, and Capt. (later Lt. Gen.) James Knight was a witness: "Upon his arrival, Colonel Brown found that a strong clique had for some time been running things at Williams Air Force Base. Miraculously, that clique dissolved almost immediately after George came in. I don't know exactly what he did, but after he had been there a short time, the clique simply disappeared. I think it was in part broken up because Brown treated everybody equally from the first day. He assumed that all were already doing their jobs, or were going to do them. He did not have any select group of friends and he played no favorites."[1]

Knight's analysis of this situation is closely paralleled by that of Col. (then Capt.) Tom Personette, who served under Brown as Pilot Training Group Commander: "Previous commanders," recalls Personette, "tolerated cliques on the base, and they had a devastating effect on morale. When George came in, the cliques were broken up, and he, with his ability to lead, soon had everybody working for him and with him in the desire to do the best job they could. He was completely down-to-earth, and his judgment was fantastic. People soon recognized this, and he got everybody to fall in line. Brown would not have any part of the cliques; he would not have anything except a single team that was totally mission-oriented. He was very much a part of everything. At his staff meetings, you came to expect (and were not disappointed) that he would make decisions, lay down policy—policy with meaning—and follow through with it without deviation.

"The pilot training program at Williams was really demanding," continued Personette. "We were always at work around seven in the morning and would never quit until after five or six at the earliest. The morale became so elevated under Brown that people were really eager to work and had no complaints about the long hours."[2]

One reason for the new high morale at Williams was that Brown took personal interest in all levels of the operation there. He quickly developed a feel for what was going on, so after taking care of the necessary staff work or paperwork in the office, he found time to get all over the base. He liked to see at first hand what the training program was accomplishing. He was in and out of his office, but somehow he seemed always to be present whenever anything critical came up. He led by example.

Brown visited the flight line daily, and made evening visits when there was night flying going on, which was most of the time. He checked out as an instructor in all types of aircraft used there, concentrating on the T-28, and made a habit of flying sorties with the students. This was altogether a different approach. "I don't think," states James Knight, "that the previous commander ever flew with the students. Colonel Brown made it a point to fly with them at least once a week. He wanted to know how they felt, so he talked with them a lot. The students seemed to admire him because of his interest in them and his ability to communicate.

"He was all over the base; he was down into every squadron on the flight line. He studied every maintenance activity. He could sense when people weren't doing all they could, were not going as far as they could, to turn out the airplanes.

"I recollect one example that especially endeared George Brown to his staff," continued James Knight. "We had been having trouble getting enough airplanes to fly each mission. The maintenance people, inspectors, instructors, and others were all wrestling with the problem. At a staff meeting one day early in 1955, Brown said to our group, 'Well you guys haven't come up with the answer yet. I'm soon going to show you how to do it.' He then proceeded to circulate to all parts of the base, talking with people and analyzing everybody's job.

"One week later, he took out his slide rule and, with the inputs he had gathered during his intensive personal inspection, calculated before us what had to be done and how many airplanes were needed to fly each day. He proceeded to go through it as the Wing staff maintenance officer should have been doing all along. When he came to the end, he announced, 'This is what we've got to do every day if we are to stay on schedule.'

"The basic problem was that the people had never figured out how many planes they needed to do the job; they did not have an exact goal and had not established a standard to meet. Brown came up with a figure of sixty—sixty airplanes for each four flying periods a day. Up to that time, they had been struggling along with fifty or fifty-five because that's all they thought they could turn out. But when the goal was established at sixty, they reached it, continued to meet it, and were never faced with that problem again."[3]

Despite overall success at Williams, things could and did go wrong. Brown's response to one such adverse instance is again indicative of why he was a successful leader. The trainees used a range at Yuma, Arizona, for air-to-ground gunnery practice. On one occasion one of the foreign students had a flameout and bellied in, landing on the desert. The instructor pilot leading the flight of four circled around, came in low, and observed that the pilot's head was bobbing in the cockpit. The instructor immediately proceeded to land on the highway and run to the airplane to release the pilot. But the pilot was all right; the head bobbing was simply due to his exertions in trying to open the canopy of his T–33.

The problem was that a pilot ordinarily doesn't land an airplane on a public highway. The humanitarian thing to have done was exactly what the instructor pilot *had* done. Brown's concern was that the pilot could have killed himself and also anyone driving down the highway. There was a small field close to where the student came down, and the instructor should have landed there.

"Brown was disturbed about this, and since I was Pilot Training Commander," recalled Tom Personette, "I was called in immediately to explain why the instructor had landed on the highway. I gave him all the details, and he said to me, 'We just can't tolerate this sort of thing.' I assured him that this was not standard policy. Brown could easily have handled me in a very severe manner, could have chewed me out or embarrassed me. But he did not. He made his point, which I well remember, and the way he did so made me more eager than ever to do a better job."

Clearly, as in the above instance, Brown asserted full authority when he felt it necessary. Nonetheless, he was also most willing to listen to recommendations of his key staff people. Personette recalls: "I recommended to George Brown that we eliminate the power-off approach with our F-80s and T-33s. The practice had been for the aircraft to come in for a 360-degree overhead, pitch out, and throttle to the idle position. I believed that procedure to be the cause of several people spinning in during the traffic pattern and killing themselves. I recommended a power-on approach, not a 360 overhead. He accepted this suggestion immediately and gave me full support in putting it into effect. From that time on, as long as I was there, we never had another accident or fatality in the traffic pattern."

When asked if he had made this recommendation to the previous wing commander, Personette responded, "I was not in a position to make it, but the previous wing commander wouldn't have had any part of this idea. He was of the old school and felt that any fighter pilot worth anything should be able to come in with height, throttle to the idle position, and make it to the runway. This may have worked for pilots with lots of experience, but we were in a training environment, and when these inexperienced students got into trouble, the results were sometimes fatal. George Brown insisted that you should have a training environment and keep it a training environment. He did not believe you should expect the young men coming in to be finished pilots.

"Another important distinction was that the previous commander had a policy that once a student had a final check flight with the section commander—when the student was up for the 'washout ride'—then that student was never returned to the training program. In other words, once a student got to that stage, the flight with the Director of Flying was merely a formality, and a washout was virtually automatic. I felt this to be a wasteful procedure," continued Personette, "because my purpose in giving these check rides to students was to evaluate them and determine whether or not they had the *potential* of becoming pilots. With Brown's support, I established the pattern of riding twice with each student, unless a student admitted that he had no interest whatsoever in continuing. But if a student was really interested, I would always ride twice with him and try to use my background and flying experience to determine whether he really had the ability to fly. With this policy we put many students back into the training program, and they went on to finish it and become excellent pilots."[4]

In addition to his attention to the specific workings of Williams AFB, Colonel Brown was fully aware of the need to keep abreast of what was going on beyond the perimeters of his own base; he perceived how necessary it was to avoid becoming isolated, ingrown, and parochial in his outlook. To that end, Brown flew numerous "cross countries" to other Air Force training bases. He wanted to learn how the other bases were doing their jobs. He was extremely good at learning from other people. He had no reservations about learning from a lieutenant colonel, a captain, another commander, or even a student pilot in training.

Here, then, is yet another insight: despite his own attributes as leader, guide, and instructor, Brown always profited from the ideas and viewpoints of others, regardless of their rank or position. Indeed, this absence of stiffness and self-pride made him one of the most unpretentious and unassuming men imaginable. For the most part, his assigned staff car and driver were employed for official functions only, and a lowly motor scooter sufficed for his personal on-base transportation. He also mowed his own lawn, an activity in which none of his predecessors had ever indulged.

It was perhaps this facet of his personality—the basic self-confidence that made strict adherence to protocol unnecessary—that led to the development of an uncommon social relationship between Brown and Captain Knight and their families. James Knight, who served on his staff at Williams AFB during the first two years of Brown's tour as commander, describes it.

"I think it all began with Brown's desire and love for outdoor life, particularly the family type of outdoor activities—hunting, fishing, camping, and boating. My family and I had been quite involved in camping in the Phoenix area, at Apache, Canyon, and Roosevelt lakes. He asked me one day about hunting and fishing prospects in the area. In the course of our conversation it soon became clear that he and I shared an interest in these outdoor activities.

"He displayed no formality or stiffness. He was an easy man for a captain to be with. When he was out fishing or camping, he really didn't want to talk about problems back at the base, unless there was something that simply had to be discussed, and that was quite rare. He wanted that time for pleasant relaxation. Although I always referred to him as 'Colonel' on these trips, he called me Jim, and insisted that my wife, Annie, call him George, which she did when we were together informally."

Brown spent many an hour in a canoe doing what he liked to do best—fishing. He would often go for an hour without saying a word to those fishing with him. It was recreation in the true meaning of the word, and the relaxation it brought helped sustain his spirits, vitality, and sense of humor.

Another contemporary of Knight and Personette who, as a junior officer, served in a position of responsibility under Brown was Frank Rogers. His personal account of the years 1954–56 shows how Brown took a personal interest in his subordinates and their welfare without sacrificing his sense of military purpose.

Rogers had appealed to Brown to give him a job at Williams, which eventually was arranged. "However," recalls Rogers, "I became disappointed immediately. I never had an opportunity to command anything, and it had appeared likely that I would be appointed an Air Base group commander at Williams upon the imminent departure of the incumbent. Unfortunately, the anticipated transfer failed to occur, so when I got there I was asked by George if I wanted to be Personnel Officer. I could sense that he didn't particularly want the present one replaced, and I told him that I had had all of that I needed, but that I'd like to do whatever he wanted me to do. He said that they were in trouble in Maintenance and Supply, and he'd like me to consider going down there as 'number two' in that organization.

"Although it seemed like a comedown for me at the time, George handled the problem well and demonstrated that special knack he possessed for reconciling an individual's needs with those of the service. He also demonstrated his remarkable ability to assuage injured pride and, in general, make all things easier whenever he could. I had enough faith in him to be able to respond affirmatively, and I said, 'You know what I'd *like* to do, and I presume you'll give me that opportunity when and if you can; until you can do so, I'll give you 102 percent of whatever you want me to take on.' So even though it was in one respect a disappointing welcome to the organization, it worked out fine in the long run, and it further cemented the relationship that had begun over two years before at Selfridge."

The integrity that Brown displayed in his personal relationships was carried over into other areas as well. "George was always on the lookout for any evidence of waste or misuse of government assets," continued Rogers. "He insisted that equipment, supplies, and property be used for the purpose and manner intended. He saw the operation of the base as a serious business, sustained by the taxpayers' dollars; he insisted that the taxpayers were entitled to their money's worth."

An example of Brown's ability to cut waste is provided by Rogers: "A new program introduced by the Air Force was an elaborate system of data keeping at the flight-line level, designed to measure the time and effort being spent by the mechanics on various types of activity, to improve maintenance through the use of statistics. The new system had been introduced at Williams shortly before I arrived and had already started to create problems, as new systems often do.

"The trouble was that nobody paid any attention to it. The master sergeant was the only one who seemed to know anything about it. The maintenance supervisors on the line and in the shops weren't enthusiastic, and most of the mechanics were cheating on the figures. It looked like there ought to be something done about all this, because it represented a considerable investment in machinery, software, and time.

"It all began with a lot of punched card machines, and Williams was one of several bases that had been supplied with them. The equipment was presided over by a master sergeant from maintenance control. The system required that virtually all of the maintenance personnel on the base fill out what amounted to a time card each day. They were turned in every day, were processed and run through the equipment, and every day the machines produced an elaborate, impressive-looking 'poop sheet.'

"The master sergeant and I came up with some simple bar charts that were easier to read than all that paper being disgorged by the computers. We were trying to make sense out of all this information. We then went up to see George Brown to get his reaction. We got the kind of reception from him that one would expect. He recognized immediately the validity of our trying to make sense out of it and utilize it.

"With that, we entered a new era in maintenance record keeping. George directed me to make sure that the people under our supervision who were providing the records from which the data were compiled fully understood their responsibilities, and that proved to be the key to the whole problem. With his backing, we were able to bring all supervisors together for on-the-job training and instruction. From then on we got full cooperation from the people providing the data, instead of lip service, because they understood that the data gathering served a useful purpose and was not just another piece of make-work. We began generating meaningful data of use to all commanders."[5]

That George Brown effectively solved as many problems as he did at Williams is a particular credit to his leadership when one considers the lack of experience of many of his personnel. A main ingredient of leadership is the ability to get the job done with the people on hand. Unfortunately, the talent with which George Brown had to work at Williams Air Force Base was extremely thin. This was because the Korean War had caused all activities throughout the Air Force to expand. Higher headquarters had transferred many people out to man new installations, and by the time George assumed command in 1953, many of the most highly qualified personnel had departed.

"I recall saying to George," said Rogers, " 'You're awfully tolerant, and sometimes you put up with things I never would.' This was during a discussion concerning an officer who was transferred to another Air Force base at George's request. 'I'm surprised,' I went on, 'that this hasn't taken place before now.' This was George's reply: 'The fact is that at times the system turns up people who really try to put out but have limited ability; perhaps they are put into the wrong job through no fault of their own, due to circumstances beyond anyone's control. You simply have to recognize that you can't punish people because of things beyond their control.' ''

Brown's rejoinder covered much ground in few words. It showed why he had tolerated that officer's poor performance, and why he had arranged his transfer elsewhere instead of removing him from the Air Force. It illustrated his fundamental decency in his dealings with subordinates and his overall concern for the service.

Brown was successful in getting optimum performance from a sometimes inexperienced staff because he attended to their personal needs. The maintenance squadron was once losing enlisted personnel, particularly specialists, at an alarming rate. The reason was that the men were working on the flight line under the most miserable conditions. In summer, they had to work on airplanes that could not be touched because the metal parts became too hot, so he found a way to provide shade for them. The men had no place to get in out of either the heat or the cold. At other times, working at night, it was extremely cold. They were working out of what amounted to packing-box huts along the flight line.

"We dug around and found some old scrap stuff," said Frank Rogers, "and got permission from George Brown to build some better-looking structures, put water containers in them, get heaters for use at night, and install electric lights to make them more usable and comfortable. We probably violated some rules, but we got the job done. George, you see, had told us to get cracking once he had been informed of the situation. Frequently, when you deal with senior officers, they'll turn you down if you propose something they didn't think of themselves, or if your suggestion is out of line with accepted procedures. But George was always willing to listen, and if he could see a good result on the other end, he'd go along with you. In this instance, we had two good results: our people started putting out as they never had before, and eventually our Armament and Electronics Squadron became the only one in the Training Command with a 100 percent reenlistment rate."

During the latter part of 1954 and early 1955, the mission of Williams AFB changed from basic to advanced flying, and more specifically, from basic single-engine to fighter bombers. This was brought about by the fact that Gen. Charles Myers, head of Air Force Training Command, became aware of a critical situation that had developed at Nellis Air Force Base, Nevada. At that base they were having a bad time with their F-86 and F-100 training. They were also flying the F-86 gunnery program, which overburdened their 430 airplanes. Myers's solution was to take the F–86 mission out of Nellis and transfer it to Williams. The effect of this change was to take Williams out of the command of Crew Training Air Force (FLYTAF) and place it under the command of Crew Training Air Force (CREWTAF). When this took place, most of the earlier problems at Williams had been dealt with, and the base was operating well. Frank Rogers recalled the final FLYTAF critique for General Disosway: "George and Disosway were seated at the head of the table with thirty or forty others in the room. A maintenance inspector from Disosway's staff began the critique and stated that we had the greatest operation he'd seen in his entire career. Halfway through his briefing, Disosway spoke up and said, 'Wait a minute. I don't understand this. A few months ago this place was under water, and now you're telling me—while I'm fighting to get more manpower and stuff down here to make it easier for you—that everything is going great. What's this all about? You wouldn't want me to look silly when I go down to see Charlie Myers.' A great silence came over the room.

"Suffice to say that by the time we finished describing the improvements that had taken place since the last FLYTAF critique, the general seemed to be satisfied. He turned to George and said, 'Well, you know, the big problem at Willy Field for years had been that it was the first jet training base in existence, and they thought that they were better than everybody else, when all the time they really weren't. It appears that you've at last got the operation of this base where it ought to be.' "

With this change in mission, Williams went under the command of CREWTAF. Prior to going under CREWTAF, Colonel Brown had flown down to see Gen. Frank Robinson, the CREWTAF commander. He informed Robinson that they were doing some things that were not quite in line with the way they were down in CREWTAF. As told me by Robinson, Brown said, "I would like to have your permission to carry on, because we've been through a period of strain and have come out of it to the point that we are satisfied and proud to stand on our record. We'd like to have a chance to continue to do things our way, rather than make a lot of sudden changes." Robinson concurred, and indicated to George that he would advise his staff people not to be too "nit-picky" with them.

At the time of their first inspection following the change of command, a visiting major picked up a discrepancy in the use of a maintenance form. The whole thing wouldn't really have been worth talking about except that the major made a "federal case" out of it. He went in to see Rogers prior to writing up his report and gave him a stern lecture on what they were doing wrong.

According to Rogers: "I related the incident to George Brown, and he said, 'Well, write it up; answer the inspection report the way you said you were going to.' I did so, and he endorsed it in the following manner: 'I concur with the opinions of this officer, and request that you let us continue to function in the way we are doing, because we are satisfied that we're doing a good job, and we like the way it works, and it makes sense to us. Why not let us just keep going?' Well, the answer was, of course, we just kept going."[6]

During his tour at Williams, Brown was to discover that not all of his responsibilities were purely military in nature. Periodic flooding of several rivers in the area had on many occasions severely restricted the base's flying mission. It also caused great hardship in the local civilian community. A flood-control effort had been going on for some time prior to his arrival, but Brown concluded that the problem needed to be tackled at a higher level. He felt that a federal flood control program was the only solution and with the approval of his superiors went to Washington to see what he could accomplish.

Through the good offices of Congressman John J. Rhodes, Brown was invited to make a presentation before the Inland Waters Committee of the House of Representatives. He emphasized that the base could not carry out its mission with floodwaters covering the runways and urged the appropriation of funds to permanently divert the waters. In the end, he obtained federal flood-control assistance and, at the same time, gained worthwhile experience through his exposure to Washington politics.

Despite the many problems that Brown encountered at Williams, the following story, recounted by Lt. Gen. Albert P. Clark, suggests that life at the base was not without its lighter side. But in this case, it turned out that the joke was on George Brown. "During my first tour in the Pentagon," recalls Clark, "while I was in charge of personnel promotions and separations, I ran across a very interesting case in which an unscrupulous but talented individual was successfully impersonating Air Force officers, writing his own promotions, and traveling around the country free of charge.

"The subject came across my desk at the time they finally caught up with him. He was then being prosecuted in a civil court, since he actually had no military status. He would bury his trail as a captain and come out a major with a new name somewhere else. He'd cut temporary-duty travel orders for himself and even took a tour of the Caribbean at the Air Force's expense. The part of his story that relates to George Brown picks up when this 'officer' was at Bolling Field cashing bad fifty-dollar checks, but not trying to draw any pay. He'd just keep a step ahead of the bouncing checks. While at Bolling as a lieutenant colonel, he heard that there was an excellent get-rich-quick jet training course out at Williams where lieutenant colonels could get checked out in the T–33 trainer in a one-week course and come back and be right up with the head of the crowd. So he decided to try it, even though he was not a qualified pilot. So he changed his name to Royal and moved over to Anacostia Naval Air Station to break the chain and then hitched a ride to Williams, having sent bogus wires ahead saying he was coming for a certain course.

"He was duly met at the ramp by Colonel Brown and given the red carpet treatment. He was assigned an instructor and was doing quite well flying the T–bird, but he had made the mistake of leaving his B–4 bag behind at Anacostia and then compounded it by wiring back and asking that the B–4 bag of Lieutenant Colonel 'Jones' be forwarded to Colonel 'Royal' at Williams. So they came out and cut him off at the pass. When the FBI arrived at Williams, he was taxiing in from soloing in his T–bird. I'll never forget the fun I had joshing George Brown about the 'Case of the Visiting Royalty.' "[7]

It is fitting that this chapter, covering in retrospect George Brown's tour as Commander of Williams Air Force Base, conclude with the words of his one-time commander, Gen. Gabriel P. Disosway in a fitness report:

"His day-to-day operation of his base is outstanding. He is ahead of the job at all times, foreseeing problem areas and taking corrective action before serious situations develop." General Disosway went on to emphasize that under Brown's leadership there was an improvement in yearly average in-commission rate of aircraft, better scheduling, more missions flown, even improved maintenance.[8]

General Disosway further commented on September 30, 1955, "Colonel Brown's sound planning and aggressive follow-up action on all aspects of the changeover, without detriment to the present mission, has been highly gratifying to me and is indicative of the type of performance which can always be expected of this officer. This required changes in personnel who had to be upgraded, establishing special training courses, changes in facilities and all support activities for the new type of jet airplanes, new pilots, new and bigger supply problems, and new type support equipment." General Disosway later wrote on January 31, 1956, that Colonel Brown "demonstrated time and again his ingenuity and imagination in problems and changes that have arisen."

"George," remembers Gen. Gabriel Disosway, "had the feel of the people. He was a straightforward, honest individual, maybe too straightforward sometimes for his own good, but it never hurt him. He was a real comer."[9]

I asked General Disosway why he considered George Brown to be a "comer." He responded, "He had integrity, he had knowledge, he had a feel for people. He had that wonderful ability that made people do what he wanted them to do, and he didn't have to force them to do it."[10]

Upon the completion of this tour at Williams, Colonel Brown was slated to attend his first formal schooling since graduation from West Point, as a member of the National War College Class of 1957, another step toward bigger challenges and responsibilities for the future.

NOTES

1. Personal interview with Lt. Gen. James Knight, USAF (Ret.), August 7, 1979.
2. Personal interview with Col. Tom Personette, USAF (Ret.), June 29, 1979.
3. Knight interview.
4. Personette interview.
5. Personal interview with Col. Frank Rogers, USAF (Ret.), July 18, 1980.
6. Ibid.
7. Personal interview with Lt. Gen. Albert P. Clark, USAF (Ret.), June 29, 1979.
8. Personal interview with Gen. Gabriel P. Disosway, USAF (Ret.), January 17, 1979.
9. Ibid.
10. Ibid.

CHAPTER 11
NATIONAL WAR COLLEGE: AUGUST 1956–JUNE 1957

In August 1956, George Brown was assigned to the National War College at Fort McNair, Washington, D.C. Other than the U.S. Military Academy and the old Air Corps flying schools, the National War College was the only service school he ever attended. Brown was one of the younger officers in the Class of 1957 but because of his exceptional career was one of the most senior in rank.

The course lasted almost a year, from August 16, 1956, to June 11, 1957. The curriculum devoted two weeks to "The World Situation," followed by four weeks on "The Conflict of Power," and a month of "The Employment of National Power." Six weeks were then spent on an analysis of the Communist bloc and a similar period of time on our allies. Next there were three weeks on "A National Estimate of the Situation," and then five weeks on "Development of National Security Policy." The course closed with a field study, emphasizing a reappraisal of national security policy.

By design, the atmosphere was relaxed and informal, and the association among faculty, staff, and students was decidedly pleasant. Everyone was on a first-name basis, and the prescribed "uniform" was civilian dress. Each year's class was made up of the most promising officers from the Air Force, Army, Navy, and Marine Corps, and senior civilians from the State Department, the Department of Defense, and other government agencies.

A special effort was made to foster an understanding of the interaction between the military and civilian fields, and the curriculum was highlighted by prominent speakers from the military services, the State Department, and the executive branch. These guest speakers' presentations were followed by an extensive question-and-answer period for the students. There was a great deal of required reading, and frequent student seminars were held. These seminars gave them the opportunity to exchange ideas with members of other services.

The impression that George Brown made on those who knew him during this period was that of an unassuming, yet quietly forceful, individual. "The then Colonel Brown was not one of our 1956 'fertile five,' " wrote Navy classmate Rear Adm. Mason Freeman. "He was handsome, young, sociable, and along with the vast majority of the group, took the rare opportunity in a military career to read and to listen in order to broaden his knowledge and outlook. He was not one of the vocal few who wanted to impress contemporaries or perhaps superiors with their brilliance as speakers.

"When called upon in small committee groups, however, he expressed his views concisely and clearly. Having given his opinion, he was not keen about debating an issue. This, I believe, stemmed from the fact that most War College topics were long-standing national problems with few, if any, viable solutions, and at that stage George Brown saw small merit in lengthy discussion to no useful end."[1]

"At the National War College we all had our work cut out for us, and while socializing was encouraged, we just did not get to see one another that much," reflected Col. John Mitchell. "However, in our committees and seminars there was a very favorable atmosphere for informal discussions. George impressed me in these discussions with his attention to others' views and with the quiet manner he always assumed in presenting his side. I found him to be above average in intelligence and in his ability to speak and persuade without causing resentment."[2]

Foreign Service officer John A. Birch remembered, "George was very direct, not overbearing or tedious, but certain of his views, perhaps a trifle impatient with seemingly oversubtle positions taken by his colleagues. As a State Department participant, I was often on the defensive when it came to international problems, especially those that were not susceptible to military solutions. George believed in direct and forceful action, and he bore the stamp of an officer slated for high command. George clearly had the gift of leadership."[3]

Another civilian member of the class, Chester H. Opal, commented, "I must impute great tolerance to his spirit because I can't for the life of me remember when my own abruptness and no doubt abrasiveness ever evoked an expression of irritation from him . . ."⁴

"Perhaps I tended to view George differently," wrote then Col. Russell A. Berg. "I never knew him to go about seeking personal accolades or indiscriminately tossing about great pearls of wisdom or carrying on a personality contest. George was always George: level-headed, poised, well-balanced, and completely in control. When he spoke out it was because he had something to say that was direct, pertinent, and to the heart of the discussion. I never did see George lose control of himself or use harsh and crude language. His opinions were transmitted quite clearly without the need for verbal blasts. He was a natural leader who led by example. His fine personal appearance and presentation, honesty, and his forthright manner compelled admiration and respect. He had a very personal and individual style about him."⁵

Despite the positive overall impression that he created, some classmates confessed surprise at the ultimate success achieved by George Brown. What to some was forthrightness and straightforwardness was seen by others as a lack of diplomacy. For example, Col. Preston Piper, USAF (Ret.), remembers this of Brown: "In those seminars when he did speak or voice an opinion he was very certain, even to the point of being dogmatic, about the subject in question. It was almost impossible to argue with him about his position because of his attitude.

"I thought that he was lacking in diplomacy as far as his relations with the other service personnel, and that this probably was due to his having had just Air Force assignments prior to coming to the NWC. Because of this I must say that he was the least likely of my Air Force classmates there to become Chief of Staff of the Air Force and certainly Chairman of the Joint Chiefs."⁶

"George was certainly not one to stand out from the others in that very able class, either intellectually or as a personality," wrote Richard Van Wagenen. "He seemed to be a steady, low-key, likable person. I can think of several others who sparkled intellectually, or at least more obviously, than did George."⁷

"I knew him only slightly during the 1956–57 school year," recalled Army Col. William L. Osbourne. "He was quiet, never had much to say or asked many questions. My evaluation of his leadership qualities at the time were rather negative. I was surprised at his later success."⁸

Other classmates predicted a great future for George Brown. "His 'service reputation,' as it developed in our National War College class, quickly revealed facts that predicted his advancement," said J. L. Stewart, a Marine officer. "He was a West Pointer, slim, neat, military, and handsome in bearing and appearance. His peers from the Air Force looked to him and treated him as being a leader among them. A 'team' player who seemed to enjoy being with those in the school and in the college itself, he was articulate as a student and tended to come directly to a point and express forthrightly rather than to conjecture alternatives. He seemed to be well read and had opinions on most of the subject matter covered. He was sincerely interested; he met people easily and warmly, a very friendly man."[9]

Maj. Gen. Gilbert L. Pritchard wrote: "Our paths crossed frequently from 1945 on—as recently as March '78. My prime recollection of George was his straightforwardness and personal integrity. I believe these attributes won the full confidence of superiors, peers, and subordinates alike."[10]

"He was a man who exhibited his professional competence in such a quiet, unassuming way that he naturally attracted the attention and respect of those who were fortunate enough to be associated with him," said then Col. Elby D. Martin. "I got to know him a little better than some of the other non–Air Force officers because of our one-on-one athletic competition. I found him very competitive. One of the strongest memories I have of him concerns both of us thoroughly tired, sweaty, and out of breath—sitting on a bench after a good squash match (which I had won) trying to muster enough strength to take a shower. His look at me said, 'Just wait 'til next time!' "[11]

George Brown also played golf and softball while at the War College. He was a man with great physical energy and stayed in excellent condition. A young Naval Academy midshipman, whose father had served with Brown at Selfridge Air Force Base, and who had become somewhat of an adopted son, recalls a weekend visit with the Browns during which the colonel demonstrated his prowess as a woodcutter. The Browns had purchased an old house near the Potomac and were in the process of restoring it. It was a house built probably in the 1800s, and in addition to working on it, they were also clearing out the woods. "He had this big field of woods," reminisced Jack Cremin, "and during that weekend I helped him cut wood. I thought I was in great shape, particularly since the life was so active at the Naval Academy. Well, we were cutting and sawing and hauling wood that Saturday morning, and I was getting mighty tired and sore. Mrs. Brown finally came out and asked, 'Would anybody like some lunch?' and I immediately volunteered. But Colonel Brown replied, 'I'm going to go a little bit longer.' So we continued for another forty-five minutes. I was awfully glad when we stopped, and I was amazed at the outstanding physical condition Colonel Brown was in."[12]

Maj. Gen. Wiley D. Ganey, Deputy Commandant of the War College during the 1956–57 year, summarized his impressions of George Brown during this period of his career in his final training report:

> A friendly, intelligent, and polished officer who is highly regarded by his associates. Generally quiet, he is, however, an active participant in discussion groups where he expresses himself clearly, with self-assurance and with persuasion. His contribution to committee work is positive and is marked by his sound judgment and alert thinking. He writes well and convincingly, a fact which was made evident by the excellent individual research paper that he submitted. Obviously interested in his work at The National War College, he enthusiastically joins in the non-official as well as the official activities of his class. He is eminently qualified for work in joint or combined staff and command positions.

NOTES

1. Letter from Rear Adm. Mason Freeman, USN (Ret.), to EFP, June 21, 1979.
2. Letter from Col. John W. Mitchell, USAF (Ret.), to EFP, June 4, 1979.
3. Letter from John Birch, retired Foreign Service officer, to EFP, May 9, 1979.
4. Letter from Chester H. Opal to EFP, May 28, 1979.
5. Letter from Brig. Gen. Russell A. Berg, USAF (Ret.), to EFP, May 10, 1979.
6. Letter from Col. Preston Piper, USAF (Ret.), to EFP, May 7, 1979.
7. Letter from Richard W. Van Wagenen, USAF (Ret.), to EFP, May 20, 1979.
8. Letter from Col. William L. Osbourne, USA (Ret.), to EFP, May 11, 1979.
9. Letter from Brig. Gen. J. L. Stewart, USMC (Ret.), to EFP, June 8, 1979.
10. Letter from Maj. Gen. Gilbert L. Pritchard, USAF (Ret.), to EFP, May 14, 1979.
11. Letter from Brig. Gen. Elby D. Martin, USMC (Ret.), to EFP, June 2, 1979.
12. Personal interview with Maj. Jack Cremin, USAF, August 8, 1979.

CHAPTER 12
WASHINGTON, D.C.:
JULY 1957–JUNE 1959

Upon completion of the War College in June of 1957, then Colonel Brown was selected by Gen. Thomas D. White, Air Force Chief of Staff, as his executive officer. I asked Brown why he was selected for that position, and he replied, "I wasn't aware that I had ever met him, but I had worked with and been associated quite closely with Gen. Jacob Smart, his Assistant Vice Chief of Staff. I think that he arranged for my selection, although he has never said anything to me about it. The only time I ever laid eyes on General White before I went to work for him was when he came to the National War College to speak and I was just one in the class. When we were about to receive orders I said something to General Smart about what he thought the future might hold and he said, 'Why?' I said, 'Well, I've got property here in this area, a house that I need to dispose of. If I'm not going to stay in this town, I'd just as soon get out.' He said, 'Don't worry, you're going to stay right here.' I think those two worked this thing out together.

"It says a lot for General White," George Brown continued, "that he'd take me on, because I knew nothing about the Pentagon or how to get anything done there. Usually a senior officer is pretty selfish about who he has on his immediate staff. He wants them to help him. It was not the normal thing to have somebody whom you can help. I think, and I don't want to sound conceited about this, that they believed that they could bring me in as the Chief's executive and push me on to other things that would benefit the Air Force."[1]

Gen. Jacob E. Smart offers firsthand insight into Brown's selection: "I recommended George as White's executive officer. I did so because I thought he was the best man for the job and that they would complement one another. I was absolutely certain that this would be a great experience for George and that this would contribute to his development for larger jobs."[2]

Brown's job required him to supervise the Chief's immediate office staff. He monitored all the incoming and outgoing correspondence, transmitted General White's orders to appropriate staff officers for implementation, and, as his job description specifically provided, "when practicable acts for the Chief of Staff or in his name," and to "resolve for the Chief of Staff those problems that do not require his personal attention."

Obviously, it was a unique opportunity for him to learn and grow. Brown observed to me of General White, "In addition to the experience and knowledge that he had of the game played in this town, that is, the work that went on, the interservice responsibilities, the work of the Air Staff, between the Air Staff and OSD, with the Congress, General White just had no fear. I may overstate this because I was quite impressionable at that time. I came to the Air Staff as his executive officer without having served previously in the Pentagon. I didn't even know where to get a cup of coffee. I also observed that General White had a perceptive mind with a quick appreciation for things others just didn't seem to grasp, but which seemed evident to those of us around him."[3]

When I asked General White's aide, Tim Ahern, about Brown's comment that he didn't know his way around the Pentagon and the Air Staff, he reflected, "I think that he knew more about the way the staff should operate than he was owning up to. He was, I think, simply modest. He was saying, 'I'm coming to work for General White, who had been everything that anybody could be on the Air Staff, so I find it difficult that with that kind of experience he could select somebody like me to come in to help him.' General White had all the expertise in the world, but George had a lot of savvy about how the staff operated, even though he might have said differently. It was just typical of his humility."[4]

When Brown came on board, Ahern had been working as White's aide for several years. If he had wanted, George could have interjected himself into the already established routine, since as exec he had carte blanche to pretty much do as he pleased. His transition, however, was a smooth one. "I briefed Colonel Brown very thoroughly on the way we operated," said Ahern. "He instructed me to continue to do as I'd been doing and just keep him informed."[5]

As exec, Brown was responsible for running the office. "He was different from previous execs," recalled Ann Fletcher, General White's secretary, who had been in the Chief's office for over ten years at that time. "He was more straightforward and businesslike, a man I could admire, so honest and straightforward in every respect. If he told you something, he expected you to do it. You could just feel that he believed in you. He expected more of you and you did more because of the type of man he was. He was also very personable. He treated everyone fairly, a sergeant as well as a general."[6]

As the Chief's exec, Brown really had five or six key contact points in the staff, the execs to the deputy chiefs of staff. For example, if there were an operations problem, Brown would call the exec to Gen. Frank Everest, Deputy Chief of Staff for Operations, and give him the necessary instructions.

General White relied on Brown to make his workload easier, more bearable. For example, if a paper came in that in Brown's judgment presented too many options to the Chief, he had the staff rework the paper and arrive at a better position so that the Chief could choose from two options rather than five. Brown worked with the execs as described by Tim Ahern: "He would say, 'Hey guys, we can't give this mishmash to the Chief. Why don't you and Plans get together? Quit pulling and shoving and see if we can't work something that's a lot closer.' There weren't very many occasions when that had to be done, but George had the stature to pull it off."[7]

Brown also screened and summarized much of the other paperwork that came through the office. The Chief in the course of a normal day would probably sign anywhere from thirty to fifty staff summary sheets or letters going to the other services, or letters external to the Air Force. Principally, the bulk of the paperwork consisted of staff summary sheets, but many of these were quite thick. Brown read each report and would write a one- or two-sentence précis, like, "This is not controversial," or "The staff's in full agreement," or "No hidden problems." General White was a speed reader, so with Brown's help, he never left a paper in his basket overnight.

General White was difficult to satisfy, a person who didn't tolerate fools gladly. But, his entire staff was devoted to serving him, with Brown leading the pack. In lessening the Chief's workload, George sent some of the papers to the aides and execs, but they would be the less controversial papers that really only needed to be checked for something other than the substance of any arguments. Brown kept the knotty ones for himself.

Another of Brown's duties was to assist in the preparation of speeches. General White would give him guidelines and George would coordinate with the speech writers. "He was kind of like the final sieve," recalled Tim Ahern. "He didn't get into the nuts and bolts of cranking it out, but quite often he would, at the outset, say, 'I think what the Chief ought to be talking about in this forum is thus and so.' The speech writers would then go off and do their thing."[8]

"I remember on one occasion General White had requested a speech on the missions and equipment of the Tactical Air Command," recalled Col. Robert G. Moll. "The Air Force was working hard to obtain a new all-weather fighter. The speech writers furnished General White with a speech that he read and sent out to George with the comment that it did not adequately express his views and should be rewritten. George read the speech, turned to me and said, 'Hell, I can write that speech,' and proceeded to do so. He finished it and sent it in to General White, who accepted it without change."[9]

On one occasion, General White was scheduled for a speech in San Francisco. He received the speech from Henderson, but said to Ahern, "You know, this doesn't say anything. You and George Brown sit down and put something in the speech so that it says something." At that time, military personnel were often quoted in the press, as they spoke with some authority. The audience was a meeting of NATO parliamentarians, and White was interested in saying something of note. Brown and Ahern decided that White should issue a call to our NATO partners to do more toward their own defense posture. They, therefore, carefully couched some words to that effect, and submitted it for necessary clearances. Donald Quarles, the Under Secretary, read and approved it. Then it went through the bureaucratic clearance labyrinth of the State Department and the Joint Chiefs and finally was scrutinized by OSD Security Review. White gave the speech, and it was picked up and quoted in San Francisco, Washington, and New York newspapers.

"We got back and were feeling pretty good about the speech," reflected Ahern. "The morning after, the telephone rang. Edith McCaffrey, the Chief's secretary, said, 'The President is calling.' It was Ike Eisenhower.

"Let me make a confession. At the assistant exec's seat they had a little mike where you could listen to the telephone conversations of the Chief. It was foot operated so that there was no click like somebody picking up on the phone. I listened to the conversation. Ike was livid. In his first burst of anger there were no preliminaries with General White. He said, 'What the hell do you think you're doing? What's the idea? What are you trying to pull? Why are you getting everybody excited?' He went on and on.

"General White replied he had gone through all of the clearance processes, that it was not something he had unilaterally taken up and spoken off the cuff on. He had touched all the bases. He made no effort to say, 'Well, sorry, no excuse, sir.' He simply said, 'I did all of the things that I am expected to do.'

"He came out afterward and said to us, 'Well, I just had a little conversation with the President.' It didn't bother him particularly. He said to Brown and me, 'You know, you just do the best you can. You win some, you lose some.' One of the things that seemed most impressive to me was there would have been other people in his position who would have taken our heads off. White did not. George and I discussed it afterward and said, 'Gee, for a foray into speech-writing activity, this one was a zinger.' It was not the kind of thing we wanted to do all the time, but White was a very fair man."[10]

When General White traveled, Brown normally stayed in Washington to "hold the fort." Detailed itineraries were left, and it was up to Brown to initiate all calls to him both in the air and on the ground, since the Chief didn't ever want to have to call in. Brown had to advise him when something had happened needing his immediate attention. The burden on Brown was a very heavy responsibility for a colonel.

When Brown got in his flying time he flew with Tim Ahern, who commented, "Brown was an excellent pilot who really knew his way around, understood the regulations and associated constraints. A typical colonel would get himself a seeing-eye major and let him do all the worrying about that sort of thing; not Brown, he stayed abreast of all that."[11]

During this period, Brown demonstrated his thoughtfulness, which throughout his career endeared him to all who served with, under, and above him. For example, he was instrumental in arranging for the presentation of command pilot wings to Charles Lindbergh while White was Chief. The Chief made the presentation, but it was Brown's idea, and he worked out the details of how the presentation would be made. Technically, Lindbergh might not have had the requirements for the wings themselves in terms of military time, but the stumbling blocks were all worked out, the hurdles overcome, and the Chief pinned them on.

During General White's tenure as Chief, his Vice Chief of Staff, Gen. Curtis E. LeMay, led a record-setting flight in a KC–135 from Westover Air Force Base nonstop to Buenos Aires, the longest such flight of its kind up to that time. No prior special preparations had been made for their return. A call came from LeMay when they were about halfway back, asking General White if it could be arranged for them to land at Washington National Airport, and that certain awards be made to the crew members. Brown immediately got certain members Distinguished Flying Crosses and others, Air Medals. This was quite a coordination problem, because in a matter of hours they had to obtain the medals, arrange for the appearance of the Air Force Secretary and Chief of Staff, gather a crowd, ask the newspaper photographers to be there, and, finally, make unusual arrangements for the military aircraft to land at the overly crowded National Airport.

It was decided that when they landed the crew would line up with General LeMay at one end and the lowest ranking airman down at the other as the medals were awarded. The Chief was to decorate people from left to right, and the Secretary of the Air Force would decorate from right to left, working toward the center. White's aide, Tim Ahern, went along carrying the medals.

"It wasn't the neatest way to do this thing," recalled Ahern, "but it did fit the moment. Anyway, after we had gone through the formalities and made the presentation, we came back and were standing there, and I felt Brown tap me on the shoulder. He said, 'They missed the sergeant in the middle.' He then insisted I get the Chief to go out there and decorate the forgotten sergeant. We went out and made a special award, and the crowd loved it. Now someone of a different temperament might have just let it slide because it could have been awarded later, but George insisted that we had to take care of that airman in the middle." [12]

When I asked General Brown himself what he personally considered to be his most significant learning experience while serving as General White's exec, he leaned back in his chair and spoke of an address White made to the cadets of the United States Air Force Academy on December 14, 1957. "The most memorable point of that speech," said Brown, "was General White's emphasis on the importance of avoiding becoming bogged down in detail." General White said in this speech:

> Leadership means many things to many men. I cannot tell you how to become a good leader—that is something you have to find out for yourselves. There is no positive check list to follow—but you must have the desire.
>
> General Freiherr von Hammerstein-Equord, who was the former head of the German War Department, Chief of Army Direction, said:
>
> "I divide my officers into four classes as follows: The clever, the industrious, the lazy, and the stupid. Each officer always possesses two of these qualities. Those who are clever and industrious I appoint to the general staff. The man who is clever and lazy is destined for high command because he has the nerve to deal with all situations. Use can, under certain circumstances, be made of those who are stupid and lazy. But, whoever is stupid and industrious must be got rid of at once."
>
> I have always considered General von Hammerstein's observations very interesting, particularly so, when one attempts to analyze the four categories he listed.
>
> It is quite clear to me why General von Hammerstein wanted

clever and industrious officers on his staff. Such men are particularly needed today. Men with imagination and the power to
comprehend the essential nature of the problems or situations,
and who are not afraid to work, are extremely valuable to a
commander.

But, what did von Hammerstein mean when he said the
clever and lazy man qualified for the highest leadership posts?
The cleverness attribute we needn't discuss except to point out
that he meant brains and experience—experience because no
man would be in a position to be considered for high command
had he not already gained considerable experience.

To me the general used the word "lazy," however, in a wholly
unusual context. The general didn't mean lazy in the true sense.
He meant, without a doubt, the ability to distinguish between the
really vital and the less consequential; he meant the attribute of
being able to grasp the essentials and to refuse to be cluttered up
with the non-essentials. Once the man with such attributes has
charted his course based on vital essentials, he delegates the rest
to subordinates—subordinates whom he has selected, whom he
trusts and in whom he can repose confidence. These men do the
"work" so the high commander can perform the major tasks.
Then this clever and so-termed "lazy" commander accepts full
responsibility for his actions. The major decisions are his alone
and he accepts the consequences as worked out in detail by competent subordinates. That's what von Hammerstein meant by the
"nerve" to deal with all situations.[13]

Brown's close friend, who also worked for the Chief, was then Col.
Robert J. Dixon (who went on to become a full general and Commander of
Tactical Air Command). I asked General Dixon: "Would you say that
General White had an impact on Brown's development?" General Dixon
replied, "There is no doubt about that. You couldn't be around White without being impressed and learning. At that stage, colonels like ourselves were
like sponges—worse than sponges, like vacuum cleaners. We'd sweep it all
up wherever we could get it. There wasn't a minute of the day that a million
impressions didn't hit us, not only with General White, but with other
senior people too. My impressions of people from those days are the most
vivid because they were formative days. Our minds were wide open. Washington was an exciting town, and we had exciting jobs.

"General White had a very firm grip on what he did and didn't do, on
what he wanted and what he didn't want," commented General Dixon. "He
had a gentle style, but there was a lot of steel in his gloves. I never saw any-

thing but the glove. General White had a conviction, shared by George Brown, that the open warfare of 'Let's bring the matter to a head and get the damned thing settled' was not the way to go about doing things. To some extent, White was criticized for that by others who were more direct. However, he believed in persuasion. George learned from that. It was his nature and approach, too. Both George and General White had tempers; George had a temper that could really flare on occasions. But, given a preference, George would prefer to conduct things in a gentlemanly fashion. George also thought that General White was an eye-opener in terms of being able to see long-range issues, being willing to let the short-range gain go and be happy with the long-range victory. General White's view on the importance of space to the nation, to the Air Force, was an example of a long-range view. It's very trivial now, since everybody knows that space is important, but then, nobody appreciated it. I think the kind of vision that General White had taught George, as it taught me, a new way of looking at things."[14]

In analyzing Brown's overall effectiveness as White's executive, Tim Ahern made the comment that George Brown stood out among the many execs he had known who served the Chief. I asked him why, and he responded, "A number of reasons: One, his war record was just superb. The only medal he didn't have was the Medal of Honor. Two, he was a hell of a handsome guy with bearing and appearance. He was articulate and had a quality awfully hard to describe that makes for great leadership. That is that you wanted to associate with him, be wherever he was, part of whatever he was doing, because you liked him as your front man, your leader. You'd like to say, 'I'm one of his guys.' Third, I think he was extremely astute in knowing the way a staff should operate, a superior staff officer as well as being an operational commander. You don't get that combination very often."[15]

General White himself was raised in an Air Force generation that did not believe in inflation in an officer effectiveness report. Thus, White checked the square on Colonel Brown's evaluation covering the period from June 18, 1957, to November 3, 1957, "a very fine officer of great value to the service," but did not mark the square on the far right of the form that stated "one of the very few outstanding officers I know." General White said in the word picture of Brown:

> I have known this officer only about four months. In this period he has fully met my expectations in selecting him for the position as my Executive. I consider him outstanding and anticipate that further experience with him will justify an even higher rating than that accorded in this report.

The next year, covering the period from November 4, 1957, through September 30, 1958, General White did check the square, "one of the very few outstanding officers I know," and wrote:

> Colonel Brown has demonstrated outstanding executive ability, exceptional knowledge of his job, and tact. He is a fine appearing officer, well educated, well mannered; he maintains the highest standards of conduct. He will be a credit to the U.S. Air Force in any assignment suitable for an officer of his age and years of service. Colonel Brown's personnel records are ample testimony to his distinguished combat record. This officer, in my opinion, deserves promotion well ahead of most of his contemporaries.

In his final year with General White, which ended June 28, 1959, a new responsibility was added to Colonel Brown's job description—"Renders advice to the Chief of Staff on request on a great variety of topics." The brief word picture written by General White stated:

> Colonel Brown is in my opinion a truly outstanding officer and gentleman. He is effective in dealing with superiors and juniors alike; he is courteous but courageous in expressing his convictions. He has a charming wife. He should go a long way in his Air Force career.

After his tour with General White, Brown was promoted to the grade of brigadier general and was selected to become military assistant to the Deputy Secretary of Defense, one of the most challenging assignments of his career, one that was extremely important for his continued personal growth.

NOTES

1. Personal interview with Gen. George S. Brown, September 14, 1977.
2. Personal interview with Gen. Jacob E. Smart, USAF (Ret.), July 17, 1979 and June 10, 1980.
3. George S. Brown interview.
4. Personal interview with Maj. Gen. Timothy I. Ahern, USAF (Ret.), July 2, 1981.
5. Ibid.
6. Personal interview with Ann Fletcher.
7. Ahern interview.

8. Ibid.
9. Letter from Col. Robert G. Moll, USAF (Ret.), September 9, 1980.
10. Ahern interview.
11. Ibid.
12. Ibid.
13. *Air Power Historian,* vol. 5 (April 1958), pp. 75–79.
14. Personal interview with Gen. Robert E. Dixon, USAF (Ret.), June 10, 1980.
15. Ahern interview.

CHAPTER 13

WASHINGTON, D.C.:
JUNE 1959–AUGUST 1963

George Brown's next assignment was most challenging and meaningful, as in June 1959, he became military assistant to Deputy Secretary of Defense Thomas S. Gates, Jr. I asked Secretary Gates why he chose Brown for this position, and he responded, "Well, when I went over to the Department of Defense from the Navy Department, I thought that I ought to have an Air Force officer as a principal assistant. I didn't want anyone to think I was partial because of my Navy background. So I asked both General White and Gen. Lyman L. Lemnitzer, the Chief of Staff of the Army, for recommendations. Tommy White sent me down the background papers on three officers, and after reading all three, I decided to look at George Brown first. I had always had a bias in favor of people with combat experience, because I found that they usually knew more about what was going on than other officers. George Brown had a remarkable combat record in World War II," Gates continued. "I talked with him and was greatly impressed. We hit it off well, and I selected him."[1]

On December 2, 1959, when Gates became Secretary of Defense, Brown, who had been promoted to brigadier general on August 1, 1959, continued to serve him. "George Brown did a remarkable job for me," said Secretary Gates. "He was a fine officer with a fine record, but it never occurred to me when I hired him that he was as bright as he turned out to be. He was a very good thinker. On many of the difficult policy questions I had to settle as

Secretary, I worked out the decisions with him. We didn't often have unanimity within the Joint Chiefs, so the decision on many issues had to be mine. I'd come back with Brown from these JCS meetings and we'd sort out the questions when we had to make a decision between them or a policy decision of some importance."[2]

When asked to give an example, Gates said, "The most important decision I made during the time I was in Washington—perhaps the most important decision I ever made in my life—was to establish an Integrated Targeting Strategic Plan, which was ultimately set up under SAC in Omaha. This took the place of what was called the 'coordinated targeting plan,' which had been in effect between the Air Force and the Navy, a plan under which they attempted to coordinate the strategic missiles of the Polaris submarines with the Air Force missiles and bombs. We had a split decision within the Joint Chiefs on this, and they couldn't agree at all. In fact, Adm. Arleigh Burke, Chief of Naval Operations, protested the decision all the way to the President in a two-hour meeting involving Jim Douglas, the Deputy Secretary of Defense, Gen. Nathan Twining, Air Force Chief of Staff, and myself. George Brown helped me make this decision, helped me to determine that this was the right way to do it. He helped me more than the prejudiced Joint Chiefs did."[3]

Did George Brown show any favoritism toward the Air Force in the formulation of this decision? Secretary Gates answered, "No, George was always objective, very objective; he was an unprejudiced officer. The whole process took several months. George sat in on most of the many meetings relating to it. It was a weapons, targeting, and command problem all rolled up together. George was of immeasurable help to me in its resolution.

"He was also helpful in advising me whenever he felt I could make a decision that would clear up accumulated paperwork in the Pentagon," Gates continued. "The Pentagon was famous for papers lying around for years because no one would make a decision. George was constantly urging me to *make* a decision, even though a lot of people weren't going to like it, which was much better than having it hang there to be brought up five years later. So, at his urging, we cleaned up a lot of backlogged stuff that was festering in the works because nobody could get general agreement on it.

"Some of the issues resolved were relatively minor. There was one, for example, concerning who would command a possible African action; that is, who would be the commander and which service would be the dominant one in an invasion or action in Africa if we ever had one. It all seemed rather silly to me. It came up one day when I was down with the Chiefs. It had been up there for years. There was a planning document, and after some discussion, I said, 'Well it ought to be the Army. Africa is a land mass, and the Navy's got to get them there, but the Army certainly ought to be in command.' They finally agreed with that, and coming back upstairs from the meeting, George said, 'Do you know what you did this afternoon?' I said, 'No, what did I do?' He said, 'You cleaned up about three years of paperwork and now they can put this behind them and forget it.'

"George was wise in his judgments on how to get things done," continued Gates. "He was a prodigious worker, putting in long hours. As I said, when I met him initially, I didn't realize what an incisive and analytical mind he had. He did his job quietly and was a great reader. My Army aide had a lot to offer also, but he did less of the policy work and more of the personnel and administrative work. George was most helpful to me in the area of policy."[4]

General White wrote of Brown's nineteen months of service under Secretary Gates: "Brigadier General Brown has distinguished himself and reflected great credit upon the Air Force by superior service as Military Assistant to the Secretary of Defense. I have personally observed this officer's performance of duty, demeanor and appearance. I am convinced that he has proven his ability to contribute greatly in positions of higher command and staff duty and should be promoted at an early date."

One of Brown's great challenges during this period was the problem of remaining loyal to the Secretary of Defense without offending his own service. White perceived this problem and commented further in his evaluation, "General Brown retained the respect and full confidence of the Secretary of Defense by the objectivity of his views with relation to other services and at the same time was of inestimable value to me and the Air Staff."

When President John Kennedy's administration took over in January 1961, Gates was succeeded as Secretary of Defense by Robert S. McNamara. "As I remember," recalled Gates, "McNamara came down around the first of the year, maybe three weeks or a month before the Inauguration, before he was to take office and reviewed with me everything we did. I gave him all my files and let him sit in with me in all my meetings in that period. During that time, he got to know the secretaries in the office, the aides, George Brown, everybody. He made up his own mind as to what he wanted to do. In some cases, he made changes. I recommended to McNamara that he keep George and he did."[5]

There were also other inputs into McNamara's decision as to who should be his military assistant. "I was then Deputy Chief of Staff for Air Force Personnel in Washington," recalled Lt. Gen. Edward J. Timberlake. "McNamara wanted an Air Force assistant and I suggested he retain George Brown. Some people on the staff said that that was a dirty trick; anybody who got the job, they said, was going to get his head cut off. I said, 'No,

Brown is so good that he'll be able to satisfy both McNamara and LeMay. If you can satisfy those two divergent people, you're doing well.' And sure enough, George stuck it out with McNamara for two-and-a-half years, and was promoted to major general at the end of it."[6]

I asked McNamara himself why he selected George Brown. "I inherited George from Tom," responded Robert S. McNamara, "who put him in that post, and I'm deeply grateful to him because George proved to be an extraordinarily able man. I primarily kept George because Tom Gates had suggested him. Now of course I looked at the record, but I learned long ago that I can't tell nearly as much from a simple interview as I can from hearing the opinion of somebody whose standards and values I know, such as Tom Gates."[7]

I then asked, "What was the quality you were looking for in an assistant?" "Well," he commented, "I wanted integrity above all else, because to be an Air Force officer in the office of the Secretary of Defense who was dealing with issues having high emotional content to the senior Air Force staff, including the Chief of Staff, required integrity on the part of the military assistant, and Brown had it. He also had high intelligence, broad experience, and sensitivity to military–foreign policy issues, but most of all he had absolute integrity.[8]

"He illustrated his integrity by advising me that he thought I was right in taking certain positions contrary to those taken by the Air Force Chief of Staff. A specific example was the B-70; he believed that we were right in canceling the program, whereas Chief of Staff Gen. Curtis E. LeMay was determined to go to the Congress in support of the plane, contrary to the President's decision. I was impressed by Brown's integrity time and time again because in a very real sense promotion decisions to higher military rank were made in the service, not in my office. He had every reason to believe that taking positions contrary to his own service might affect adversely his promotion prospects. Yet he was willing to take positions because he believed in them and thought it his responsibility to the Constitution and to the President and me. I admired him immensely for it."[9]

Then I asked Mr. McNamara, "How would you define what role you wanted your assistant to have? What did you expect of your assistant?" He answered, "I expected him to advise me. I don't want to suggest that I looked to him instead of the Chairman of the Joint Chiefs for advice, but I wanted him also to advise me based on his experience as a senior officer in the service on issues in particular matters put before me, on judgments that were beginning to form in my mind, on further avenues of investigation that I should undertake before I came to a decision. He was never reluctant to disagree with me, which he did often. I have always wanted the best and the

brightest people around me, and I have never wanted them to try to anticipate what my wishes were, what my decisions were likely to be, but rather to
present their own views and leave it to me to accept or reject them. I never
had any hesitance in rejecting them, overruling them, or going contrary to
their views. But I sure as hell wanted to know what they thought."[10]

I related to McNamara that Secretary Gates had said that often at a
meeting of the Joint Chiefs, without unanimity among them, the decision
had to be his as Secretary of Defense. He would then go back to the office
and sit down with Brown and discuss it back and forth. George would
always be candid and not show any service bias in advising him of what
should be done. "That's exactly the way he behaved with me," said McNamara. "There were discussions on particular matters, such as the Tonkin
Gulf, for example. We were being shelled by, or thought we were being
shelled by, the North Vietnamese. I said to George, 'What do you think?
Can we accept at face value the reports that the North Vietnamese shelled
us or were they attributed to a response by some action of ours that we don't
understand?' That kind of exchange would take place after such a meeting.
But other big issues, force structure, strategy, what have you, would normally come up outside of meetings with the Chiefs, from papers that had to
be sent to the Chiefs for their views. Their views would come back on these
fundamental matters, not simply reflections of discussions in the Chiefs'
tank, on which I thought George's judgment was so valuable. I used the
B-70 as an illustration. That is not a subject that would have been discussed
in the tank.

"During the early years in Vietnam," continued Secretary McNamara,
"allegations were made that we were short of bombs or other supplies. I
would ask George his opinion, and invariably he would find that requirements had been overstated. He could look at it from the point of view of a
professional Air Force officer and could recognize that there were other
ways of dealing with the problem than saying that either we couldn't move
forward because we didn't have the logistical support or that in order to get
it we had to engage in a huge munitions production program, which really
wasn't feasible under the circumstances. He was an extraordinarily wise,
very intelligent, extremely hard-working individual."[11]

The Chairman of the Joint Chiefs of Staff under Mr. McNamara was
Gen. Maxwell Taylor of the United States Army. Secretary to the Chairman
was then Lt. Andrew Goodpaster, also an Army officer. "I can tell you that
there were many occasions when I called George Brown," reflected Goodpaster, "to ask about key issues and decisions, where matters stood, what
further action could be expected, whether anything further was needed from
the Joint Chiefs of Staff. That's the kind of thing that I did with him. We all
thought that George had that inner strength, that inner fiber, so that he was

going to tell Mr. McNamara the honest facts of the matter whatever they might be, that there would be no distortion, there would be no glossing over, there would be no dropping out, there would be no selectivity of service positions in his presenting the situation. I guess there was also a bit of personal chemistry that worked in it because we knew that when certain issues arose, decisions were made in response to higher considerations. We knew that he had an understanding and appreciation of the military, what the military impact would be. If that was adverse, he felt as bad about it as we did. But he had a job to do, too.

"We had a system, for example," continued General Goodpaster, "for learning of the status of Joint Chiefs of Staff recommendations sent up to the Secretary of Defense. If we found that one of our recommendations had been hung up for a long time in ISA (International Security Affairs) and nothing had come of it, I'd get in touch with George and find out who was acting on it. George was a steady, sensible, straight, honest, able man there in OSD. He was a man you could transact business with in full confidence. We were able to work together quite effectively." [12]

Serving under Defense Secretary McNamara was probably the greatest challenge of Brown's career to that point. To say that McNamara was controversial is an understatement; to say that he was hated by many military men is a fact. The Secretary was widely regarded as a brilliant but cold and machinelike personality whose hard-line stewardship over the Defense Establishment resulted in a bristling relationship between him and the Joint Chiefs and in competitive and difficult attitudes and relationships among the military services. George Brown was required to promulgate his unpopular decisions and action papers downward to the Joint Chiefs and the armed services. That George, duty-bound in loyalty to his superior, was able not only to survive in this environment, but to perform his duties without incurring either the enmity of the military service chiefs or the displeasure of the Secretary is an everlasting tribute to his diplomacy, honesty, and integrity. He emerged from this "hot seat" with McNamara's highest recommendations and the admiration and respect of each of the military services. His reputation was now firmly established, and it became evident that he was destined for leadership positions of the highest order.

A senior Air Force officer, Gen. Gabriel Disosway, said of the relationship between George and Secretary McNamara: "Brown would come down and tell General LeMay, the Air Force Chief of Staff, or General McKee, the Vice Chief of Staff, 'Look, here's what McNamara is going to do whether you like it or not; this is what's going to happen, and you better adjust yourself to it.' This is the type of man he was. He didn't mince words. And he was just as frank with McNamara as he was with everybody else." [13]

"I was in War Plans when McNamara and the Kennedy administration came in," commented Lt. Gen. George S. Boylan, Jr. "I don't know what motivated McNamara, vis-à-vis his younger years in the Air Corps. He probably had some fixed opinion about the quality of the Air Force, but in any case, we were inundated with studies the first month or so, and mountains of work that had to be done and hours spent with only a few people to do it. Certain echelons in the Air Force got stiff-backed. 'Who the hell is this guy McNamara?' George impressed an opposite philosophy on me. 'You work for the guy,' he said to us. 'Let's do it. Let's do it right and do it superbly well. Then next time he'll notice.' George rapidly gained McNamara's confidence. He never let McNamara down and never sold him short. When George came to the Air Staff to visit us, he'd say, 'Get straightened out. You're going to have to do these things.' He respected McNamara's ability and was loyal to him, openly defending McNamara. He defended McNamara on the basis of McNamara's own individual intelligence—own individual capability—and McNamara's position as Secretary of Defense."[14]

The Secretary of the Air Force at that time, Eugene M. Zuckert, said of General Brown, "Despite his relatively junior rank, he had no hesitation in giving me and the senior Air Force officers the frankest appraisal of our difficulties in communication with Secretary McNamara. He and Col. (later Lt. Gen.) Jack O'Neill in Defense Research and Engineering were invaluable in helping the Air Force with their savvy and calling them the way they saw them even when they were calling attention to serious deficiencies in Air Force philosophy and tactics."[15]

This quotation from Secretary Zuckert was read to Secretary McNamara for comment in a personal interview. Mr. McNamara replied, "I don't know what George Brown told them. He didn't discuss with me what he told them, and I didn't really ask him to carry live bricks to the Air Force. But the Air Force was so parochial at times they weakened their own case. They were acting contrary to both their own interests and the interests of the nation. I think George very possibly may have pointed that out to them, in which case he was acting in the interests of everyone. The bearer of unpleasant tidings is not often welcomed with open arms, but I know Brown spoke up and said what he thought."[16]

"I think the first time I really met George Brown was in Dave Burchinal's office (then Deputy Chief of Staff for Plans and Operations)," reflected Gen. Russell E. Dougherty. "George, as assistant to McNamara, was very loyal to him, but at the same time, he never compromised himself. At this first encounter, he was 'explaining' McNamara to us, almost as if he felt that parts of McNamara needed to be explained. I guess they really did, because we considered McNamara some sort of unique fellow who didn't really exist. George did a remarkable job of teaching us what made McNamara tick, how he operated, and how we could best adapt to his methods."[17]

"I remember when I would go see George during the period," recalled his World War II comrade Ramsey Potts, "I disagreed intensely with some of Secretary McNamara's approaches to his taking unto himself the responsibility for knowing everything and being, in effect, the sole spokesman on the Hill, his decisions to run the war in Vietnam, controlling so many of the fine details of operations from the Pentagon. I went to talk to George two or three times about my concern. He would try to explain to me what his boss was doing, why the approach, but it was clear that he had reservations himself and that he was trying to express those views in the right way to the Secretary. I thought maybe George would damage his reputation in the Air Force because he was associated with Secretary McNamara, but again, I think you have to realize that here was a man who was not only professional, not only clearly dedicated to duty and always regarded as being truthful and straightforward, but perceived that way by everybody else. So nobody thought he was up there in McNamara's office turning favors and trying to get some special favors or appointments for himself. Nobody thought of him that way because of his character and his personality. That's why his contemporaries and the people who were ahead of him in the Air Force who had to make decisions about his appointment and assignments never penalized him."[18]

"My first contact with Brown," reflected Lt. Gen. William Y. Smith, "was in 1962. I was a major at the time, and what impressed me most about General Brown was that he was interested in one thing—doing his job and doing it the best that he could. He did not appear interested, as a lot of other people were, in trying to sell himself or impress people. He focused on what needed to be done and did it in a professional and effective way. Brown knew what he was doing and had confidence in himself."[19]

Smith's comment was read to McNamara, and the Secretary commented, "That's exactly my view. I never saw him try to advance himself by taking a position that his service wanted him to take but in which he didn't really believe. I never saw him push himself forward. He never spoke to me about promotion."[20]

"During the period of our association, I also saw his ability to deal with people," continued General Smith. "He treated them as individuals, accepting them as they were and not in terms of rank or position. There were people with great ability working for and with him, and Brown had the ability to perceive their worth.

"Regarding his personal interest in individuals, I particularly remember the first evening that a group of us went out together. Within the group was everything from an assistant service secretary to plain secretaries and stenographers to generals and others. At that dinner he treated everybody as a social equal. He was really a great believer in the quality of people simply as people."[21]

Gen. Frederic Smith was Vice Chief of Staff of the Air Force when Brown was military assistant to McNamara. Smith, an outspoken critic of Secretary McNamara, finally resigned his appointment over a disagreement with the Secretary. I asked him how George Brown survived the McNamara assignment. "I think," said Smith, "it was probably due to his genius. He was thoroughly able and clearheaded. In spite of McNamara's idiosyncracies, he was impressed with George."[22]

Secretary McNamara was indeed impressed, as shown in his first written evaluation of George Brown in his Officer Effectiveness Report on June 1, 1962:

> During the past 17 months, I have worked very closely with General Brown. He is an outstanding officer, one of the very few general officers who have the potential for promotion to Chief of Staff of the Air Force.
>
> His judgment on political military matters is excellent and he has an unusual ability to grasp the potential effects of military strategy on foreign policy decisions. Further, he understands, more clearly than most officers in the Department, how to translate general military strategy into force requirements and, finally, into effective applications of existing forces.
>
> His loyalty to and perception of general interest, as contrasted to the interest of a particular service, is extraordinarily high.[23]

I asked McNamara to elaborate on why he thought Brown had the potential for promotion to Chief of Staff. He replied, "He was highly intelligent and wise, with a clear strategic sense and a clear sense of the relationship of military and foreign policy matters, which I think is absolutely fundamental in a Chief of Staff; he had a very high sense of integrity. As an illustration, there was a school of thought, particularly in the Air Force, that you could win the war in Vietnam with air power. And there was a constant exaggeration of the potential use of air power in Vietnam, with a constant overstatement of the results of air power. During World War II, I had served under LeMay at one point, in the Eighth Air Force when they only had four bomb groups early on, and I had been doing operations research work, and I followed the strategic bombing survey at length. I'd been part of the 50th Bomb Wing in the Twentieth Air Force and followed the air war in the Pacific. So I knew something about air warfare, and something about its limitations. I was skeptical about some of these claims. George had had experience in the Korean War and had studied other applications of air power, and he was very strong in his belief that one should approach this skeptically. He wasn't saying there's no place for air power. That's not the point. But he did say that we should examine the results carefully. It was on that basis that I asked the President to allow us to go to the CIA to have them set up a unit to evaluate what air power was accomplishing in Vietnam. This is a perfect illustration of why I thought he should be Chief of Staff, or was capable of being Chief of Staff. You've got to be realistic in your appraisal of what you have done and what your potential is."[24]

Another point of view was expressed by Gen. Jacob Smart, Assistant Vice Chief of Staff of the Air Force during part of the time Brown served under Secretary McNamara. General Smart emphasized, "It was George Brown's full intellect, his capacity to see merit in both sides of an argument, his realization that the world was not all black and white. He tried his best to find logical, sensible courses of action that would satisfy the concerns of widely divergent forces."[25]

"I saw a good deal of him through that period," remembered Maj. Gen. Richard A. Yudkin. "There was no pretense about George; he was absolutely honest, utterly frank. There was never any dissembling, deception, or anything like that, and I think he established this clearly with McNamara on one side, and the Air Force and the other services on the other. I think McNamara was made to understand very early in the game that George would serve him loyally, that he would never betray him or his confidence. But in his advice to McNamara, the background he came from would inevitably be reflected. On the other side, I think that he would listen to people like myself, like others who would come to him attempting to sell points of view; but he would never leave anyone in any doubt that he was working for McNamara."[26]

When his close friend Lt. Gen. James Knight was asked why, in his opinion, George got along so well with Secretary McNamara, he responded, "That's just the kind of man he was, the ideal man in uniform to fill that job. He could present to McNamara the military view, George Brown's view, and the Air Force view, and many times convince him that he was right. McNamara would listen. When McNamara said, 'No, this is the way we're going to do it,' Brown would tell the Air Force what the consequences might be if there were a revolt." But perhaps Knight's most significant point was made when Brown told him of his service under Secretary McNamara,

"I can do a lot more good by staying in here and working on the problem from the inside than I can by quitting."[27]

Inquiring of many of his contemporaries, both superiors and subordinates, as to why George Brown was so successful as military assistant to Secretary McNamara, I found that the consensus was on Brown's loyalty. George Brown himself said of this quality: "Loyalty to superiors is important. Your commander must be able to rely on you. If you don't give loyalty, you can't expect to get it. I believe you must make sure that your boss is completely and accurately informed about your area of responsibility so that he can make decisions based on facts. I express my ideas freely to him until a decision is made, then I carry out that decision to the best of my ability, whether I agree with it or not. Whatever I do, I don't show doubts to the subordinates.

"When my loyalty to subordinates conflicts with loyalty to superiors, duty and discipline demand that I support my superiors. Undisciplined acts and attitudes do not lead to an effective military unit—or to promotion. If I don't know how to follow, I don't know how to lead."[28]

Secretary McNamara was asked if Brown ever showed any service loyalty. "George Brown was never disloyal to his service," said McNamara. "The fundamental point is that I never saw him put his service ahead of the country. You asked me about service loyalty. I'm not absolutely positive of my memory of this, but when we came to the problem of the F-104, which the Air Force was just having a hell of a lot of trouble with, I had the idea that the F-4, a Navy plane, could be used by the Air Force with advantages compared to the F-104. Therefore, we should stop its production and produce the Navy plane for the Air Force. Initially there was absolute hell to pay in the Air Force, and the Chief of Staff was absolutely opposed to it. My recollection is that George said, 'Well, that's worth looking at.' We did look at it, and we ultimately went ahead with it and it proved to be tremendously successful."[29]

Another perspective was offered by Gen. David C. Jones, who was an action officer serving on the Air Staff as a colonel at the same time Brown was on McNamara's staff. "I think he did it, number one, by never trying to wear the mantle of the Secretary of Defense's office. I've seen throughout my career people who have worked for someone, whether they were an aide to a general or an executive assistant to a senior officer or senior civilian, trying in dealing with others to act as though they were the principal. George never tried to wear the coat of the Secretary of Defense. He was honest, straightforward, candid. He never worked back door with the Air Force in being disloyal to Mr. McNamara. He tried to smooth the relations. It was a difficult time in the relationship between McNamara and the Air Force because there were so many Air Force programs being cut and canceled. There was a lot of ill will and not much of a dialogue. George was able to fill that gap in trying to smooth things over or at least trying to make each side understand what the other side was trying to accomplish, even though the face-to-face dialogue between the principals was not good."[30]

Things did not always fall into place for George Brown, and while he was working for McNamara he received a major disappointment in his career. "An interesting side of George was revealed," said Burt Andrus, "over the selection of the commandant of cadets at the Air Force Academy to succeed General Sullivan. George and our classmate Bill Seawell were the finalists in the competition. Each was called in by General LeMay, and when it was over, he had chosen Seawell. I think for the first time in George's career, something that he really wanted eluded him. George had flown in on a cross-country when I was wing commander at Dyess Air Force Base and discussed his not having been selected as commandant. He wasn't distraught or anything like that, just a little disappointed. I remember him saying to me that I had one hell of a good job and that he hoped that I appreciated it. He said to me he envied me being out in the boondocks commanding a wing and flying airplanes."[31]

When Brown began his role as military assistant to the Deputy Secretary of Defense in June of 1959, he was a colonel. When he left in July 1963 as military assistant to the Secretary of Defense, he was a two-star general. Secretary Robert S. McNamara wrote on July 27, 1963, "In terms of intelligence, energy, and integrity, George Brown is, I believe, the most outstanding two-star officer whom I have met. His assignments should be such as to prepare him for consideration for appointment as Chief of Staff."

After spending two years as exec to the Chief of Staff and over four years as military assistant in the office of the Secretary of Defense, altogether more than six years in the Pentagon, it was time to move on, back to the operational Air Force. Some officers who served in the office of the Secretary of Defense were really not welcomed back by their services. Gen. Howell M. Estes, Jr., was Commander Materiel Air Transport Service (MATS) during Brown's tenure with the Secretary. "Secretary Zuckert told me on a visit to Washington," recalled Estes, "that Brown was going to leave the position as assistant to McNamara. Would I like to have him in MATS? I replied, 'You bet I'd like to have him.' One of my subordinate Air Force commanders in MATS was being moved to another job, so I had a two-star general's position open. I told Gene I'd like to have him run the Twenty-first Air Force at McGuire. I got him."

NOTES

1. Personal interview with Thomas S. Gates, Jr., January 17, 1980.
2. Ibid.
3. Ibid.
4. Ibid.
5. Ibid.
6. Personal interview with Lt. Gen. Edward J. Timberlake, USAF (Ret.), July 18, 1979.
7. Personal interview with former Secretary of Defense Robert S. McNamara, March 18, 1981.
8. Ibid.
9. Ibid.
10. Ibid.
11. Ibid.
12. Personal interview with Lt. Gen. Andrew J. Goodpaster, USA (Ret.), July 22, 1980.
13. Personal interview with Gen. Gabriel P. Disosway, USAF (Ret.), January 17, 1979.
14. Personal interview with Lt. Gen. George S. Boylan, Jr., USAF (Ret.), April 27, 1980.
15. Letter from Eugene M. Zuckert to EFP, February 22, 1980.
16. McNamara interview.
17. Personal interview with Gen. Russell E. Dougherty, USAF (Ret.), March 15, 1979.
18. Personal interview with Ramsey Potts, April 15, 1980.
19. Personal interview with Gen. William Y. Smith, USAF, April 21, 1979.
20. McNamara interview.
21. William Y. Smith interview.
22. Personal interview with Lt. Gen. Frederic H. Smith, USAF (Ret.), July 6, 1979.
23. Officer Effectiveness Report, June 1, 1962.
24. McNamara interview.
25. Personal interview with Gen. Jacob E. Smart, USAF (Ret.), July 17, 1979.
26. Personal interview with Maj. Gen. Richard A. Yudkin, USAF (Ret.), July 30, 1979.
27. Personal interview with Lt. Gen. James A. Knight, Jr., USAF (Ret.), August 7, 1979.
28. Letter from Col. Willis B. Sawyer, USAF (Ret.), to EFP, November 21, 1979.
29. McNamara interview.
30. Personal interview with Gen. David C. Jones, March 31, 1980.
31. Personal interview with Col. Burton C. Andrus, USAF (Ret.), June 28, 1979.

CHAPTER 14

McGUIRE AIR FORCE BASE, NEW JERSEY: AUGUST 1963-SEPTEMBER 1964

In August of 1963, Brown reported for his new assignment as commander of the Eastern Transport Air Force. His commander was Gen. Howell M. Estes, Jr. "The Twenty-first Air Force, with headquarters at McGuire Air Force Base, was the Eastern Transport Air Force, abbreviated EASTAF. George had responsibility for anything that happened in the strategic airlift force from the Mississippi eastward to the border of India, the airlift support for all the forces in Europe, anything that happened in the Mediterranean, in Africa, all through the Middle East. We had the responsibility for MATS becoming an all-jet Air Force, getting rid of all the propeller-driven aircraft. It was a challenging job, and George had to supervise this transition for our mission for half the world."

Although Brown had had transport experience at McChord Air Force Base from 1950 to 1951, EASTAF was a complex challenge, the largest command he had held up to this time. It was made up of 37,000 military and civilian personnel, 375 heavy aircraft, an overseas air division, and five wings. As EASTAF commander he had responsibility for the movement of troops and cargo to support the activities of the United States Air Force, including the movement of troops to Europe and the shipping of supplies necessary to support overseas establishments, particularly engines to support our aircraft overseas.

Under Brown the staff at EASTAF Headquarters had two daily meetings. One was at 10:00 with his deputy chiefs of staff in the War Room. In it they would review the operation of the prior day plus the activities that had occurred during the night; it lasted only thirty minutes. They discussed delays, why the delays happened, and all operational matters. When there were exercises going on, the meetings were more frequent because they had to keep current on how they were supporting the various exercises, many overseas. They might be going to the Philippines, to Turkey, or to Europe. At the second daily meeting Brown heard from staff people for personnel, intelligence, supply and material, maintenance, and the judge advocate.

One of Brown's strengths as a leader was his ability to delegate his authority when appropriate. At his first commanders and staff meeting, he established his delegating policy when he told all his deputy commanders and staff officers, "Goewey is my vice commander, and when he says something or gives an order, he represents me. If he gives an order it is the same as if I gave it. Don't come running to me and questioning it."[1]

Delegation to others was a necessity for Brown since his responsibilities required frequent traveling to all the EASTAF bases located throughout the world. Although this extensive traveling may seem glamorous to some, when he traveled it was business only. He had bases in both France and England. "Yet he never went for the pleasure of going to Paris, London, or Istanbul. He went to work," said his deputy. "He'd normally do his traveling at night, flying all night to his destination. Then he'd start to work as soon as he got there."[2]

While on these trips inspecting his bases, he would always chat with the men who had anything to do with crew duties—the whole crew, not just the officers. He talked with men like the loadmaster and the engineer, and always in a very natural sort of way, getting acquainted with all his aircrews. He never seemed to be running a popularity contest, but nonetheless the socializing made him popular with his people.

This personal interest in his people would continue once Brown reached his destination. One of the wing commanders he inspected on the visits, for instance, was then Brig. Gen. James C. Sherrill. "He would come and talk with you. He wanted to know what your problems were. He listened to our briefings, talked with my people, socialized with me. He always left it to me to determine what I wanted him to see and what I wanted to talk to him about. He never was a pushy guy, but you always felt with him a strong demand that you'd better get on with the job. But I never heard him be sharp or abrupt with anybody. He was a good guy to work for, easy to be around, always very thoughtful of everybody. George had a pleasing personality, but you could sense a firmness about him, a determination in what he wanted to do and what he wanted you to do. You always felt that he had a mission and he wanted to get on with it, but he was never rude, overriding, or overbearing with people.

"He called his commanders in for a conference about every six months," continued Sherrill. "They were always informal. He was there to try and get us all together and get us working on the problems we had; no axes to grind, but get on with the problem; do the job the best we could, but improve all the time; no flimflam. Oh, sure, he liked to have a drink and play golf, do that with all of us. But he always dealt off the top of the deck. I don't know of any guy that George Brown ever stepped on. I never heard him poor mouth anybody."[3]

Brown's sense of mission and ability to listen were appreciated by others in his command also. "The first thing he did that impressed me, which was a big plus sign for anybody coming in to take command, was that he listened," said his deputy, Brigadier General Goewey, who had been in place as EASTAF deputy several years before Brown's arrival. "He didn't claim to have all the answers. I recall his telling me on the day we said good-bye to him when he went elsewhere that up till the last day he was still learning, which is an indication of a man who doesn't think that because he has two stars he's got the answers, particularly where everybody else surrounding him is junior to him. In the Pentagon, two stars aren't overpowering, but that was a lot of rank to us at EASTAF. But he never acted that way. For the first two or three weeks he asked questions when somebody would finish his briefing. I felt that he didn't want to come in with the idea that 'I know it all and I'm going to tell you how it is done.' Instead he had the attitude 'I'm going to listen to you.' I think this was a smart thing to do, but I don't think it was done in a contrived sort of way. That was the first impression. Here was a man who wanted to listen."[4]

Even though he listened, Brown had no trouble making a decision. For example, at the base in Charleston there was a central heating plant fired by coal which was damaging the automobiles of those stationed at the base. In that part of South Carolina there was always some heavy morning dew, which, mixed with the coal soot, took the paint off the vehicles, even causing damage to the airplanes. To replace it, however, would have been extremely costly. "Every three months," said Sherrill, "I'd send a report forward asking that we be permitted to use natural gas. George finally said, 'Please don't send those reports forward any longer. You know we're not going to do it.' The decision was made."[5]

Brown was always aware of where his decisions fit into the chain of command, and he insisted that his subordinates recognize this as well. The EASTAF wing commander for the base in the Azores, then Brig. Gen. George Boylan, learned this the hard way. "The weather in the Azores was bad in the wintertime," Boylan recalled. "During my first year our problems were aggravated by an earthquake on St. George Island. After the destruction by the earthquake, the Portuguese governor asked me for U.S. assistance, which I tried to get to him, initially going through Air Force channels. They turned me down, but I had a friend, Phil Hilbert, on the Secretary's staff in Washington. Hilbert was a pillar of strength for many Secretaries, and a man well known in Washington who knew how to get things done. I got in touch with Phil and he picked up some debts over in the Navy Department. As a result, the Navy sent a supply ship which delivered some quonset huts, supplies, and a Seabee team to erect replacement buildings. The Portuguese were grateful and I was happy about it all, but I got a brief note from George that said simply, 'I applaud your results, but your method is leaving a lot of people on the Air Staff upset. Get back in channels.' "[6]

On another occasion Brown's reaction to violating the chain of command was much stronger, when he learned that a wing commander was bypassing him and going directly to higher MATS Headquarters in Illinois because he had entrée there. Brown called him in and simply said, "The next time you go out of channels, and I will hear about it if you do, you will be no longer useful to this command. You can find a job somewhere else." In short, Brown didn't fool around where discipline was concerned. If there was a serious personal problem, he was always ready to listen, but he was quite impatient with carelessness and laziness and strongly disapproved of anyone going outside the chain of command.

When Brown cracked down he pulled no punches, but he never berated or disciplined anyone in front of others. For example, a directive came from higher headquarters that on overseas personnel flights, Turkish exchange officers on the way from the United States to Turkey were not to be bumped. It seems that this had been done frequently to make room for higher ranking U.S. officers and was upsetting a strong U.S. ally. It was an easy way out since certain operations personnel thought a Turkish officer had little influence or importance.

One senior officer at EASTAF had continued to bump Turkish officers in violation of the order. Thinking that perhaps there was confusion because of a lack of communication, Brown's order was written out quite specifically, spelling out in the operational book at all EASTAF bases that no Turkish officer was to be bumped without the authority of his headquarters.

This required the specific approval of either Brown or his deputy Goewey.

That same senior officer bumped a Turkish officer in spite of the very specific instructions. General Brown at the staff meeting the next day was being briefed on the previous day's operations and was informed of another bumping of a Turkish officer. This really upset him. The officer who violated the order was there, so Brown waited until the meeting was over and called him into his office and then really let him have it, saying, "I will not tolerate disobedience. If it happens again I will relieve you of duty and you will be reassigned with an appropriate comment in your records." It never happened again.[7]

Although Brown was tough, he was also a compassionate and understanding man. For example, courts-martial in the wings came up for review to Brown. The Headquarters Judge Advocate, of course, reviewed the court-martial records and brought them to the commander, often a big file. Most commanders would not read the whole file, but Brown had a different philosophy. He believed if he were going to send a man to prison, he had to read the file and be assured in his own mind that it was not just a staff recommendation. On several sentences he reviewed, for instance, he was concerned and decided to talk with the prisoners, most of whom were quite young. This was typical of how he operated, trying to get as much information as he could. He'd try to get these young airmen to explain the circumstances of their offenses. On occasion, he'd find somebody who really had some mitigating circumstances, and he would either remit or lessen the sentence even though this didn't always please the staff and his lawyers.

"He didn't get bogged down in detail," said General Goewey, "but military justice was important to him. The future of a young person was involved, so he was willing to go into those details. I can tell you that it was unusual. I'd been the number two man for a lot of commanders, and I hadn't run into any of them that would go to that length. It was a great tribute to his type of leadership."[8]

Brown's sense of compassion is evidenced in still another instance. A master sergeant got drunk at an EASTAF overseas station. He was barred from the NCO Club for an indefinite time; then his superiors wanted to court-martial him for the offense. Brown learned, however, that the NCO Club was selling drink tickets at a price of twenty drinks for a dollar. He felt very strongly that this was an outrageous thing to do, to let a man get a strong drink for five cents. To him, that contributed to that sergeant's problem and many others'. After he had talked with the sergeant, he felt that there were mitigating circumstances, so he would not take any further action, leaving the man's otherwise excellent record intact. The blame, he felt, should have been placed in part on the command that allowed him to buy hard liquor for a nickel a drink. He ordered that the cheap drink policy be stopped.

Brown's concern for others extended to the dependents of his men as well. One of his senior colonels had an alcoholic wife who was often picked up by the Air Police and brought home. It became pretty well known, so Brown called the colonel in and went over the problem with him. The colonel said, "Well, it's menopause that's causing these aberrations, not alcoholism." It was said in defense of his wife, but he was incorrect. The doctors said it was indeed alcoholism. Brown said to him, "Look, every time you go TDY she is charged with driving a car under the influence of liquor, so why don't you take the next six months and don't go on any trip. I want you to stay around here on base." That in itself didn't cure her alcoholism, but with the loneliness at an end she was not charged again.[9]

A further example of Brown's attention to the needs of his men's family members is provided by Col. Edward B. Rasmussen: "I remember an occasion when George Brown was commander of EASTAF and I was in Italy. My wife had returned to the States when her mother died in the Washington, D.C., area. I had told her that if she had any trouble getting back to Italy on space available to call George Brown. Janet had been reading the papers and saw that Exercise 'Big Lift' was going on and that all airplanes were full of troops and supplies going to Europe. So she called George and asked, 'Is there any point in my coming to McGuire and sitting around waiting for space available with what's going on?' He said, 'Janet, by no means. Don't come here.' He said, 'As a matter of fact, I'm leaving for Europe tomorrow myself.' Then he said, 'Wait a minute, I've got an idea. I think I can get you on a State Department flight. I'm leaving, but my sergeant will call and make arrangements.' The next day the sergeant called Janet to tell her she was being placed on a presidential airplane taking Secretary of State Dean Rusk, Senator Hubert Humphrey, and other big wheels over to Europe. Needless to say, my wife was very surprised at the royal treatment. To me this is another indication of General Brown's willingness to help others, of his thoughtfulness. Here was a man in the midst of a big upheaval because of an exercise in his own command, leaving soon to fly to Europe to direct this big operation, who yet took time to think about helping a friend's wife. How many other men would do something like that?"[10]

Jim Sherrill summed up his evaluation of Brown by saying, "He was just George Brown, straightforward and on the surface all the way. I never saw George any other way than as George Brown, never out of character, never any deviation. George was—I don't exactly know what to say about it except that he was always himself. I don't think he ever tried to be anything but George Brown, period. And to me that's awfully important. There are a lot of people who try to be a lot of things other than themselves."[11]

"I used to come back to Washington about once a month," reflected Gen. Howell M. Estes, Jr., "to talk with the Air Staff, the Chiefs of Staff of the Air Force and Army, to find out how we were coming along in providing the services my command was responsible for. I was back on one of these trips and was having lunch with Air Force Secretary Eugene M. Zuckert. I'd known Gene for a long, long time. He told me at this lunch, 'We've got an opportunity to get Brown promoted to three stars by sending him to work on a project to evaluate weapons systems, working for the Chairman of the Joint Chiefs of Staff.' My response to Gene was, 'Boy, that's terrific. If you can get George his third star, you've got him tomorrow. No one is going to have any problem taking a man from me if he can give him a promotion that I couldn't get for him.' "[12] Thus, George Brown was ready for a new challenge.

NOTES

1. Personal interview with Brig. Gen. Robert J. Goewey, USAF (Ret.), September 9, 1981.
2. Ibid.
3. Personal interview with Lt. Gen. James Sherrill, USAF (Ret.), October 3, 1981.
4. Goewey interview.
5. Sherrill interview.
6. Personal interview with Lt. Gen. George S. Boylan, Jr., USAF (Ret.), April 27, 1980.
7. Goewey interview.
8. Ibid.
9. Ibid.
10. Personal interview with Col. Edward B. Rasmussen, USAF (Ret.), August 9, 1979.
11. Sherrill interview.
12. Personal interview with Gen. Howell M. Estes, Jr., USAF (Ret.), March 14, 1980.

CHAPTER 15

SANDIA BASE, NEW MEXICO:
SEPTEMBER 1964–MAY 1966

In September 1964, George Brown was selected to organize Joint Task Force-2, a Joint Chiefs of Staff unit formed at Sandia Base, New Mexico, to test weapons systems of all the military services. Initially it was a temporary duty assignment, but ultimately he was to spend eighteen months in the job.

"I came," recalled then Lt. Col. Howard M. Lane, "after the plans were formulated and while the organization was still being manned, but from my involvement in making plans for some of the major tests that they conducted, I could see it was obviously an organization designed to exploit the joint operation of forces, particularly in a low-level environment. In those days, we didn't know all that we could or should know about recognizing targets at high speed at low level, coordinating attacks on targets once they were recognized. One concept of our operation was to design tests of camouflaged targets at selected locations."[1]

The mission of JTF-2 was summed up by George Brown: "One of the greatest pluses of our joint-service operations is the identification of any weaknesses in our systems and tactics; finding the 'soft spots' gives us an immediate opportunity to correct them—or develop something better to replace them. We wanted to know how pilots would react to very low-level flying over extended periods and varying terrains. The heart of our objective was to evaluate low-altitude penetration and how to defend against it to insure the security of the United States."[2]

In addition to testing to determine the advantages and disadvantages of low-level penetration of enemy targets, the Joint Chiefs wanted to test our own defensive weapons against low-altitude attacks by hostile aircraft, and also to test tactical and strategic air offensive and surface-to-air defenses. Before they started, however, a study was made by Brown's newly formed group of the testing previously done by the Air Force's Eglin Air Proving Group, the Navy's "Chinalake," and the Army's White Sands Missile Range to avoid duplication of effort.

Tactical and strategic aircraft from the Air Force, Navy, and Marines, plus Army ground weapons all took part in this joint service testing—the B–52, B–58, RF–101, F–105, RF–4C, RA–5C, the A–1, A–4, and A–6 and their crews from all the military services. The base of operation was Sandia with one hundred of the seven thousand employees of the Sandia Laboratory assisting in the testing and support of JTF–2.

The Airman described JTF–2 as "an all-star team. Every one of its 106 officers, 54 enlisted men and 84 civilians was handpicked for a starring role in its activities. Air Force Major General George S. Brown, who works directly for the Joint Chiefs of Staff, commands and coaches these professionals."[3]

Select operational crews were taken out of operational units, not professional test people, but line crews who were to have their performance evaluated in recognizing and attacking low-level targets. A difficult task was to balance the requirements of the analysts and the statisticians against operational realism. How many trials were required to reach a level of confidence, and what confidence level? How many times was it necessary to expose people to an environment before the norm could be seen? Because of his experience in the Office of the Secretary of Defense, Brown understood analysts and their requirements. He understood what had to be presented in analytical form to support operational judgments.[4]

"I was among the first fifty or so people who reported at Sandia," said Howard Lane. "We commenced operations in an old dining hall full of desks. Our first requirement was not to fall into the trap of becoming just another study group; we were there to produce results. So even in the initial stages we became deeply involved in planning our first tests. There was a lot of work to be done, and everybody pitched in and didn't worry about whether they were getting credit for it or not. There were no prima donnas. If I remember correctly, it was thought it would take about two years to produce our first results. We had some results within a year, but not because we were driven by George Brown. He led by example. That doesn't mean he didn't force a little bit every now and then, but we weren't driven."[5]

Part of the success was the way in which Brown worked with the news media. "Brown hired me as his information officer," recalled Col. Albert Cochrane, "and I worked with him for two years. I set up a news conference when we first arrived at Sandia Base. All three of our senior generals and a flag officer were present, with General Brown taking the questions. As always, he was honest and straightforward in his answers. There were some dumb questions, but he handled them beautifully, never embarrassing the newsmen. He sometimes groaned about meeting with news people, but he was always a hit with them."[6]

Since JTF-2 had no operational force of its own, the low-level missions were all flown by pilots assigned from all the services. They flew so low that barrels placed for directional purposes were slashed by the airplane pods. But, with a total of 464 sorties flown, there were no accidents of any kind, an amazing safety record.

General Brown maintained excellent rapport with the local citizenry. To promote understanding, they were fully briefed on the coming supersonic flights and the importance of the mission. Although damage was limited, Air Force lawyers from Sandia even assisted home owners to file damage claims for such things as broken windows from supersonic booms. A team of officers traveled to communities throughout all the test areas, covering portions of New Mexico, Louisiana, Oklahoma, Texas, and Arkansas to brief the residents on what to expect. All flights were restricted to specific hours, and hundreds of road signs were placed to warn drivers of low-flying aircraft.

"One of our first major projects was low-level testing in the hills of Arkansas. I was chief planner for those tests," continued Lane. "I was also one of the pilots, although this was not the normal procedure. There was extensive orientation of people living along the route when we were out building targets in remote forest areas and farmlands. Each of the four routes was some fifty miles long. Brown wanted to make sure that the people along the route understood what we were doing. During this six-month test, we did receive telephone calls, but relatively few concerning the few supersonic booms and a lot of low-level noise. We had normal problems with the mink and chicken farmers, but I don't think we ever had a claim submitted for damages to livestock. I attribute this to the advance work we did in letting people know what we were going to do and in following up their complaints. Our great success in this public-relations area was attributable to our immediate response to potential problems. When an individual called in, he was not handled in a bureaucratic way. Every call was followed up by a personal visit, and that visit would often result in a representative of JTF-2 staying with the individual and observing the problem from his viewpoint."

What was General Brown like as a leader? "In the mid-sixties I was an F-105 wing commander, associated with General Brown," said Col. Ed McGough, USAF (Ret.). "I attended many meetings with him at higher headquarters and with his own staff. At higher headquarters meetings, his leadership was evident. His thoughts, ideas, and requirements were eagerly sought, and even in disagreement, his position was highly respected. At his own meetings, he was always in command: brief, informal, humorous, and yet demanding. He tolerated no 'yes men'; he respected very highly the opinions of others. I was impressed by his ability to have a 'controlled' free-ranging discussion and yet to keep it on target. Staff officers felt at ease and consequently were not afraid to speak their piece. He seemed to get each to perform to his capacity."[7]

"Our staff meetings," wrote Albert Cochrane, "were the places where his simple, firm, common-sense leadership really came to light. As a junior officer, I loved his staff meetings—simply because he insisted they be conducted at a level that everyone could understand. He always got down to the basics. If a member of the staff couldn't do that, he simply didn't last. A few Sandia technicians learned that the hard way.

"Like all good leaders I've known," he continued, "Brown had an uncanny sense of sorting things out quickly and getting to the heart of the matter—a talent that was invaluable in those early days at Sandia when we didn't have many clearly defined goals."[8]

Brown's ability to delegate responsibility also stood him in good stead at Sandia. As Howard Lane stated, "The people who formed JTF-2 were carefully picked by George Brown. He put people together and then exercised his knack of knowing exactly what level of detail he should be involved in and where he should cut it off. He clearly understood that he didn't have all the brains, that he had to depend on his subordinates, and he had confidence in them. He had a broad objective that some people didn't really understand, but he did. I don't really know exactly what his instructions were from higher command, but he had constant interface with the Secretary of Defense. He gave us broad guidelines and then said, 'Use your imagination.' He didn't want to know all the details. He wanted results."[9]

"In my judgment, one of his important characteristics was the real confidence he placed in others," commented Ed McGough. "He knew the capabilities and limitations of each person and assigned with a faith that tasks and responsibilities would be completed properly and in a timely manner. He did not harass or continually check for progress. In today's political and military environment such a practice takes courage. His subordinates and associates respected him for his vote of faith and responded accordingly. No one wanted to let him down."[10]

"There was a personal touch which I think was most representative of General Brown. You could not work with that individual without feeling as if you were the only person in the world as far as he was concerned. It was still a military relationship, but with warmth."[11]

As he did throughout his career, George Brown made a point to become personally acquainted with all phases of the operation there. And, as always, he was discreet in pointing out shortcomings that he observed to his subordinates. "He didn't stay in the office very much," said Howard Lane. "He moved around where things were going on. He was very scrupulous of the authority he had delegated to subordinates. I never knew him to undercut a subordinate performing some job that was a subordinate's responsibility. The way he addressed problems was to wait until he got back to Sandia, call in the appropriate subordinate, and say, 'Here's what I saw and I think you ought to look into this.' There was rarely any on-the-spot correction. He was not a detail man; he understood the details, but he knew the amount of time that he could devote to a subject. He knew the demands on his time, and although it might have been rewarding for him to go out and turn the nuts and bolts personally, he clearly understood that his responsibilities were of a higher order."[12]

The challenges were even greater since JTF–2 was a "purple-suit" staff composed of units from the Air Force, Army, Navy, and Marine Corps, including a recently frocked rear admiral and an Army officer who had been an old hand in Air Defense. There was a mixture that represented every shade of opinion and experience on low-level penetration. His civilian experts from Sandia included a number of scientists who had trouble speaking in anything but scientific jargon. Somehow, Brown got this unlikely conglomeration pulling in the same direction at the same time. He made it clear from the beginning that parochial service opinions were out and open minds were in. And he was often the best example. Blue suiters were often stunned when he directed, "Let's try it the Army way. It makes better sense."[13]

"I don't think they could have picked a better-prepared officer than General Brown to organize and get JTF–2 off to a good start," said Howard Lane. "He had all the joint experience required to put a joint command together to produce solid results. He had all necessary contacts, the command experience, and the operational background. He had superior understanding of the purpose, objectives, and limitations such an outfit had to operate under. There were still conflicts between the services, and you had to be very careful that you didn't step on service toes by exploiting one service to the detriment of another. George functioned as a purple-suit individual. He had absolute dedication to the idea that he was doing something for the good of the Department of Defense and the country, and not just for the Air Force.

"He was careful to balance the supervisory levels to perfection, putting together the right mix of the different services, and thus never faced the problem of service parochialism. It was a completely integrated and operating outfit in the joint area. The Army major general was an air defense type; the Marine was his Chief of Staff; and a Navy rear admiral was deputy commander. There was never a time that one of these deputies was unable to move right in and fill in as commander. In everything he did, from his social life to his duty performance, there was never any perception of favoritism at all. The example he set was the best thing going for him." [14]

When General Lane was asked, "Did Brown have enough operational background with Tactical Air Command to know what he was doing?" Lane responded, "I certainly think so. I'm not a very firm believer in the idea that you have to have been one to be one. He had the broad background and experience that permitted him to take complete advantage of the expertise of others. He knew his shortcomings, knew when he had to rely on others. He was not a tactical fighter pilot and most of our work was with fighters. But, he was not the commander of a flying organization since we brought in all of our test subjects from operational commands. So other than overall safety responsibility, he had no requirement to participate in tests; but he did fly the routes.

"In addition to my primary duty in the planning end, I accompanied him on all his trips. I was supposed to be his T–39 pilot, and he and I flew together frequently. He flew; I rode. You still have to have an instructor pilot for a general officer to fly, so I was his. As a pilot, he was absolutely super, no doubt about that. We flew some six or seven hundred hours together. Despite our familiarity with each other and his own familiarity with the T–39, he never failed to give proper attention to the preflight checklist. There was no such thing in his mind as kick the tires, light the fire, and go. If there was an established Air Force procedure, we were going to follow that procedure, and at no time did I ever have to remind him that we might be violating some rule. He abided completely by all the rules at all times— for weather, for fuel reserve, for everything.

"I am a graduate of the Experimental Test Pilot School at Edwards Air Force Base, California. In the 1950s I ran the fighter test branch there. I was involved in all the Century fighter series testing, so I consider myself to be fairly critical of people in the way they handle airplanes. I guess my classification of General Brown, if I can say this and be understood, is that he was extremely smooth. He was not a ham-fisted pilot. He was a part of the airplane and although he clearly understood that the airplane could withstand g's and hard-turns and everything, his always was a smooth, professional job of flying, a soft touch on the stick and just a pleasure to fly with, a pleasure to be with." [15]

The job was demanding, but "George was a firm believer in time for work and time for relaxing," recalled Lane. "He always found a tennis game. His philosophy was that if you can't get it done during normal duty hours, you better take a look at how you're doing it because you're not doing something right. It was a ten-hour day, but if you didn't have something to do, don't hang around, get your job done and go."[16]

As stated earlier, the JCS thought it would take two years to get results, but under Brown's leadership, only a year was needed. "An important question, as far as the Army was concerned," said Lane, "was how effective their ground camouflage was. There were different kinds of camouflage to prevent pilots from seeing targets. Also from an Army air defense standpoint, results were in on the detection and identification ranges of airplanes approaching targets. From the Air Force, Navy, and Marine Corps standpoint, extensive information was developed on how low you could fly and still be able to detect targets, and what target indicators you should be looking for in the different types of targets—ground air-defense installations, tank parks, truck parks, bivouac areas, for example. Many of these indicators are still in use today."[17]

One of the most meaningful evaluations of Brown's career was made by the Chairman of the Joint Chiefs of Staff, Gen. Earle G. Wheeler, USA, covering the initial period of Brown's tour as chief of JTF-2:

> General Brown is without doubt one of the most able Air Force general officers I know. Although JTF-2 was established only four months ago, General Brown has accomplished a thorough organization of assigned resources, secured an approved budget, established a headquarters facility, worked out an extremely complex arrangement for technical support of his test program with the services and military laboratory facilities, and has initiated the first phase of his test program. These accomplishments represent outstanding results and were due largely to General Brown's personal initiative and involvement at every step along the way. He has earned the respect and liking of subordinates and superiors alike—both military and civilian—and is an outstanding leader. In my view, General Brown has unlimited potential and should advance rapidly to staff or command positions involving greater responsibilities and increased rank. He is one of those rare individuals to whom you can assign a job, regardless of its difficulty, and know that it will be done thoroughly, with dispatch, and with no loose ends.

General Wheeler wrote of the period from May 1, 1965, to April 30, 1966:

During the period of this report, General Brown has displayed outstanding ability as a general officer, commander and administrator. Organizing a new headquarters and a completely new staff, he established a comprehensive test program which has already produced needed operational data and which should provide further information of value to the services in the future. With only 50 percent of his authorized staff assigned, he planned and implemented the first test in program within five months after the organization became established at Sandia Base. The personal initiative and the negotiations conducted by General Brown with agencies such as OSD, the FAA, Sandia Corporation, the FCC, the Services, AEC, DASA and industry made this possible. Through his personal efforts, test programs have been planned, submitted and approved for FY 1967 and FY 1968, together with the five-year program through FY 1972. These programs propose the most comprehensive test schedule and test instrumentation ever attempted by any military test organization. Additionally, he has had the foresight to provide flexibility within each individual test plan in order to utilize economically minimum operational forces without jeopardizing the test objectives or delaying the deployment of such forces to other areas. The scope of the program, which initially was estimated to cost about 300 million dollars has, through his efforts, been reduced to approximately 150 to 180 million dollars without any degradation or deletion of test objectives as directed by the Concept of Testing for JTF-2. General Brown has unlimited growth potential, the capacity to accept positions of increased responsibility, and is ready now for promotion to Lieutenant General.

Equally significant in its way is this somewhat more personal testimonial by Albert Cochrane: "Unlike some generals, George Brown always had time for the little guy. A fellow named Benny, a Spanish-American, was the building custodian for Headquarters JTF-2. Benny and the general became close friends—often sharing fishing tales. I think the general put more faith in Benny's recommendations about Albuquerque than all of the chamber of commerce delegates who called on him. Benny got more time with the general than some of his staff, especially those who had trouble getting down to basics.

"Total honesty and an ability to set his priorities and stick to them were the two most outstanding leadership qualities with General Brown," continued Cochrane. "He was always firm but fair and always unpretentious. When some of his staff were coming to work in chauffeured staff cars, he, the boss, drove his own car, an old Ford that was in bad need of a paint job. Often when he went camping or fishing, it was with his junior officers, not an entourage of senior staff. While I never called him George, I never felt uncomfortable in his presence. To those who knew him well, the only thing awesome about him was his dedication, wisdom, and total honesty. It may seem like great hindsight, but I was among many who knew beyond a doubt, back in 1965, that Major General Brown would someday be Chief of Staff and, perhaps, Chairman of the Joint Chiefs."[18]

NOTES

1. Personal interview with Lt. Gen. Howard M. Lane, May 16, 1980.
2. *The Airman,* vol. 10, no. 7 (July 1966), p. 21.
3. Ibid, p. 20.
4. Lane interview.
5. Ibid.
6. Letter from Lt. Col. Albert C. Cochrane, USAF (Ret.), to EFP, April 9, 1980.
7. Letter from Col. Edward McGough, USAF (Ret.), to EFP, August 27, 1979.
8. Cochrane correspondence.
9. Lane interview.
10. McGough correspondence.
11. Lane interview.
12. Ibid.
13. Cochrane correspondence.
14. Lane interview.
15. Ibid.
16. Ibid.
17. Ibid.
18. Cochrane correspondence.

As Air Force Chief of Staff with Gen. David C. Jones.

The adjutant of the Cadet Corps in first-class year with Skip, his future wife.

Polo player, as a cadet at USMA.

A major in World War II.

Just after World War II (Official Photo U.S. Air Force).

In B-24 gear.

144

In Korea, being decorated by Lt. Gen. Glenn Barcus.

With General LeMay and Secretary McNamara, receiving first star.

Pinned with third star. AF Chief, General McConnell on left and Brown's wife, Skip, on right.

Impromptu promotion ceremony for fourth star. Red Gideon and Brown on their way to Vietnam to command U.S. Air Forces.

PART FOUR
TO THE TOP OF THE
LEADERSHIP LADDER

CHAPTER 16

WASHINGTON, D.C.: AUGUST 1966–AUGUST 1968

On May 1, 1966, it was announced that George Brown had been selected as Assistant to the Chairman of the Joint Chiefs of Staff. The position of Chairman was then held by Gen. Earle G. Wheeler, United States Army, who was first appointed on July 3, 1964.

Wheeler had been Brown's superior from September 1964 through May 1966, since Joint Task Force–2 came under the direction of the Chairman. Wheeler had said of Brown's performance as commander of JTF–2 that he was "an outstanding leader" and had "unlimited potential and should advance rapidly to staff or command positions involving greater responsibilities and increased rank." His rank did indeed increase since the Assistant's position was a three-star billet, and George was therefore promoted to lieutenant general on August 1, 1966.

Was General Brown selected only because it was the Air Force's turn for the position? Lt. Gen. Andrew Goodpaster, whom George replaced, was an Army officer, although in the Chairman's office one was considered a "purple suiter," that is, no longer belonging to one's service of origin. Goodpaster moved on to become Director of the Joint Staff for Wheeler. "George Brown was my number one recommendation to succeed me as assistant to General Wheeler," reflected Goodpaster. "I thought he was a superb appointment. He would be strong, honest, and straight. He was able and had had extensive experience in varied assignments."[1]

I asked General Goodpaster for more details on the responsibilities of the job. "It grew out of my old job, which had been upgraded to full Assistant to the Chairman," he said. "We had to read and advise the Chairman on every document that came into the office. The documents that the Chairman worked on were mostly JCS documents to act on. We had to advise him on methods of operating the JCS and supervise the operation of the Chairman's staff group. We had to represent the Chairman in meetings around Washington and in the Pentagon. This was always a very delicate area because the Chiefs were reluctant to have just anybody represent them without a set of written instructions to participate in the kinds of meetings that we had. The Chairman had to have someone as assistant who knew the thinking of the Chiefs, and who would be right nine times out of ten."[2]

"I first really began to work closely with George Brown when he became assistant to the Chairman," recalled Maj. Gen. Robert Ginsburg. "At this time I was liaison officer between General Wheeler and Walt Rostow, the President's foreign affairs advisor in the White House, so nominally Brown was my boss. But, in fact, 90 percent of the time, I worked directly for General Wheeler. There was a small portfolio that I had in staffing JCS actions on which I worked directly for General Brown, but mainly I simply had to keep him informed on things that Wheeler and I felt that he ought to know about what I was doing. He walked in to succeed General Goodpaster and within five minutes had the loyalty of all the people there. Not that they had been disloyal to Goodpaster, but the new boss came in and immediately established himself."

I asked General Ginsburg how General Brown established himself. "It was a small office," he said, "only about a half dozen people. During the course of the first hour General Brown met each of them; he either went by their offices or they came to his office. He showed that while he was a very businesslike guy, he had a great smile and he always would find time for a pleasantry. We felt he had an interest in us as professional officers and as human beings. He did personal kinds of things, but without being overly personal. He'd have a quick joke to tell. He would take people into his confidence. If he felt there was something that he knew that we needed to know to do our jobs better, he'd tell us about it."[3]

Brown's selection was initiated by the Air Force in that Brown was a comer, that is, he had had so many key jobs and had done so well in all of them. Thus, the Air Force person put forward to be the assistant to General Wheeler was recommended by the Air Force, but Wheeler, of course, had the final say. Brown's selection was, therefore, a mutual thing between Air Force Chief of Staff J. P. McConnell and Wheeler. It didn't follow that because General Wheeler was Army he had to have a man from another service as assistant. It was simply a good idea to have the Chairman and his assistant come from different services.

One of the major responsibilities for Brown as senior assistant was to be chief of staff of the Chairman's personal staff group. It was an informal arrangement with no titles and covered the various areas of the world, with one individual having Europe and another, the Far East.

As senior assistant, Brown made certain that the Chairman's position was laid out and reviewed and that he was briefed on any position taken. It might be something the Secretary of Defense had requested. For example, if the Secretary asked for the Chairman's view on a problem, the staff would work it up, monitored by the senior assistant.

This personal staff group did independent analysis for the Chairman and handled matters that he didn't consider suitable for wide dissemination and staffing. There were sensitive things going on with political overtones, such as a telephone call from the President asking for the Chairman's position.

How did Brown perform these duties? He would call one or more of the staff in and say, "Here's a problem." It was a very informal arrangement, with all five of his people in the next office. The key was service to the Chairman. Brown's group had to stay ahead of the issues so that the Chairman never was surprised.

Brown was really an alter ego for the Chairman, a sounding board, somebody with whom the Chairman could discuss his ideas. He could tell the Chairman, "I think that's weak," or "Boss, I think it's great." The personal assistant was always the last man to talk to the Chairman on any problem. Also, he usually stood in for the Chairman on interagency meetings when he was not available.

Brown would generally go in about five o'clock in the afternoon, and sit down with General Wheeler, and talk about everything that went on that day. He would brief him on the various things he hadn't bothered Wheeler with, decisions Brown made himself. They would talk about major problems, giving Wheeler a chance to tell Brown how he felt.

Since none of his job responsibilities were laid down in writing anywhere, Brown was a conduit to many people who wanted to get the Chairman's outlook on a project, paper, or problem. George was a conduit not only to the Joint Staff, but also to the Secretary of Defense and his people, and the Chiefs themselves.

The Director and the Joint Staff and Brown's personal staff were totally separate entities, so he did not get into the JCS routine, although he sat in on meetings. He also was present often for the Director's briefings to the Chairman. "In preparing a number of positions," recalled former Director of the Joint Chiefs, Lt. Gen. David Burchinal, "if they were crucial positions, I'd talk them over with George to be sure that we were putting out exactly what Bus Wheeler wanted, could handle, and could be effective using. It was very important that George and I work closely together since the Chairman had a wide variety of problems. George would prepare him for meetings with the Secretary of Defense and at the White House as well as a number of other things not strictly in the Joint Staff's arena.

"It was just always evident," continued General Burchinal, "if we had a problem or a tough issue needing handling, we went to George about it and he would sort it out. He was very close to the Chairman on a personal as well as a professional basis and had considerable influence on him, too. They had a team arrangement that didn't separate out into cubbyholes."[4]

Another member of the Joint Staff had a similar feeling. Then Maj. Gen. James Sherrill, USAF, was Special Assistant for Strategic Mobility. "I sometimes used George to sound out a problem or two because of our personal relationship," remembered Sherrill. "He was always a good sounding board, a good listener. If he thought you had something out of kilter, you could just ask him, 'George, what do you think?' and he'd come back and give you a good, straight, honest answer. If he didn't have an answer he would tell me, 'I don't know.' Then, if he thought about it and he had any further input, he'd get the word to you. Wheeler and Brown together were a great team because they were just super people. You just couldn't find a more pleasant atmosphere to work in."[5]

Lt. Gen. DeWitt C. Smith, Jr., who as a colonel served as Wheeler's speech writer, recalled, "General Wheeler used Brown in a range of ways that would be hard to cover in a job description. He felt that Brown was an extension of himself. They understood each other and took the same basic approaches toward interservice cooperation as opposed to parochialism. They took the same basic positions in expressing and defining fundamental service interests up to and including the highest civilian authority. At the same time they tried hard to understand the point of view of the civilian authority. Wheeler used Brown in his preparation to talk to the President, the Secretary of Defense, the Secretary of a service, or the Chiefs, or to convey directives, orders, requests, and instructions on important or urgent issues to members of the Joint Staff. Wheeler would test out ideas on Brown. 'What do you think about this?' 'How can I get this done?' 'If you were doing it, what would you do?' It was immensely valuable to have a man such as George with the Chairman, who was so pressed."[6]

DeWitt Smith further commented that "George could have set himself up as a super chief of staff under the Chairman, but he did not. Brown didn't intervene between the Chairman and my group. He didn't try to run me. Sometimes just to keep informed, he would bounce ideas off us or solicit ideas for things with which he was concerned. His principal function was to serve General Wheeler himself, and it depended to a marked degree on a personal relationship and was person-to-person and not through any channels.

"When I did deal with Brown," continued Smith, "we got along well together, first because I had known him before, and secondly because he tried to keep himself informed. I saw his principal role to be that of serving as a very knowledgeable and senior assistant to the Chairman who with three stars had enough rank that he could talk turkey to the members of the Joint Staff or go down the hall and talk to any of the Chiefs of Staff. In other words, he was an alter ego for the Chairman in doing Joint Staff business and in serving the Chairman directly. He was obviously well fitted for that by his own personal qualities, but beyond that, by virtue of his prior experience in somewhat the same role as a senior military assistant to Secretary McNamara."[7]

I then asked Smith what he meant by Brown's "personal qualities." He responded, "George Brown was candid. He could be very blunt. He had a sense of humor and was most likable, but at the same time he was tough. He was diplomatic in getting things done. He had a remarkable blend of things, which sometimes seemed to conflict with each other. In him they worked well together. He wasn't stuffy or worried about rank. You always felt at ease with him. I think that was true of senior as well as junior officers, and of course, in those circumstances, in my judgment, you can elicit much more from people."[8]

"I was a colonel at this time," remembered Brig. Gen. Alan Edmunds. "I traveled with the Chairman many times when George remained in Washington. We traveled mostly to Vietnam, but also to President Johnson's Guam meeting with the Vietnamese, and another Johnson meeting in Hawaii. As a result, much of my guidance and most of my task assignments came to me direct from the Chairman or his executive officer, Col. John Elder. I tried to keep George posted on all that took place between the Chairman and me but was not always able to. When lapses did occur, Brown was not overly concerned. He had enough self-confidence to provide an inner security and an ability to perform his job, which was remarkable, particularly in view of the visibility of his position to civilian and military— to the Army, Navy, Air Force, and Marines."[9]

"George was always willing to listen to advice," recalled Adm. John "Blackie" Weinel, USN. "Indeed, if you had good advice, he was the first guy to tell you. More important than that, and this is something I really liked about George Brown, if I came up with a good idea, he'd come back to me and say, 'OK, Blackie, let's go in and see General Wheeler.' On one occasion we went in on a Nike X project idea he had. Brown did the talking, and he then said, 'Now, this is Blackie's idea. When you present this to Secretary McNamara and he gives you the comeback that nobody could win a nuclear war, you tell him that it might be true that nobody's going to win it, but somebody's going to lose it worse. Now here is Blackie's idea on this issue.' "[10]

The Director of the Joint Staff was responsible for preparing all the Chairman's agenda with the Joint Staff for the Joint Chiefs of Staff and for briefing the Chairman. Brown and his staff group did not influence that activity directly. They handled more of the "external" problems of the Chairman, such as with the Secretary of Defense and his staff. "He was extremely effective in working with the Office of the Secretary of Defense," said Burchinal. "He had the patience to listen to them, and those guys in OSD liked to talk. Yet George never lost sight of what he was after, and gradually he brought them around to his way of thinking. He had an easy way about him that encouraged a discussion and he was effective in getting the OSD people to see his point of view.

"I tried to insulate myself a bit from the OSD," continued Burchinal, "from the lower level of OSD, not from the Secretary or the Deputy Secretary. When you got down into the whiz kids, the systems analysts, they took all your time and gave you nothing in return, so I just didn't bother with them. We used to get all kinds of problems. Those were the things I'd tell George about and see if he couldn't get the heat off. There was a strict rule that only the Secretary or the Deputy Secretary of Defense could disapprove a JCS recommendation. We found suddenly that JCS recommendations were being disapproved at a much lower level than the two top men. Sometimes the papers never even got to the Secretary or his deputy. The people at the lower level were doing it and just sending papers back that never reached the Secretary as they were supposed to. On those things I'd say to George, 'Now, this is the policy, this is the procedure, and this is what's happening. We got the paper returned but we shouldn't have gotten it back. Can you get it in the channels where it counts?' He was able to go over to that lower level and get the paper back."[11]

On one occasion there was a meeting of the NATO Defense Ministers and Military Committee in Europe where the Chairman was scheduled to make a presentation. However, a crisis developed in Vietnam and the Chairman had to stay in the States, so he sent Brown in his place. "George," said one of those who attended that meeting, "being both broad and versatile, had a great comprehension of the worldwide political and military situations. He did a fine job of presenting the Chairman's views and handled the question period beautifully."[12]

Brown also substituted for the Chairman at the National War College where he would discuss worldwide issues. He understood not only the Joint Chiefs' views, which, of course, reflected the Chairman's, but he also had his own thoughts.

"The political-military problems were extremely intricate," reflected Lt. Gen. John McPherson, a member of the staff of the Joint Chiefs of Staff, "but Brown could sort out the issues. He was good at eliminating all the extraneous matter and focusing quickly on the key issue. He could come up with a fast and sharp decision, and he wasn't shooting from the hip either. He simply had the confidence and know-how to decide what had to be done. He had native intelligence and quite a background. Obviously, he was able to accept responsibilities, assimilate lots of information, and sort out what was important and what wasn't. He was a smart worker and knew how to get things done and get them done quickly. He didn't waste time, and he was also very supportive of the Chairman."[13]

A constant challenge throughout Brown's tenure was the Vietnam War. "I was J–3 and worked for the Director," recalled McPherson. "We were involved with the air campaign and the troops and naval forces to be used against North Vietnam. Our staff interfaced with George's staff. It was a case of everybody working together to try to move the political authority to do something. The gradual escalation, of course, was the worst way that you could do anything in combat. This would be a national decision made by McNamara and the President. Of course, the President had final responsibility, but we all felt terrible frustration. We were searching for ways to let the North Vietnamese know that we were serious about the war. We weren't, however, because we rarely did anything that reflected any seriousness. When we did, the North Vietnamese would get to the worldwide press and scream bloody murder and the President would begin to back off."[14]

George Brown didn't get into the actual selection of the targets in Vietnam at the beginning. The J–3 did that, but he was very conscious of it. He had been operations officer in Korea and understood tactical bombardment. Thus, he became completely familiar with what was going on in the air campaign in Vietnam, what the problems were, and what needed to be done to get on with the war. "You didn't have to draw him a picture," said McPherson. "He had been there before in Korea."[15]

"During this peak period of the Vietnam conflict, we maintained frequent contact with General Wheeler," reflected meteorologist L. Dayton Blanchard, "and General Brown was always at his elbow. Being an Air Force officer, Brown was extremely interested in weather and its effect on daily operations in Vietnam. So in addition to the daily JCS briefing, he set up a private weather briefing in Wheeler's office where we provided in-depth coverage utilizing a portable vu-graph device that we placed on his desk. We even provided weather satellite coverage of Southeast Asia only a few hours old. Brown provided valuable advice to General Wheeler during this period, as he always carefully digested and evaluated what we had to say. My own observations of Brown are based solely on these daily contacts, although he was always in the background when we briefed in the tank during military exercises and during crisis periods such as the short war between Israel and Egypt. He was a quiet man, always deep in thought. His mere presence in a room always inspired and motivated me to put forth my best. He never intimidated, but I got the impression that he was forceful. When he did speak, he was eloquent."[16]

A crisis occurred in June 1967, during the war between Israel and Egypt. A U.S. intelligence ship, the USS *Liberty,* was sunk by the Israelis off the coast of northern Egypt. There was a breakdown in command and control that permitted the ship to get too close to the war zone. "I was designated by the Chairman," said Maj. Gen. J. R. Russ, USA, "to head up a board to determine where the breakdown occurred. George Brown discussed the matter with me and said that it was possible the breakdown could have occurred within the Joint Staff. He directed that I pull no punches and 'let the chips fall where they may.' He said he would back our findings 100 percent, which he did, even though it caused some 'heartburn' within the Joint Staff. This is an indication of the type of man he was. I thought him a great leader, a man of great integrity, and a tower of strength."[17]

A further crisis took place on January 23, 1968, when four North Korean patrol boats seized the *Pueblo,* a United States Navy intelligence ship, off Wonsan, taking the vessel and eighty-three crew members. The reaction to this crisis was handled by the Joint Chiefs of Staff, the Secretary of Defense, the Secretary of State, and of course, the President. Acting upon the advice of his Chairman and his National Security Advisor, on January 25, 1968, President Lyndon Johnson ordered 14,787 Air Force and Navy reservists to active duty as support for our diplomatic efforts to recover the *Pueblo.* He also appealed to the United Nations Security Council for action. The Soviet Union brusquely refused to act on a United States request that Moscow use its good offices with the North Korean government for the return of the *Pueblo.*

It was a tense and critical situation in which George Brown was to play a key role. Brig. Gen. Alan Edmunds, USAF, put into perspective Brown's part in the handling of the crisis: "Since my responsibilities covered the geographical area starting at the West Coast and extending through Burma, George and I found ourselves working together in the almost daily crises which occurred during that period—Vietnam, including the Tet Offensive; reversion of Okinawa to the Japanese; the ongoing 'cultural revolution' in

China; negotiation for U.S. presence in the Philippines; the *Pueblo* incident; and many others. We found ourselves in many late night and/or early morning sessions trying to put together a coherent package for the Chairman on the crisis of the moment.

"The situation in which George displayed his skill, coolness, and diplomacy," continued Edmunds, "was during the *Pueblo* crisis when he was appointed by the Chairman to be 'the man' with the services, the JCS, the executive branch and congressional committees. He also had to face the press during the early days of the crisis. I marveled at his ability to keep up with a rapidly changing situation, information of questionable accuracy, the President wanting instant response to his queries, congressional committees or individuals demanding George's appearance with very little notice, and the Secretary of Defense constantly on the phone. George put on quite a performance, one that has stuck in my mind over the years."[18]

During this crisis Brown remained calm in handling the daily crises, but he also could look ahead. "I was on duty in the NMCC the night the *Pueblo* was captured by the North Koreans," recalled Maj. Gen. William Shedd. "That night was characterized by anger, impatience, and finally frustration on the part of the senior people in the White House and the Department of Defense. General Brown, instead of succumbing to all this, calmly discussed with me what steps must be taken in the future to insure no repeat of such an incident. He immediately knew we could not change this one, but we'd better be sure of the future."[19]

In spite of all the pressures, Brown retained his sense of humor. An example is recalled by Blackie Weinel: "I had a good reputation with General Wheeler for being very brief and to the point. If I reviewed a paper I would write on my memorandum, 'Paragraph one—a rather stupid idea, recommend we kill the whole thing.' Then I would put my initial under it. That would be it. When George Brown replaced General Goodpaster he had heard about my reputation for brevity. One of the first papers I sent forward was a short, one-sentence analysis. It just said, 'Not a very brainy idea. Suggest we just let it die a natural death.' George read this and sent for me. He said, 'Blackie, I got this memorandum from you. I find it pretty wordy.' He already had a leg up on me, so I said, 'You know, General Brown, with all due respect, if I had known you were going to read my memorandum, I'd have shortened it more.' That was the kind of guy he was. Immediately, I felt a real rapport with him, and from that day on whatever George Brown wanted, he got. I thought he was one of the greatest guys that ever came down the pike, particularly with his sense of humor."[20]

Brown did not claim to have all the answers but sought advice and listened. "I was very impressed with George's work in that he was very decisive," said General McPherson. "He obviously had confidence in himself, and he expressed himself well. He elicited your confidence in him in that he knew what he was talking about. He'd thought the thing through and he'd had experience. You realized that he knew what he was doing and could be counted upon to do the job right. At the same time I disagreed with him on a few things. He was open to criticism and to discussing it."[21]

DeWitt Smith commented that in his discussions with Brown, "I'd say, 'I don't think that's a good idea.' He'd say, 'Why not?' I'd tell him. We'd talk it out. It was a good relationship to have. I understood that after we talked it out and he made a decision I would support him, but you had open season to lay it out without any penalties being exacted until the decision was made. That in my mind is the way leadership ought to work among good people."[22]

"Although I was a naval officer, I didn't work on naval matters for General Wheeler," reflected Blackie Weinel. "We broke down into functional tasks, not along service lines. One day, however, a paper came through and I had an opportunity to plug naval aviation. Normally I wouldn't have done it. You really had to stay purple suited down there, but I couldn't pass this opportunity up, so this time I didn't write a short memo. It had to do with carriers, and to me as a naval aviator, we were the saviors of civilization. Well, George got it before the Chairman, so he called me in. He said to me, 'Blackie, you know I'll send this thing in to General Wheeler if you want me to, but I ought to remind you of something. He has to listen to Admiral McDonald (Chief of Naval Operations) three times a week in our JCS meetings. Admiral McDonald is a naval aviator like you. There isn't a meeting that goes by that McDonald isn't plugging aircraft carriers. Do you think this little nudge from you as a Navy captain is really going to have much effect when the CNO is selling those things three times a week?' I said, 'You've got a point,' so I withdrew the memorandum, which was probably smart, because I think if it had got into Wheeler, he'd have thrown me out on my ear."[23]

In numerous personal interviews and many letters, I found a quality that received much attention in discussions of Brown's leadership: he always seemed to be under control. "He invariably appeared calm, even though those around him might be agitated by an ongoing crisis," was the comment made by Brig. Gen. Donald Stout. "I had contact with him only in crisis situations," said William Shedd. "He was always the coolheaded, unflappable professional."

"With all of the volumes of paperwork being circulated, he always seemed cool and calm, never frustrated," recalled Lt. Gen. Ray Peers, USA. "He maintained a sense of humor; he was never too busy to sit and talk."

Blackie Weinel made another observation about Brown: "To be a leader, you have to have intelligence, but there's a danger when you have too much. Sometimes I've noticed among our senior military people that when they're very smart, when they're tremendously intelligent, they pay a price for it in some other category, that is, they may not have a lot of common sense to go with it, and they normally don't have too much humility either. George Brown, fortunately, was not endowed with what I call a brilliant mind. He was above average in intelligence, but more important, he was above average in common sense and also in humility. George was the complete man, a self-effacing man. I don't think that he ever worried about his career. Promotion with George was not a driving factor in his personality. I saw other officers devote 90 percent of their time to making sure that somebody was chalking up good marks behind their names for promotions and saw them go out of their way on every issue and on everything to make sure they looked good rather than making the Chairman or the military in general look good. George carried the opposite almost to an extreme. He never worried about where he stood as far as promotion was concerned."[24]

An excellent summation of Brown's leadership was provided by Brig. Gen. John Donaldson, USA: "What was most characteristic about him was his self-confidence and unpretentiousness. He was always accessible, and he always had a clear, uncluttered mind. He listened to what you had to say and gave you an immediate decision or guidance. On the other hand, he was impatient with incomplete analysis or staff work and could politely but firmly send you back to the drawing board.

"I was impressed by his natural approach to problems and to his civilian and military associates and superiors in the Pentagon. Having previously worked under Secretary McNamara, he knew the ropes and the people at that level of decision making, and he felt at home at that level. He would not hesitate to go up and do battle on any matter of importance, and he was tremendously liked and admired by everyone with whom he came into contact. His reputation among the action officers and division chiefs in the Joint Staff was the best I have seen in three tours with the Joint Staff. His loyalty to the little guy who wrote the 'flimsy buff and green,' endeared him to all of us."[25]

On April 11, 1967, after approximately a year, General Wheeler wrote of Brown's performance as his assistant, "In dealing with the complex problems he encounters at this level of government he has exhibited sound and mature judgment, the capacity to evaluate data, the ability to analyze alternatives and the intelligence to formulate logical solutions. Lieutenant General Brown's advice has been valuable not only to me but to other administrative officials."

On July 25, 1968, General Wheeler said of Brown, "As my principal assistant and advisor, General Brown has performed outstandingly and has been of invaluable assistance to me across the spectrum of my responsibilities. His exceptional professional competence, broad experience in dealing with the highest governmental levels, sound judgment, capacity for logical analysis of complex problems, objectivity, loyalty, and deep sense of responsibility—all of these qualities General Brown brought to bear effectively in this highly important and sensitive position.''

Glowing as General Wheeler's comments were, they might have been an understatement. "I recall a situation," commented Alan Edmunds, "involving a lengthy period of absence by General Wheeler when he had his heart attack. Normally, one of the other chiefs would have presided over the meetings in the tank. For some reason, George substituted for the Chairman. What impressed me was the smooth, absolutely fearless way he ran the meeting. He defended the Chairman's positions and successfully closed the issues on the Chairman's terms. Considering that his opposites were the chiefs of their services and that the Air Force Chief of Staff was in a sense his boss, he waded into the agenda, as the citations say, 'with no thought for his own safety.' It was impressive, and I guess a thinking person would at that point have said, 'There is our future Chairman.' "[26]

Although Brown had learned much as exec to the Air Force Chief of Staff, this was a greater opportunity for exposure and growth. His responsibilities involved him in decision making at the highest level and put him in contact with our country's most important leaders. It was an extremely important assignment in his development and ultimate selection for even greater challenges.

NOTES

1. Personal interview with Lt. Gen. Andrew J. Goodpaster, USA (Ret.), July 22, 1980.
2. Ibid.
3. Personal interview with Maj. Gen. Robert Ginsburg, August 4, 1977.
4. Personal interview with Gen. David Burchinal, USAF, August 15, 1981.
5. Personal interview with Lt. Gen. James C. Sherrill, USAF (Ret.), October 3, 1981.
6. Personal interview with Lt. Gen. DeWitt C. Smith, Jr., USAF (Ret.), August 14, 1981.
7. Smith interview.
8. Ibid.
9. Letter from Brig. Gen. Alan C. Edmunds, USAF (Ret.), to EFP, February 3, 1981.
10. Personal interview with Adm. John P. Weinel, USN (Ret.), October 18, 1981.
11. Burchinal interview.

12. Personal interview with Lt. Gen. John McPherson, USAF (Ret.), July 8, 1981.
13. Ibid.
14. Ibid.
15. Ibid.
16. Letter from L. Dayton Blanchard to EFP, July 18, 1979.
17. Letter from Maj. Gen. J. R. Russ, USA (Ret.), to EFP, April 2, 1981.
18. Edmunds correspondence.
19. Letter from Maj. Gen. William E. Shedd, III, USA (Ret.), to EFP, April 3, 1981.
20. Weinel interview.
21. McPherson interview.
22. Smith interview.
23. Weinel interview.
24. Ibid.
25. Letter from Brig. Gen. John W. Donaldson, USA (Ret.), to EFP, October 9, 1981.
26. Edmunds correspondence.

CHAPTER 17
REPUBLIC OF VIETNAM: AUGUST 1968–AUGUST 1970

During the spring of 1968, while still serving as Assistant to the Chairman of the Joint Chiefs of Staff, George Brown had taken it upon himself to make a recommendation on behalf of a fellow officer that would ultimately prove beneficial to both of them. "Spike Momyer," commented Tim Brown, "was in Southeast Asia as a three-star general commanding half of the United States Air Force in Vietnam. George felt that this was a stupid state of affairs, that there were four-star generals sitting around command-ing much less than Momyer was and doing much less of a job. So George told me that he had gone to see the Chief of Staff of the Air Force and said, in effect, 'This is wrong; you ought to make command of the Seventh a four-star slot.' His visit must have had some results, because before long it was changed to a four-star position. Then, as it turned out, George himself was selected to succeed Momyer."[1]

I asked General Wade, then Deputy Chief of Staff for Personnel and later Vice Chief of Staff of the Air Force, "What role did you have in George Brown's succeeding General 'Spike' Momyer in Southeast Asia as Seventh Air Force commander?" He responded, "I guess General Disosway probably had more to do with his selection than anybody else. We knew George was highly respected by the people on the second floor and the Secretary of Defense's office. We knew that he was a capable commander. General Wheeler was still down there then. General Disosway had TAC at the time.'' I then asked, ''Why would General Disosway have so much say?'' ''Because of the TAC operation,'' said General Wade, ''and because he had known George Brown so well.[2]

''It was on a personal basis,'' continued Wade. ''Disosway and I visited back and forth on the telephone. He was getting ready to retire and 'Spike' Momyer was going to replace him at TAC. We talked about who should go out there and who shouldn't. It would be a mistake to send some officers, but George Brown would be best of all. Disosway recommended that George Brown be the replacement.''[3]

''He was promoted to full general, had his fourth star pinned on while en route to Southeast Asia to assume command of Seventh Air Force from General Momyer,'' recalled his first aide in Vietnam, Col. Lee Butler. Butler was then a captain. ''He was authorized a colonel as an aide,'' continued Butler, ''but he selected a captain. This was part of his style. He didn't want to 'waste' Air Force resources by having a colonel as an aide and didn't think he would be able to fully employ a colonel. He told me as I started the job, 'I would prefer that you use this as a learning experience. I will take you to every meeting and place that I go, whenever it is appropriate. I would like for you to learn and listen as well as to advise me on what you see, think, and hear.' ''[4]

Brown did not permit the simultaneous achievement of four stars and command of the Seventh Air Force to go to his head. ''I was a captain at the time,'' recalled another aide, Maj. Jack Cremin. ''I left the house one day when General Brown was going back to his office. I ran to the car to get there first to open the door. General Brown said, 'I'm a big boy and I know how to open doors.' I said, 'Yes sir, okay,' but I held the door while he got in. That time, General Brown decided to leave a little earlier than usual, so the driver was not there when he wanted to go home. I buzzed for the driver to meet me at the car, but he had a longer way to go, so when Brown went out the back door, zap, he was in the car. So I got out as soon as we arrived at his quarters, ran around, and again opened the door. Brown stopped and said to me, 'I told you once, I'm a big boy. I know how to open the door.'

''I never opened another door for him when there was just the two of us. Of course, if there were another general officer around or some other VIP, or if it would be inconvenient for him because he was talking with someone, then I would open the door.''[5]

As one might expect, Brown spent much time traveling throughout Vietnam to insure the effective operation in all areas of his command. When on such a trip, he followed a policy of letting the local commander show him those areas that he wanted him to see. Then, Brown would make it a point to look at the motor pool and salvage yard. He liked to do this because they were areas that affected a unit's efficient operation. He wanted to make sure that every unit had a good motor pool and salvage yard. He also wanted to ensure that the materiel in the salvage yard was properly accounted for.

"He realized, of course," said Jack Cremin, "that almost everyone would show him through the maintenance shop. There he would talk with the crew chiefs and maintenance supervisors. About 80 percent of a fighter operation is the maintenance operation and its associated equipment, so it was extremely important. Because of this, a lot of people spent more time on maintenance than they did on the motor pool, so he thought it was a good indicator."[6]

On one occasion, Brown was inspecting the base at Cam Ranh when he asked Cremin if there was anything there that he wanted to see. "Well, the 12th TAC Fighter Wing had left Cam Ranh," said Cremin, "and returned to the United States. An airlift wing came in to take their place and took over the facilities that had been fixed up by the fighter pilots. Col. Abbott Greenleaf was the wing commander, and I requested the opportunity to see the condition of the BOQs. I knew how immature fighter pilots could sometimes be. Colonel Greenleaf said to General Brown, 'I didn't want to bring this up, but I do want to show you the BOQs.'

"We went into the BOQs, which were quonset huts that had been fixed up with wood paneling. There were square mirrors with gold veins in them. We found that the mirrors had all been smashed, and that hatchets had been used on the wood paneling. Everything was hacked to pieces. They had left nothing but trash and ruins. General Brown was livid. Greenleaf explained that the fighter pilots had spent their own money to fix things up, but in General Brown's eyes that still didn't give them the right to destroy everything. When he returned to headquarters, he issued instructions that in the future, before any group left its base, its quarters were to be inspected by a general officer."[7]

When making his inspection trips, Brown asked questions of various people, particularly enlisted personnel. He would ask them what they were doing, what their housing was like, and other questions relevant to their morale. One instance that typifies Brown's concern for the morale of his troops is recalled by Jack Cremin: "On another inspection trip, General Brown was in the field, and a colonel asked him to talk with the people involved with the controller school and the controller mission. In his introductory comments, he said to them, 'You're doing a super job. I see you are all second lieutenants, and I understand you've never seen a four-star general. Your commander has asked me to get in front of you and say a few words, and I accepted because you are second lieutenants who have never seen a four-star general. The reason I accepted was that I've never seen a second lieutenant!' Well, he really brought down the house. He then went on to say to them, 'You men really have an important job; you may not think it's important, but unless you put in a mark, the fighter guys can't do their job. The fighter guys think they're important, but they are helpless without you.' It really made those fellows feel good. Here he was, concerned enough to talk with them, and it obviously meant a great deal."[8]

Another way in which Brown demonstrated his concern for the feelings of subordinates was that although he was a four-star general who commanded thousands of men, he never belittled their responsibilities by pulling rank. Cremin recalled the following incident: "At Ban Me Thout we had viewed the area and seen most of the base. We were driving down a road and came to a guard, an Army Green Beret private, standing before a barricade. We started to proceed when the guard said, 'Sir, this is a closed post.' Well, I got out of the jeep and went over and said to him, 'Get the roadblock out of the way because we're going through.' The guard replied, 'Sir, no one is allowed on this post without the permission of the captain.' I said to him, 'Buddy, you've got a four-star general who is the Deputy Commander of U.S. Forces in Vietnam sitting right over there. Now get the damn thing out of the road.' He said to me, 'No, you don't have any business in there.' Then General Brown came over, and when he learned what the altercation was about, he simply said to me, 'Well, if we've got no reason to be here, let's leave. Hop in the jeep, let's go someplace else.' So we turned around and went someplace else. It was just another example of his unpretentiousness."[9]

Sometimes Brown's lack of pretentiousness could be a real thorn in the sides of his aides, particularly where his personal safety was concerned. "One time," said Cremin, "a general officer was showing him his new shoes. He told General Brown that he had them handmade for him in downtown Saigon and that they were the most comfortable and best-fitting shoes he had ever owned. So he gave him the shoemaker's address. General Brown turned to me and said, 'Let's go.' I proceeded to make the arrangements and started to call for a jeep with a machine gun and a guard. He said to me, 'We don't need any of that stuff.' So we just hopped in his car and told the driver to go downtown. Brown was in uniform, and the Viet Cong were constantly running around blowing up cars in downtown Saigon and generally harassing everybody there; thus, I was quite nervous. The only weapons we had in the car were a five-shot .38 that I carried in my briefcase and the driver's gun.

"Gen. Creighton Abrams usually had gun jeeps in front and back of his vehicle. Brown just never thought he was that important. He thought he was not important enough that anybody would try to kill him. But they were killing majors and lieutenant colonels regularly, so when he went downtown and parked, I told the driver to stay with the car. Otherwise, the Viet Cong might come by with a magnetic mine and stick it underneath. We then went into the shoe store, which was probably half a block from where we had parked, and if I hadn't had an ulcer before, I was sure going to get one then. He wandered around, and I was trying to watch all the people and make sure they didn't make any threatening moves. He would say to me, 'What do you think of these shoes?' and 'Don't you think if I bought these, they would be good golf shoes?' Golf shoes were about the last things I was interested in; all I wanted to do was get him out of there. But he continued to talk to the Vietnamese shoemaker as though he didn't have a care in the world and were simply in downtown Washington."[10]

On his frequent inspection trips, Brown never forgot that there might be military personnel needing a flight, and he extended this courtesy to them even under the most trying circumstances. "On one occasion," said Cremin, "a courier plane was flying out at about the same time we were leaving in our T-39. I always went into base operations, at the general's direction, to see if anyone needed a ride in the same direction we were going. On this day, no one needed a ride with us because the courier was coming by and would pick up everybody. So we drove out to the T-39. General Brown and I got in, the crew chief closed the door, and we got ready to taxi out. Brown was up in the pilot's seat, preparing for the takeoff.

"Suddenly we heard an unusual noise, and I saw an Army master sergeant with a duffle bag banging on the door, thinking we were the courier plane. General Brown told the crew chief to open the door, so the man climbed aboard, threw his duffle bag down and started swearing. He said, 'You guys were about to leave me and I'm supposed to get to such and such a place, you blankety-blank sons of bitches!' I was sitting near him, so I suggested to him, 'Why don't you go up and thank the pilot for stopping to let you on?' He said he thought he would do that, and went on up to the front of the aircraft. Then General Brown turned around, with four stars on each shoulder, and you should have seen that sergeant's face. General Brown, who had heard the foul language and the upset, did not chew out the sergeant. The sergeant came back and for the entire ride just sat there quietly and perspired."[11]

Brown's self-effacing manner is seen in yet another incident recalled by Jack Cremin: "At the conclusion of an inspection at Da Nang, there was a period of twenty minutes before General Brown was scheduled to leave for

the next base. He said to me, 'I want to see the PX.' When we got there, I
went in and said to the first salesgirl I saw, 'Get the manager and bring him
here.' She disappeared, and in a couple of seconds the manager came to
General Brown and asked, 'Is there anything I can do for you?' General
Brown said, 'No, I've never been here and I just want to look around.' So
we wandered around and he picked up a tube of toothpaste. Then he went
back to the front of the store and said to the manager and the sales people,
'This is a nice store, well stocked, and it looks like the men can get almost
anything they want.'

"He then proceeded to get in line to pay for his purchase. There were
five or six people in front of him, and the first two or three were soldiers
who had just come in from the field. They had mud up to their knees, and
they were soggy and wet. I scooted in front of them and said, 'Excuse me;
I've got a general officer, and we need to cut in front of you.' I turned
around while doing this, and there was General Brown still standing in the
back of the line. So I went back to him and said, 'General, would you care
to come up front?' He said, 'No, I'll just wait here, just like everybody
else.' Well, of course, I was getting beet red. The whispers were going
around that here was this general waiting in line, and you could see the other
people at the different cash registers saying, 'That's the general.' He simply
waited his turn, paid his money, and then went to the car.''[12]

In his travels, Brown dispensed with the fanfare normally given to general officers. Cremin states, "On one particular inspection trip to several
different bases, he had me send out a message advising of our arrival time
and requesting that no military honors be rendered. We arrived at Kadena
at about 2:30 in the morning and saw standing below us a major general
with four young men at present arms. Brown turned around to me and said,
'I told you to wire that there were to be no honors.' I was about to answer
when the major general said, 'Well, General, I just happened to be driving
down the taxiway and heard you were coming, and I had these four members of the honor guard with me anyway. Needless to say,' he continued,
'we wanted to welcome you to Kadena.' General Brown didn't particularly
appreciate the idea of these enlisted men having to turn out at 2:30 in the
morning to render him honors. He simply didn't want people to go out of
their way to do unnecessary things for him.''[13]

"I was the Chief of Intelligence in Vietnam under Momyer and under
Brown, Westmoreland, and Abrams," recalled Maj. Gen. George Keegan.
"George Brown was very different from the other commanders in a number
of very specific ways. Momyer, his predecessors, and Brown's successors in
Vietnam all viewed themselves as tacticians, getting directly involved in the
prosecution of the war on an almost daily basis. They made decisions on

how many sorties, which targets, load of effort, weight of effort, direction, tactics to be used, considerations of air defenses, and the penetration problem. Momyer specifically was the greatest of them all in terms of his direct involvement in the conduct of the day-to-day air war.

Brown relied more on his very competent staff. He gave them more to do with air operations. They were to go to him when serious differences of opinion or problems arose with orders from the higher chain of command. His role was more to support and fight for them in conflicts between the Air Force, Army, and Navy, and the political chain of command in the White House, because, he said, "That's where I'm most competent." He acknowledged that his combat experience went back to Ploesti, where he was just a pilot, and to the Korean War, where he was a director of operations at Fifth Air Force and deeply involved in the conduct of day-to-day operations. He reminded his staff that their greatest problems in the prosecution of the war in Vietnam were in relationships with senior Army commanders at MACV, CINCPAC, the Joint Chiefs of Staff, the Secretary of Defense, and the White House. They were not being understood; the cause of aviation was not being heard fairly, and "we were not being judged objectively for our contribution to the war," he said. "I'm going to concentrate on improving relationships throughout that entire mixed-up level and chain of command. So, I expect to spend most of my time not with you in the staff, but with General Abrams, for whom I am Deputy for Air; he needs me on his staff more than you need me supervising you because he is empowered by the President with the conduct of this war."[14]

"When we had staff meetings in Vietnam," said Jack Cremin, "General Brown was patient and could listen to everything you had to say, even if you were blowing smoke. Then when you got through, he would ask a couple of questions which, if you did not know what you were talking about, would quietly make the point you weren't prepared. But he was always courteous enough to listen to what you had to say. Others had quite a different technique. If you had something to say and they didn't want to hear it, they might snap, 'Get off the stage; shut up; I don't want to hear it.' Brown would not do this; he would listen to everybody. His attitude was that by the time a briefing reached a four-star general, it had gone through a number of people. A man just doesn't originate a briefing as a captain or a major and say, 'Hey, I'd like to give this to the general.' So I can't help but think that part of General Brown's approach was out of respect for the other people in the chain of command who had listened to that briefing. But after it was over, he would ask the necessary questions to get the information he wanted. If you weren't on top of it, it could be a shattering experience, and sometimes he could be very rough."[15]

Besides Brown's own staff meetings, there were also formal meetings with General Abrams. "There are many people," said Gen. Robert J. Dixon, "who thought George sold out to McNamara or to the Army or to Abrams. None of this has any basis in fact. George Brown never gave an inch to anyone. In fact, he made some rather idiotic positions magnificent positions by force of character, logic, and good sense. On the other hand, Abrams was a pretty tough guy. The formal meetings that Abrams conducted lasted three or four hours, and I would sit in the back of the room, listening to Abrams make speeches about air power that no airman before or since had made, partly because George educated him, but partly because Abrams understood air power. He couldn't have learned it that quickly without some prior understanding. He got along so well with George. Some pretty touchy issues would arise about use of air support. Abrams would say things that we couldn't have written any better in the back room back here; we couldn't have written them as well. Abrams said it all, and said it to better effect, precisely because it had not originated with us."[16]

"One of George's greatest gifts was a human gift," reflected General Keegan. "He was warmhearted, wonderful with people, never mean or petty. He established the only time in that war that we were not all on edge, biting our nails from day-to-day wondering which of us was going to get a savage verbal assault from the commander. Our normal relationships with our commanders were as adversaries. With George it was a relationship of trust from the outset, complete ease of communications, and as a consequence, although George was not in the bowels of the air war as much as some of the other commanders, more of us approached Brown because his door was open. He never discouraged frank conversation.

"There were differences of opinion between the members of Seventh Air Force staff—operations, intelligence, logistics, plans—throughout the war. In our daily planning meetings we fought like savages to portray our own views of what was necessary. It was vicious. Brown simply didn't get involved in that. Yet, he was so approachable that if one of us had an irreconcilable difference, we could go see him. When this began, Brown imposed a salutary rule: he insisted that the man with whom we disagreed come along too for a real discussion. Brown, with all of his commitments, was never so busy that he didn't hear both sides of an issue fully and harmoniously, while drinking coffee and exchanging pleasantries. This caused the heat to be quickly dissipated and objective discussion achieved, with the result that a more able war was fought because more rational and thought-through decisions on how to use air power were made."[17]

The purpose of all staff meetings, of course, was the business of war. "The rules on conduct of the Vietnam War," pointed out Cremin, "permitted that if the Viet Cong fired on our reconnaissance flights, we could fire back. At one of General Brown's staff meetings, he was informed that our reconnaissance aircraft had been fired on, so at the end of the meeting, he wanted to talk to General Dixon, the Vice Commander; General Kirkendall, the DO; and General Bevans, who worked with General Kirkendall. He turned around to me and said, 'Jack, I want you to stay.' General Dixon said, 'Sir, this is a very sensitive matter.' Brown replied, 'Yes, but it's good for his education.' So the four of them sat at the table, and I sat in the background. It was interesting to observe how different minds worked. Brown first asked Bevans and Kirkendall what they thought we should do. They thought we should go in with four airplanes, drop some bombs, and let the Viet Cong know that if they shot at us again, we'd come back and drop more bombs. Then he asked Dixon's opinion. He said, 'I don't think four is enough; we ought to have about ten or twelve, about three flights, to let them know we mean business.' This was one of the few instances where I really saw some emotion on General Brown's part. He banged the table and said, 'Four? I want every damned airplane we can get airborne. I want them to know that if they shoot at us, the world comes down on them. The door is open, and now is the time to get some stuff in there while we can still do it.' They had shot at our reconnaissance planes, and we had twenty-four hours to retaliate. He wanted everything he could get loaded with bombs to go there and drop."[18]

Indeed, as mild-mannered as he could be at times, he was always strong in carrying out military objectives. "We destroyed this SAM site in the pass below the 20th parallel; I still have the picture of it," recalled General Dixon. "It was the only SAM site ever destroyed completely and totally. George wanted it hit because they weren't supposed to put it there. It was illegal and also immoral. There were certain rules, and this act was contrary to the rules. We had a hot pursuit rule, wherein if fired on from the passes below, we could go in. We were fired on from that pass where that SAM site was. We destroyed that SAM site, and it made George extremely happy."[19]

Although Brown was tough when the occasion demanded it, he was nevertheless a most considerate man. "Let me give you an illustration of his sensitivity," said his aide, Lee Butler, "and tell you a lesson I learned. An important aspect of the electronic war of Southeast Asia was Secretary McNamara's 'invisible wall,' and the 'Igloo White' operation at Nakhon Phanom. There were various aircraft units associated with flying it, sensors buried in the ground, and tape recordings in which you could hear trucks driving up hills.

"In the course of our travels, we had visited one of the F-4 outfits used to strike truck parks and other installations identified by the sensors. During this visit, we heard a tape recording which demonstrated the sensitivity of the data they were capable of picking up. We heard a Viet Cong truck being driven up a grade, with the driver changing gears. Some weeks later we visited Nakhon Phanom where they had set up a briefing for us which included, coincidentally, that same tape. It was included by a young airman who was obviously anxious for General Brown to hear it. But it was at the end of a very long day, and I started to say, 'General Brown has heard that before, so we can dispense with it,' when he stopped me and said, 'I would be interested in hearing whatever it is you have to tell me.' He took time to listen to the same thing over again so as not to disappoint a young airman who was very proud of his role in the war." [20]

There were times, however, when he was not patient. "I can remember," said Gen. James Knight, "when the war was going hot and heavy, and mostly bad for us. The intelligence staff briefing that morning was on the next season's expected rice crop in North Vietnam. Brown just blew his top. It wasn't what he wanted to hear that morning—about rice crops for the next six months from then. He listened to the briefing and then launched into a very stern lecture on what intelligence people ought to be doing. That was probably the most vocal I have ever heard him." [21]

There was another incident when Gen. John Roberts had made a mistake. Roberts had taken some action, but had not informed Brown what he had done. When Brown learned of it, "he was not very pleased," related John Roberts. "He gave me a dressing down in his own style. I emphasize his style, which was not ranting or raving, but a quiet admonition that was really quite effective." [22]

"George Brown," reflected George Keegan, "was the best commander I saw in all those years on using his staff. He knew how to use his staff organization, how to get a great deal out of it without coercing, terrifying, or intimidating them. That is not meant in any way to demean Spike Momyer, whose knowledge of the war was unsurpassed. He knew more about air-ground coordination than any man who ever went to Vietnam. Momyer ran every aspect of that war and hardly used his staff. He was so powerful at the staff planning meetings that very little discussion occurred."

I asked General Keegan, "What difference does it make if you approach it in Spike Momyer's way rather than George Brown's way?" "It makes a fundamental difference in this context," he replied. "Brown's way encouraged young staff officers and commanders to really become commanders and become distinguished staff officers. He brought the best out in initiative, zeal, and growth. Brown's approach, as I look back, is more likely to produce great young commanders, to allow this potential to be realized.

"Under Momyer the environment was much more suppressed. Really, no one was allowed to think about that war except Momyer. He contained it all within himself. Had he not been so extraordinarily gifted and accomplished and experienced, it could have been a disaster.

"Where Brown didn't know, he was very careful to get the best use out of his staff, which, I think, in the long run, is a more reliable way of achieving the proper direction and conduct of a complicated air war. Brown must be evaluated in a completely different light from all the others, because he had less combat experience in Vietnam. His style and approach were different, as was his use of the staff. His understanding of the division of labor, the limitations in span of control that preclude one man doing everything, made for a healthier operational environment; not more effective, perhaps, than it was under Momyer, but I think it was fundamentally healthier."[23]

George Brown always recognized that the people in one's command are the key to its success. Col. Kenneth Tallman, as officer in charge of Colonels' Assignment Branch, was responsible for coordinating with Brown on the assignment of wing commanders to Vietnam. "I had a verbal request from Brown before he left Washington," recalled Tallman. "In essence, it was 'keep the good guys coming.' He was a people man; he believed in delegating authority, and he wanted to have people in whom he could place confidence. He knew there were many such people in the Air Force, but he didn't know them personally because he hadn't been associated with a command in some time, or with TAC for many years. Because of the nature of the war, TAC had the largest supply of colonels for Southeast Asia, so he felt that this was the area that I could help him the most in.

"There were very few colonels I nominated for jobs in Vietnam not accepted by General Brown. I think this was because of our earlier conversation and my assurance to him that I would pick the best people available and make sure they had some recent experience in TAC."[24]

Brown was concerned for the lives of his men and made a practice of sending a personal letter to the next of kin of everyone who died in his command. "The only time I ever saw George lose his cool," said his brother, Tim Brown, "was one night when George and Skip and I had been to a party in Washington, D.C. I was stationed at CINCPAC and had come back from Vietnam after my first tour. One of my duties in CINCPAC was to publish a magazine on the air war. The thing that bothered me was that anytime you'd lose five pilots in a week, the roof would come off at CINCPAC and the Pentagon. So we were driving along that evening, and I said, 'George, I don't understand this. Why is it you lose five airplanes in a week, everyone gets so excited? Yet every day we're losing two to five hundred infantrymen, and nobody says a word?' George really got mad. I don't know why. I figured out later that the roof came off because they were all flyers. They could identify with the airplane pilots. But it did seem strange to me then, and it still does. And I asked George, 'Is it the cost of the airplanes? Is that what bothers you guys?' I thought it was a good question, but he sure did get mad.''[25]

Brown also required that he be thoroughly briefed anytime there was an accident. ''I was commander of the 3rd TAC Fighter Wing in Bien Hoa,'' reflected Howard Lane. ''We were flying F-100s and A-37s. My direct interface with him was limited to standing before him at staff meetings whenever there was an aircraft accident involving anyone in my wing. At these briefings he would let me talk to him. He understood what I was telling him, and as long as I was honest and straightforward, it was not a grilling session at all; it was an information session. We did not go down to brief him on an incident or accident on our installation to incur his wrath and permit him to relieve his tensions; we went to provide him with information. Some of his staff members didn't understand it that way, and on one occasion, he told a staff officer attempting to 'grill' a wing commander to be quiet, saying, 'That's not what the colonel is here for; he is here to inform us.'[26]

''The procedure was this: within twelve to eighteen hours following a major incident such as an airplane accident, the wing commander was scheduled to brief General Brown and his staff personally on the situation, before any investigation was finished or even started. At that point, we would simply give our impressions. We were expected to know our operation and people and what was wrong. He always wanted straight answers, whether it was against you or not. If you had to call yourself bad, you had to call yourself bad. I felt comfortable with General Brown in saying, 'I screwed that one up, boss' and in being ready to take my licks for it. You never worried because you knew he would be fair.''[27]

Another wing commander, John Roberts, said: ''I talked on the telephone with General Brown twice in Vietnam, calls I had initiated. On one occasion there had been a midair collision between one of the F-4 fighters in my wing and a civil airliner on final approach into the air base, killing eighty-three people. The pilot of the F-4 was able to come around and land his airplane safely, but the airliner crashed. I said to him, 'General, I've got some bad news. One of my F-4s just had a midair on final with an Air Vietnam airliner.' General Brown said, ''What in the world—who was the stupid—no, wait a minute; I shouldn't say that. You find out what happened and let me know.' Everybody's first reaction, including mine, had been how could an F-4 hit an airliner? As it turned out, the F-4 pilot was blameless. Brown initially reacted the same way I did, just couldn't see how it could have happened without our pilot being at fault. But Brown recovered his balance quickly.''[28]

When I asked Roberts what it was like to serve under George Brown, he responded, "I remember so well that the first thing he said to me was 'If you want me, call me; otherwise,' he said, 'I'll see you at commander's conferences.' The commander's conferences were held approximately every three or four months. He was good in holding to that principle of letting you alone to do your job."[29]

Although he wanted his commanders to call him if necessary, Brown wanted them to use good judgment. He particularly did not like to receive telephone calls in the middle of the night, unless it was an emergency, a matter needing his personal attention. Howard Lane was a wing commander at Bien Hoa and was attacked by rockets one night, some of them hitting the fuel dump. It appeared the base was going up in flames, with explosions all over the place. This occurred at about four-thirty in the morning, and Lane thought it imperative that he call General Brown. Brown simply came back to him and said, "Mac, what do you want me to do?" Lane answered, "Well, nothing, I just wanted you to know." Brown then responded, "Well, call me later in the morning and tell me about it."

A similar rocket attack occurred with another wing commander. "One morning," reminisced Robert Dixon, "George came in, sat down, and said, 'I've got to tell you. I did something awful last night. About twelve o'clock I got a call from a wing commander who said, "Sir, I'm calling you from mobile. Just a minute, I have to get under my jeep!" You could hear the noise and everything. He said, "Oh, oh, there goes another gasoline tank. We're under rocket attack." I said, "Yes," and the wing commander responded, "Well, I wanted you to know." So, I said, "Well, call me back if there's anything you want me to do for you," and hung up.' Well, I (Dixon) subsequently had a conversation with the wing commander, who knew instantly, the minute George said, 'Yes,' there was nothing he could do about the fact that they were under attack. I construed the anecdote as 'What does a young colonel do when they start shelling his base? Call his daddy. What can daddy do? Not a thing.' "[30]

"Brown always told his commanders," said John Roberts, " 'If you want me to do something, call me. If you are calling just to give me information, don't bother me.' He never carried a 'brick.' The 'brick' was the two-way radio that some commanders carried with them all the time. I asked him once why he didn't, and he said to me, 'That's why I've got an assistant. You know, there's a chain of command, and it works. If it doesn't work, we're in trouble. That's why I never carry a brick.'[31]

"The second time I called General Brown," continued John Roberts, "was to respond to a terse wire I received one night. I considered it unlike General Brown to sign such a message as this, since it instructed me to do something I didn't think appropriate with my wing. I called him and said

I'd like to come down and talk to him about the wire if I could. He said, 'Okay, see you tomorrow at ten o'clock.' So I flew to Tan Son Nhut and explained my side of the issue and talked to him about five minutes. He said to me, 'Have you talked to Colonel X about this?' Colonel X was the author of the message. And I said, 'No, sir, I haven't.' He said to me, 'Well, just stop where you are and let's get the colonel down here; I want him to hear this.' The issue involved transferring people and airplanes between my wing and that of another wing commander. I had set it up one way with him, and he did not like it. He got the support of this Colonel X on Brown's staff, so I was instructed not to do it my way. After I briefed General Brown, he said, 'Forget the message. I shouldn't have sent it to you until I had talked to you about it. You go up and talk to the other wing commander and tell him that we're going to do it exactly the way you want it done.' Well, this took me completely off the hook from a very terse message that colonels don't like to receive from four-star generals." [32]

Although General Brown was not always tolerant when it came to unnecessary phone calls, "he tended to be somewhat more forgiving than some commanders," recalled Kenneth Tallman. "By this I mean that if he felt an individual had made an honest mistake and still had the potential to do the job, he was more inclined than most commanders to give him a second chance. This doesn't mean that he didn't sometimes replace commanders, but he'd take a little longer to assess individuals if he felt that an individual had potential. I know of two cases where this happened. The mistakes were somewhat minor in nature, but under previous commanders they might have resulted in the individuals being fired.

"One of them," continued General Tallman, "had to do with an accident, and the wing commander came in to brief him. Brown, in his wisdom, saw that this commander was trying to protect his crew, but clearly the crew was at fault and should have been disciplined. Brown did not want to replace the wing commander for something like that. The wing commander probably should have been a little more firm in his corrective action with his crew. Brown thought this provided a good learning experience for the wing commander, but it wasn't sufficient for him to fire him. I think this is an indication of his forgiving nature. That wing commander turned out to be one of the most successful in Southeast Asia and was later promoted.

"Another incident involved a base commander," continued Tallman. "It had to do with his strong desire to support the mission, and in a wartime scenario, this is to be admired. I think General Brown admired it, but in so doing the base commander had taken several shortcuts uncovered by the inspector general from Brown's headquarters. The IG report of the base commander's shortcut methods had to do with improper accounting. The

IG write-up made it sound as though he had committed several unpardon-able sins in managing his resources.

"The base commander, of course, was responsible for all support ele-ments on base and he was the type of individual that wanted to provide a hundred percent support of the mission. Brown considered it so, too, but at the same time couldn't condone the shortcomings in the other areas which had been uncovered by the IG on this base commander. It was a learning experience for the base commander but also for the representatives of the IG office, since there was room, as General Brown saw it, for compassion."[33]

"One of the roles General Brown expected his aide to fill," recalled Lee Butler, "was that of chief of diversionary activities when his work was done. I learned a great deal from him in terms of surviving under pressure and stress. We worked a standard twelve-hour day, including Saturdays, and about half a day on Sundays. So when we left the office, usually around seven in the evenings, and came home, the only phone calls he would take were from higher echelons or calls concerning major enemy activity or air-craft accidents. He did not bring work home from the office, never brought a briefcase home. We either played bridge or I showed movies. He did not want to see movies with a serious message. It was strictly something to take his mind off business. During breaks in the day, he played tennis, weather permitting.

"I had at breakfast one morning reflected on a phone call from the night before and told him that I had spent several sleepless hours worrying about the context, to which he responded, 'You've got to learn to do better than that; you'll never survive in this business if you don't.' I asked him, 'Are you able to go back to sleep when you're interrupted by one of those calls?' He said, 'Yes, I am.' He continued, 'That's simply a trait you're going to have to acquire.' That advice served me very well in my subsequent career. I came to the Pentagon from being the DO of a bomb wing where I was interrupted by phone calls throughout the night, and it was having been mentally practiced and prepared for that responsibility and that work style that allowed me to get through those two years in reasonably good physical and mental shape. I learned a very specific lesson from having watched that man operate."[34]

While in Vietnam, Brown wanted to stay in good physical condition, and therefore took up the game of tennis in earnest. It was his attitude to-ward and during these tennis games that also exhibited his leadership quali-ties. "He always could separate the office from everything else," recalled Cremin. "If it was office business, it stayed at the office. When he left the office, he rarely discussed anything that related to his work. Normally, he would take a two-hour lunch break each day and would spend an hour and a half on the tennis court. Initially there were those other general officers who played with him, but it was sort of 'pitty-pat' that really did not supply the challenge he was looking for. When Lee Butler was his aide, he asked to see if he could not find some stiffer competition. When I became his aide, he also kept after me to see if I couldn't get some better tennis players for him; he simply wanted more of a game. He didn't like to lose, of course, but when he did, he never said anything disparaging about his partner (we normally played doubles) but would say such things as, 'Come on, let's get after that ball,' or, 'We've got to win.' If he missed a shot, he would always say he was sorry.

"I especially remember the Australian commander, a General Hay; back in 1940 he was so good that he was slated to represent Australia in Davis Cup competition, but World War II came along and he was never able to. But that Australian was still quite an accomplished tennis player. He and Brown decided to take on two younger tennis players. One was a young man who had been Iowa State tennis champion before coming into the service; the other had won a tennis scholarship to the University of Southern California. They were very good tennis players, but they lost to the two older men.

"On another occasion," reminisced Cremin, "he was playing in a doubles match, and one of the opponents was Admiral McCain. McCain was small and hunched over a little bit when he played. He had as his partner a man who had formerly been a tennis pro. So if you hit it to the pro, you could hit it in a more vigorous fashion. I was out there watching one day when McCain was there, with a big black cigar in his mouth while he was playing. The ball came to Brown and he evidently forgot he was playing Admiral McCain, and he just whipped this ball right at him as hard as he could hit it. McCain simply said to Brown, 'Goddamn it, George, nice shot.' I noticed thereafter, however, he tried when hitting it so vigorously to hit it to McCain's partner. The real reason behind it was that McCain had a great deal of pressure on him with his job, and did not get out to play tennis so often and was not physically as able as Brown. But General Brown just did not like to lose."[35]

Tennis was a good way to relieve frustrations, and certainly Brown had them in Vietnam. "One time," said Jack Cremin, "there was a great deal of activity in and out of his office. We were leaving at the normal time to go home for lunch, and I noticed that he did not say a word. This was unusual for him; usually he had a little smile, a twinkle in his eye, or some comment when we left. We went to the house and I went out and made sure everybody was ready for the tennis game. General Brown came out and the others had already warmed up. They asked him if he wanted to warm up and he simply said no. So they started play and everytime the ball was hit to him, he hit it as hard as he could, so hard that five or six times it would simply stick in the fence. None of the balls were well hit, and I noticed when he served that he was consistently double-faulting, unable to get the ball in he was hitting it so hard. This was very rare for him. At the end of the first set the score was six–love with Brown on the losing side. I didn't know what to expect, but after that six–love loss, he said, 'All right, now I've got that out of my system, let's play some tennis.' From then on, he was back playing his usual game. I sensed that the problem then was that some further restrictions had come out of Washington regarding the bombing. Normally this did not get to him, or if it did, he never showed it. But that day, it was just his way of getting rid of his frustrations."[36]

General Brown was unpretentious as part of his everyday life, including his tennis. "The tennis court that he played on in Vietnam had sort of a tough acrylic coat on it. It rained often, and then would clear up. When that happened, we would use rubber squeegees to clean up the water. This would not clean up all the water, so we then had to use towels to mop it up. On many occasions," said Cremin, "General Brown would be out there dragging a towel in order to get the courts dried off. There he was, working like a farmhand, dragging a towel with the rest of us."[37]

Brown had social gatherings as well as tennis matches. John Roberts, who had been a wing commander as a colonel under Brown, was promoted to brigadier general and became commander of the Tactical Air Control Center (TACC). "In my capacity as TACC Commander," remembered John Roberts, "I got to know him personally quite well. I used to play bridge with him and had dinner with him once a week. He had a policy of getting his key people together for dinner every Sunday night. It was kind of a ritual. The only thing we did was play bridge and go to dinner. This dinner included all senior officers in the Seventh Air Force. We would go to the MACV mess, often with General Abrams. These were good social evenings listening to and talking with Brown and Abrams. We worked hard over there, starting at six-thirty in the morning and normally going until at least seven o'clock in the evening. We did this seven days a week, but on Sundays we would stop at five-thirty and go over to the MACV mess and relax and have a steak. This policy of General Brown was really meaningful to all of those that worked for him."[38]

Brown backed his people but was tough when the need arose. "I've got to tell you a revealing story," recalled Howard Fish. "One of the fundamental problems we had in our tactical analysis shop had to do with civilians, civil service types, who were assigned to Seventh Air Force. When they came to Vietnam, they'd usually get a promotion. It wasn't that they weren't qualified, but they got a little higher rating than what they would have been able to compete for stateside.

"That wouldn't have been a major problem by itself," he continued, "except that there was no specified tour for civilians. They could stay just as long as they wanted, like other civilians anywhere else. We tended to have some people overgraded in civilian capacities and at the same time the more normal guys who came over for a year's assignment with retreat rights to some job in the States in order to get the experience that the war provided. The real good ones would come over for a year and then leave. The least qualified would stay on and on. Over time we had a large number of high-rated civilians of limited capability. Additionally, they not only got paid their normal salaries and got 25 percent differential for overseas, but were on a forty-hour week and got overtime for anything over forty hours. Everybody was working at least twelve hours a day. My choice was either to have them work and run up enormous salaries or have them get up and leave after an eight-hour day, five days a week. I had young captains working for me with advanced degrees who were often better qualified than these civilians. It got to be a terrible morale problem with the high-grade civilians in supervisors' jobs.

"I decided the only way to handle this thing was to eliminate the jobs, because I could get by with the military primarily, and with the very limited number of civilians who were real good sharp guys. So I went to George Brown and said, 'I want to eliminate this GS–16 and three 15s, a total of ten people, GS–13 through 16.' George said, 'My God, what will that do to the operation?' I said, 'Improve it.' He said, 'Oh come on now. I can't believe that.' I explained it all to him and he said, 'Go ahead and do it. We'll take the heat.' Sure enough, they wrote their congressmen, complained to the IG, complained to the Civil Service Commission, and in retrospect, I don't even know if it was worth it. George, of course, recognized immediately when he agreed to let me do it, because he was more experienced, that I was going to have some trouble. One was sent back to PACAF. We were able to eliminate the rest of their jobs and eliminate them. It was the right thing to do, without question."[39]

An excellent summary of Brown's leadership style was provided by John Roberts, who said, "It was a great joy working for the man, nine months of seeing Brown twice a day in staff meetings, then perhaps once or twice during each day individually about something, and several nights a week playing bridge or the like. The better you got to know George, the more you admired and respected him. My leadership style was patterned a lot after his, the cardinal point of which was to put a competent man in charge of an operation and let him run it; leave him alone, go out and see how he's doing once in a while, have Commanders' Calls, and ensure that the headquarters staff is always helping. To me that was the right way to do things. When he gave someone a job to do, he also gave him the tools with which to do it. There are few commanders who can do this and do it effectively. I believe nearly everybody who served under him in Vietnam loved working for him."[40]

Another significant achievement was Brown's rapport with the Army. "His relationship with General Abrams was the finest between a ground theater commander and his air subordinate that I have seen since 1941," said General Keegan. "There was complete trust, rapport, an end to gamesmanship between one service and another. It was clear from the outset that Abrams understood finally that in George Brown he had a personal friend whose life and resources were wholly committed to fulfilling the theater job and responsibility that Abrams had upon his shoulders. The consequence was that the constant dogfighting among colonels, who are usually the perpetrators of the problems, the constant bickering and fighting that went on throughout that war, about which very little has been written or disclosed publicly and which was vicious beyond anything that I have ever seen— George Brown managed to put that fire out. Abrams before had never for a moment entertained the slightest doubt that those air assets were his and that the air commander would follow the Army's bidding to a tee. Under all the other commanders, it was a case of the Army specifically laying carefully specified tasks on the Air Force, then judging the Air Force on the results. The relationship was so close with Brown, however, that Abrams allowed Brown to use his air force in whichever way he felt would contribute most significantly to the solution of the Army's problems. The result of this was that Abrams got out of Brown much greater results with more effectiveness, because he let the air commander really do his thing.

"Under Momyer," Keegan continued, "when the issues of how do you use air power best came up, he usually won his case. Usually he was allowed to use his air power the way he wanted, but the relationship was vastly different. In Momyer's case it was his intense knowledge of air-ground coordination, of which he is the foremost disciple and student in the armed services. It was a different technique, but under Abrams it blossomed, and it flowered under George Brown, who used to say to Uncle Abe, 'I'll handle it. You let me worry about the details.' Abrams never had an occasion to be unhappy about the total commitment of the Air Force."

The Pacific Air Force Commander at the time was John Vogt. He commented, "George's ability to win the confidence of people, to let them feel that he was working with them and not against them, is the key. He worked hard at this. I saw this everywhere George's path and mine crossed. When I got down to the Vietnam theater and saw General Abrams, a great combat commander, a tough, combat-seasoned guy who had been there now some six years fighting the war, it was apparent to me that the highlight for him was that Air Force aid and assistance had saved the day for him militarily. And he attributed this not to the Air Force, but to George. He was a great admirer of George. This tells you something. Abrams was not the kind of guy you could fool. I think he, better than anybody that I can talk about, was an evaluator and a judge of men. He had a good feel for both the phonies and the capable men. His esteem for George was unbounded."[42]

General Abrams' Chief of Staff was Andrew Goodpaster. He reflected, "When George took command of Seventh Air Force, he was in charge of the thing from the first moment. He was a fully competent and able commander, a wonderful man to work with from our Army standpoint. We knew that we had somebody here who shared with us the overall goals and had the ability to put the air operation into that context and did, I would say, a crackerjack job of it.

"Brown and Abrams were like two brothers who liked each other and worked very well with each other," continued Goodpaster. "But there was no doubt who was in command. It was Abe. He was tough and hard when he had to be. He was decisive and intolerant of shoddy work of any kind. There was absolute cooperation between them.

"Abe and I would often say to each other that we really had a winner there in George Brown," said Goodpaster. "He was everything that you could ask for in that job, a perfect solution to the need, outstanding in every aspect of command. His strong points were his ability to get high-quality intelligence and generate high-quality plans that were consequently very professional in the way they were worked out. He made excellent command decisions as to how the forces were to be used, supervising maintenance and the manner of performance—all of the things that make a really first-rate commander. He could see what the operation was, to give judgments on things that came up such as the negotiations we were having with the North Vietnamese and some of the proposals that were made for replacing the role of the Americans, at least in part, with Vietnamese forces. In all of that, he was first-rate."[43]

Brown realized he would not always be in Vietnam. Thus, he tried to remain current in all aspects of the Air Force so that he would be prepared when he returned to the States. "He knew I was fresh from the seed," recalled Howie Fish, "and he wanted to stay up with knowledge rather than lose touch. I think that what some people do is immerse themselves in a new assignment, which is a worthy thing to do, but if you're going to be a great military leader you've got to maintain your interests—be more catholic than that. You can't get so caught up in what you're doing that you no longer understand the world, the larger world into which your piece fits. He kept track of what was going on in Washington with care."[44]

It was good that he did, for after his tour was up in Vietnam, he was again to be assigned to the Washington area, this time to take over Systems Command, a completely new and different task.

NOTES

1. Personal interview with Brig. Gen. Thomas W. Brown, USA (Ret.), August 8, 1979.
2. Personal interview with Gen. Horace Wade, USAF (Ret.), November 17, 1981.
3. Ibid.
4. Personal interview with Col. Lee Butler, USAF, October 30, 1979.
5. Personal interview with Maj. Jack Cremin, USAF, August 8, 1979.
6. Ibid.
7. Ibid.
8. Ibid.
9. Ibid.
10. Ibid.
11. Ibid.
12. Ibid.
13. Ibid.
14. Personal interview with Maj. Gen. George F. Keegan, USAF (Ret.).
15. Cremin interview.
16. Personal interview with Gen. Robert J. Dixon, USAF (Ret.), June 10, 1980.
17. Keegan interview.
18. Cremin interview.
19. Dixon interview.
20. Butler interview.
21. Personal interview with Lt. Gen. James Knight, USAF (Ret.), August 7, 1979.
22. Personal interview with Gen. John W. Roberts, USAF (Ret.), March 6, 1980.
23. Keegan interview.
24. Personal interview with Lt. Gen. Kenneth L. Tallman, USAF, June 18, 1980.
25. Brown interview.
26. Personal interview with Lt. Gen. Howard M. Lane, USAF, May 16, 1980.
27. Ibid.
28. Roberts interview.
29. Ibid.
30. Dixon interview.
31. Roberts interview.
32. Ibid.
33. Tallman interview.
34. Butler interview.
35. Cremin interview.

36. Ibid.
37. Ibid.
38. Roberts interview.
39. Personal interview with Lt. Gen. Howard M. Fish, USAF (Ret.), March 8, 1980.
40. Roberts interview.
41. Keegan interview.
42. Personal interview with Gen. John Vogt, USAF (Ret.), September 9, 1981.
43. Personal interview with Lt. Gen. Andrew J. Goodpaster, USA (Ret.), July 22, 1980.
44. Fish interview.

CHAPTER 18

ANDREWS AIR FORCE BASE, MARYLAND: SEPTEMBER 1970–JULY 1973

Upon completion of his tour as Commander of the Seventh Air Force, and Deputy Commander for Air Operations of MACV, George Brown, in September of 1970, became commander of Air Force Systems Command, with headquarters at Andrews Air Force Base, Maryland.

When General Brown was asked by the author, "Why do you think you became Chief of Staff of the Air Force?" he responded, "Oh, I never thought about it. I have no idea. Perhaps I was the best choice among my contemporaries. I started out in bombardment, you know, and I got into everything else except Logistics Command and Systems Command. I'd been in Vietnam a year when Ryan visited us. He was then Vice Chief and had been nominated to be Chief. He told me that I was going to follow him as Chief of Staff."[1]

The author responded, "He told you that *before* he became Chief?"

"Yes, before he became Chief; and I said, 'Jack, look, don't say that, because you don't have to make a decision now. Keep your options open.' He said, 'No, your selection is obvious assuming you don't stub your toe and your health is all right. But I want you to know now, because I want you to start thinking about it, and to think in such a way that you prepare yourself mentally for it.'

"Considering the jobs I had held and the exposure I had gained, it appeared quite evident that I *was* being prepared, although I had never thought about it until he mentioned it; it had never occurred to me. But, I had been executive to the Chief of Staff and executive to the Secretary of Defense for four years. Then I went to MAC, MATS, the Joint Task Force, and here as assistant to the chairman of the JCS for two years, and finally to Vietnam. So I knew the game around this town pretty well, on the Hill and in the Pentagon, and at State, and the National Security Council from my experience here with the Chairman. And I'd been on the Policy Planning Board at State, where I was thrown in with a lot of people in high government positions today, like Brzezinski.

"But I really don't know what caused Jack Ryan to do it. Anyway, I said, 'Don't even talk that way; that's silly.' Then, when I finished in Vietnam, I wanted to go to Europe, because I figured it was time David Burchinal left and then that job would be open. We were in Washington, D.C., for a conference, and Jack Ryan got me in a corner and said, 'You're coming home and you're going to Systems Command.' I replied, 'I don't know a damn thing about Systems Command,' and he said, 'That's precisely why you're going.' "[2]

I discussed the Systems Command assignment with Gen. John Ryan. "I visited George Brown quite often at Seventh Air Force," said Ryan, "and was very impressed with what he was doing there. He was thorough, he knew what was going on, and he was able to influence his Army superiors. His assessment of application of force was extremely good. He could pull the F–4 outfits from Da Nang and Cam Ranh Bay off in-country and move them out of country without causing a big uproar in MACV. He stood up for his convictions without antagonizing people.

"So we pulled him back when he finished his tour in Vietnam, and I put him in charge of Systems Command, because I thought it needed an operational type. I thought it might be wise to bring some new blood in, and a top-notch man at that; and, of course, I was also thinking of my successor. Brown was logical, and I felt it would do him good to get some Systems Command experience, because weapons acquisition is one of the big jobs that the Chief of Staff has. This assignment would let him learn that side of the job and still be in the Washington area. So I told George I would recommend him to be my successor sometime in the fall of '72."[3]

The Under Secretary of the Air Force at the time of Brown's selection as commander of Systems Command was John McLucas. He said of Brown's appointment, "We all agreed that George was the right man to be the next Air Force Chief of Staff, and that the Systems Command would provide the best background he could get for the job."

That Brown's initial reaction to his new assignment was not overenthusiastic is not surprising. As John McLucas pointed out, "One difficulty the Air Force has had over the years is that it has tended to give rank and status to people in the operational side of the house. An officer is really excited if he can be head of TAC or SAC, less so if he's going to be in Systems Command. Status is in the operational areas. However, I feel that a Chief of Staff who has been in Systems Command is bound to take a different view of things and feel that more emphasis should be placed on the procurement and research side.

"I'd read the *Washington Post* every morning," he continued, "and see headlines on page one that seemed to say, 'Air Force Screws Up One More Time.' It didn't matter what the topic was, the Air Force always screwed up, according to the newspapers. And a lot of 'screw ups' they were talking about were at Systems Command. Most had to do with weapons systems procurement.

"They weren't saying that our pilots couldn't fly, or the Chief was a fink, or whatever; they were saying, 'You guys don't know how to build or buy anything.' For example, we had a colonel in charge of the C-5 program, and his bosses, two-, three-, and four-star generals, were all too busy running some air base or something. Thus, this poor colonel was carrying the load on the thing that was causing us all the bad publicity. The procurement side obviously needed leadership.

"I had a conversation with Mel Laird, Secretary of Defense, shortly after I came to Washington, and he said, 'John, I want you to tell me one Air Force program that's not in trouble.' And I said, 'Well, Mel, I'll have to work on that.' I went back to my office and called in a couple of assistants and said, 'Can't we think of something, anything, that we're doing right?' It turned out the only thing was the C-141, a program started seven years before."[4]

Brown began preparations for the new assignment while still in Vietnam. "As the Systems Command Liaison Detachment Commander on Brown's staff," reflected then Col. Gerald Hendricks, "I was called at midnight and told that the AFSC commander was having him send me the command briefing, which contained very sensitive information that I was to quietly present to him. I perceived, as we started the briefing, that Brown was disappointed to have gotten AFSC instead of USAFE as his next command. As it progressed, however, he saw the number of bases, people, and programs, the dollar values, and the overall responsibility and seemed to reconcile himself to the assignment."[5]

From its headquarters at Andrews Air Force Base, Maryland, Systems Command directed the operations of many divisions, development and test centers, ranges, and laboratories. It included six field commands with division status: Aeronautical Systems Division (ASD), Electronic Systems Division (ESD), Foreign Technology Division (FTD), Aerospace Medical Division (AMD), Air Force Contract Management Division (AFCMD), and the Space and Missile Systems Organization (SAMSO). There were five separate research centers: Arnold Engineering Development Center, Air Force Civil Engineering Center, Armament Development and Test Center, Air Force Special Weapons Center, and Air Force Flight Test Center. The laboratories that reported directly to AFSC included Rome Air Development Center, Weapons Laboratory, Rocket Propulsion Laboratory, Armament Laboratory, Human Resources Laboratory, Cambridge Research Laboratories, the Frank J. Seiler Research Laboratory, Office of Scientific Research, European Office of Aerospace Research, Aero Propulsion Laboratory, Materials Laboratory, and Avionics Laboratory. The command organization also included two schools, the Test Pilot School, located at Edwards Air Force Base and the School of Aerospace Medicine at Brooks Air Force Base.

During the first fiscal year that Brown was Commander of AFSC, the Air Force received more funds than either the Army or the Navy in the 1971 Appropriations Act, although the differences were not large. The Air Force received $21.4 billion, the Army $19.6 billion, and the Navy $20.4 billion. AFSC alone received $7.4 billion, or 34.6 percent of the total Air Force appropriation.[6]

Although its budget was still substantial, during fiscal year 1971/72, the Air Force Systems Command personnel authorizations continued the downward trend caused by the phasedown of the Vietnam War. In consonance with President Richard M. Nixon's stated objective to trim the military budget, Gen. John D. Ryan, Air Force Chief of Staff, stated:

> Like the other Services, we are also taking a substantial cut in personnel. People are not only our most important and valuable asset, they also represent the largest single Air Force expenditure. This fact, by itself, accounts in large degree for the provision in the FY 71 budget and for an Air Force with a projected total officer and airman strength of 762,000–well below the 857,000 we had on board at the start of the Vietnam War.[7]

Despite these cutbacks, the scope of AFSC's mission was enlarged. Prior to September 10, 1971, the mission was to "advance aerospace technology, adopt it into operational aerospace systems, and acquire qualitatively superior aerospace systems and material needed to accomplish the Air Force mission." The second proviso of the new mission statement on that date required the command, in accordance with Air Force Regulation 23-8, to "apply it [aerospace technology] to aerospace systems development and improvement," thus bolstering AFSC's research and development program. "The change was initiated by the merger of the Office of Aerospace Research, which had been a separate Air Force operating agency since 1961, into the Air Force Systems Command on 1 July 1970. This merger brought basic research into the total acquisitions spectrum of a single manager."

Several new responsibilities were also added in 1971 and 1972. Among these was conducting research activities to insure that ecological considerations be reflected in mission activities, a result of increased pressures for federal emission standards. Another important addition was the maintenance of superior quality laboratories in-house to conduct necessary research.

The broad scope of his new command was not the only challenge George Brown faced at AFSC. He also had a service reputation to live down. "Brown was very concerned," recalled Gerald Hendricks, "because the word going around Washington was that the Air Force couldn't do anything quickly. He therefore asked the Chief of Staff to take a few high-priority defense suppression projects and run with them to demonstrate that AFSC could meet high expectations.

"Preparation for the final approval meeting with Secretary of Defense Packard included AFSC staff preparation of a complex briefing by Brown. But he kept rejecting the staff briefing charts and finally produced his own single simple version, which read approximately as follows:

To Get the Job Done I Need
- The authority
- The resources
- Minimum staff interference

I Will
- Ask for help if I need it
- And keep you informed

"Packard responded to this request by saying, 'George, I don't see anything wrong with what you've asked. Go ahead, do the best you can, and if you see one that's not going well, cancel it. And periodically let me know how things are going.'

"This request for real autonomy and authority on the part of the AFSC commander in December 1970 was a new way of doing business, contrary to normal HQ USAF and OSD staff practices, particularly the authority to unilaterally cancel a program that did not appear to be going well. Packard and Brown were both straightforward men. They had had a meeting of the minds, and Brown got what he wanted—clear, simple authority, from the top, to get the job done."[8]

Brown had no trouble getting started. "When George Brown assumed command of AFSC," recalled Lt. Gen. Edward O'Connor, his deputy commander, "everyone knew immediately that he was in charge. George came in a great man, clearly the chief executive officer of the organization. He showed it, first, by his presence, and secondly, by jumping right into the job. He identified our major problems, and plunged in and tried to understand them. He tried to do what he thought was right with them, popular or not. He represented a type of officer who had not grown up in the R & D business and therefore wanted to know why things were the way they were. He had a high degree of intellectual curiosity. He engendered a spirit of confidence within the organization which seemed to say, 'Look, we can do this as well as anybody can.' "[9]

Despite his high confidence level, however, Brown was not arrogant. "When General Brown got to Systems Command," recalled Maj. Gen. Jerry Cook, "the first thing he did was to assure people that he did not know their business, that he was there to be their commander and a channel to handle their business when they had run out of clout. 'But I do not know your business,' he would say. 'In fact, I'm ashamed to be here and not know your business.' He was very humble and very open about it.

"But he used that as a strength," continued Cook. "When the experts would come in to brief him he would very often say, 'Now, I can't quarrel with any of the engineering details or the specifications you're talking about or production data or timing. But I can quarrel with the *feel* I have of the *way* you're telling me these things.' He would sometimes say, 'There's just something wrong about that,' picking out obvious mismatches. For instance, where he observed a conflict as when a man with 'clout' on a configuration control board had a conflicting interest in engineering, Brown would jump on it in a flash. But when he did pick up on something like that, he would always give the briefer a chance to correct it right there. He'd let the man build himself up after being caught.

"He traveled extensively," Cook went on, "particularly to visit all fifty installations of Systems Command. He wanted to meet all his commanders. He always had a personal touch with them, talking freely with everybody. He would say, 'Everyone is authorized to make mistakes; the only thing that people are not authorized to do is to sit on their hands.' "

Despite his lack of knowledge of detailed scientific technology, Brown nonetheless became successful in his new position. He had a feel for the mechanical and physical principles behind airplanes and weaponry, certainly, but in those years AFSC was moving out of the mechanical and linear age. As Cook put it, "This was an area for which most of us were not really equipped. Brown's great strength was in his approach: There could be a bundle of complex scientific technology you'd have to study for twelve years to understand, but he realized that it didn't make any difference. The flow to get to a military objective was the same whether it was raisins or avionics."[10]

Brown's view was that being a program director was important and challenging. "On several occasions he reminded his staff and program managers that he had personally served in a variety of operational capacities in the Air Force," commented Hendricks, "and in several operational commands; but now that he had gained some insight into the R & D side of things, it was clear to him that the program director had a significantly more difficult and challenging role in life than his wing commander counterpart. 'The operational counterpart has rules, procedures, and checklists clearly laid out for him,' said General Brown, 'and is graded on how closely he follows them. The program director, on the other hand, has to make judgments continually, invent solutions, innovate—break trail every day on how to get his job done. There are no pat, cookbook solutions in the acquisition management game.'

"As part of preparing for requesting Secretary Packard's authority, Brown asked for a slate of candidate program directors. He said to me, 'Jerry, I want you to go over and have a chat with Dr. Seamans. I've selected you to run these defense suppression projects and he wants to meet you before we go to Mr. Packard.' General Brown gave me no lengthy interrogation, no instructions on how to handle my first meeting with the Secretary of Defense. Although I had a good record, I was still surprised at how simply and directly I was given the job—without any threats, charters, or detailed instructions. I felt totally responsible for the projects and to him as I headed across the river to see the Secretary. In any event, the Secretary seemed satisfied, and I was announced to Secretary Packard as the program director by Brown at the meeting with Packard.

"After the Packard meeting, I rode back to AFSC with Brown. He said, 'Well, they gave us what we asked for; now it's up to us. You pick yourself a small, first-class team, whatever you need, and get going.' Shortly after we had returned to the headquarters building, Major General Kronauer, our Chief of Staff, called me and said, 'Let's take a walk.' He led me to a fully occupied office suite one story above and fifty feet east of Brown's private office and asked, 'How would that be for *your* office?' I said, 'I don't need anything that good, and it doesn't have to be near the front office.' 'Look,' he replied, 'the boss just said to me, "I told the Secretary we'd get Hendricks set up running those projects—right outside my office," and he pointed up here. General Brown also wants to announce at tomorrow morning's staff meeting that your office has been established and who some of the people are working with you. So give me the names of those you want—anyone in the headquarters—and I'll get the folks in this office cleared out this afternoon so that you can be moved in by the time we announce you and your team tomorrow morning.' By next morning, the office suite was cleared, my team members announced, and Brown had his defense suppression show on the road.

"Shortly after we got the office established, George said he would like to come up, meet my team, and chat a bit. He came, all four stars and alone, sat on our two-drawer office safe and told our six-officer, two-secretary organization how important our task was to the Air Force and how he was depending on us to do what he had promised Secretary Packard. The management philosophy he expressed to us at this meeting included:

- Do whatever you have to do to get the job done.
- Ask me for help if you need it.
- Keep me informed.
- Get yourself some milestone charts so that if the Secretary should come over we can explain how we're getting along.
- Don't let Headquarters USAF or OSD staffs bother you—but on the other hand why don't you go over and 'buy them a cup of coffee' now and then and let them know how things are going.
- If we come up with a sick program, let me know and we'll cancel it.
- If you want to come to my morning staff meetings, fine; if not, and you have something to do, don't.

"That was the first and last time he came to our office, but he left our team completely and totally dedicated. We knew we had his full support and that he was counting on us to pull it off. He did not expect to offer Secretary Packard any excuses at the end of our five-project, one-year feasibility demonstration period, and we knew he did not expect excuses from us. He was also realistic and knew we might not make it all the way with all five projects.

"We soon recommended cancellation of one program, which Brown was very happy to do in order to (1) demonstrate his direct-from-Packard authority, and (2) make sure we had enough money to conclude the higher-payoff programs correctly. The remaining four programs were concluded on schedule and within budget, which gained significant praise and increased our reputation for being able to get the job done."[11]

Another significant thing Brown did to correct things at AFSC was to start a "Program Acquisition Review" (PAR) group. "Shortly after I arrived at Systems Command," recalled Maj. Gen. James Stansberry, "I attended a PAR, in which the program directors briefed the commander on their program prior to taking it to the Secretary of the Air Force for formal review. That was the first time I had seen General Brown in action; of course, I was only one among many colonels, but I got to know quite a bit about him and how he reacted, beginning at that meeting."[12]

"For one PAR," said General O'Connor, "George assembled his military and civilian talent, including practically all his general officers, in the Southwest near Albuquerque. He said, 'Look, we're going to sit and work this out for three or four weeks if that's what it takes.' He participated personally; he didn't drop in and ask them how they were doing. He sat in on the sessions and participated in the findings and recommendations for improvement, a great exercise and contribution to this way of doing business within the Defense Department.

"It was a review of our business practices as opposed to the requirements phase. It focused attention on another point which George emphasized—that in our business we had a right, a privilege, and an obligation to challenge any requirement that appeared to be stupid, unnecessary, too costly, or premature. It was a bottoms-up review of how we did business rather than what our business was."[13]

"General Brown chaired the meeting," recalled Hendricks. "He had his entire senior staff there, seated around a big U-shaped table. On the sides of the room were the chief subordinates to the people seated at the table. The briefing itself was conducted by the program director to the commander, and of course, the commander's staff joined in with questions and probed various areas on which the program director was reporting. He met with each group about once every three months for each program director, and there were on the order of fifty or sixty programs that were brought through, each about once a quarter.

"During Brown's tenure, he expanded that approach in order to have a chance to coach directors of programs which were not yet of the national significance of, say, the C–5 or the A–10. He called these sessions 'Command Acquisition Reviews' (CARs), and I always felt that they were worthwhile because they gave the young program directors a chance to interact directly with the commander and the Chief of Staff and receive valuable guidance from them."[14]

I asked Stansberry, "How did Brown approach these problems? How did he come to grips with what had to be done?"

"To begin with," replied Stansberry, "he was a man of complete integrity. Let me characterize it this way: When I first got over here, I was new to the program business, too, although I'd been in the atomic energy field. At the first PAR that I sat in on, some complicated slides started coming quickly by. I thought, 'Boy, I'm in trouble; I don't understand a damn thing that I'm being shown; it's going by too fast.' At that point, Brown spoke up and said, 'You guys must think I'm a lot smarter than I am, because I don't understand what you're telling me. You're going too fast.' I said to myself, 'It takes a man with moral courage to speak out and display his ignorance that way.'

"I also discovered that he had a great deal of plain, ordinary common sense. He could get to the bottom of problems with many technical ramifications and nuances; he was good at getting to the bottom line and making decisions based on principle as opposed to being led astray by some bureaucratic mishmash. Further, he displayed a lot of courage. Let me give you an example.

"He chartered me to go out and run a small task force to look at subcontractors because, whereas the command paid a lot of attention to the prime contractors, we didn't have much visibility in the subcontract network, where probably half the work on all major programs was done. We had a rash of problems which, when we started tracing them back, turned out to be subcontractor-oriented. So my team and I scouted around to see what we could find. We visited about fifty subcontractors and twelve prime contractors in a few months and came back convinced that the existing system had to be bucked up, that AFSC needed better visibility on where the work was being done by subcontractors.

"I talked to General O'Connor about it, and he said, 'Let's go up and see George Brown.' I was given practically no advance warning, so was apprehensive about seeing the boss without running five rehearsals by. Anyway, I talked plainly about what we'd done, but without getting into a great deal of detail. He simply wanted to know what we had seen and what we thought. He listened very attentively to my briefing and asked only a few questions. He said, 'Did you ever get below the first tier of subcontractors?' I replied that we had penetrated to the fourth tier in a couple of cases. That seemed to convince him that there was considerable depth to what we were telling him.

"I gave him our observations and made some recommendations for things Systems Command might do. He listened to each one, nodding as I talked, and when I had finished he asked, 'Are any of these things that you're asking me to do illegal?' I replied in the negative. He then asked,

'Are any of them against regulations?' I told him that they were all against current regulations. He said, 'Do you have something for me to sign to approve them?' I did, and whipped it out of my briefcase. My boss, General O'Connor, had never even seen it and his eyes were bugging out a bit. Brown read it over and said, 'Well, I'll just sign it right now.' Then O'Connor quite sensibly remarked, 'General Brown, I appreciate the fact that you have that kind of confidence in us; but maybe, just to clean up any "nicks," we ought to at least circulate it around the staff this afternoon.' General Brown said, 'Fine, but then get it back in here, because I want to sign it.'

"I, of course, was in seventh heaven. I had successfully short-circuited at least a month's work. I took the thing around the staff that afternoon, saying, 'General Brown's already approved this and wants to sign it; if you have any big problem, I guess you can go up and talk with him about it.' The not-so-funny thing about it was that nobody had any problem with it at all.

"He signed a policy letter to his command. It took four years for the ink to dry on the final set of regulations and to get it into the Defense Acquisition Regulations, but in the meantime, AFSC was following Brown's policy letter. We moved out immediately.

"This can-do and will-do approach was characteristic of George Brown," went on James Stansberry. "He figured out what to do, and then did it. For that, he always had my greatest respect. Once he decided that you were on a proper course of action, he was willing to make a decision and go along with you. Obviously, he was always careful—as he should have been —to observe the legalities. We were operating in a highly technical area in which he had no particular expertise, the contracting business. But it certainly was a thrilling experience for me, a young colonel; here I was, operating in an area that had four thousand statute provisions governing what we did, and this exalted four-star general was willing to take my word for something, sign a policy letter, and change command policy, all on the strength of a fifteen- or twenty-minute session."[15]

One of the major problems for AFSC was the F-111 aircraft. "General Brown did a very bad thing to me," reflected Gen. Robert Mathis, later the Vice Chief of Staff of the Air Force. "He assigned me to the F-111 program. I didn't know too much about it, but I had been told by Dr. Seaman's exec, Col. Frank Simokaitis, that Secretary Laird had made the comment that the Vietnam War, the C-5, and the F-111 were the three major problems for his administration, and not necessarily in that order. Then I was told by General Higgins of Systems Command all about the serious problems they were having with the F-111. The next thing I knew, I was part of the problem.

"I still remember the first briefing I gave on the F–111 in the latter part of January 1971. I came to the Secretary's conference room, and General Brown said, 'Just give it to us straight.' I had been in charge of the program from Thursday night until Monday morning. All the assistant secretaries were there, including Grant Hansen, the R & D man, and General Crow, the comptroller. I told them, first, about a wing box problem on the F–111. We had a problem with the wing box and were doing a process called cold-proofing; that's where you flex the wings to 7 g's at minus 65 degrees. If they take the stress at minus 65, then you know they'll take 7 g's at normal temperatures for a long time.

"Well, we had great success with the wing box and then all of a sudden Air Force Logistics Command decided, 'We're going so well, why don't we get some good publicity. We'll have national television come in to look at this while we're doing it.'

"Just a few days before my briefing, the television program occurred and the inevitable happened—the wing box broke. Fortunately, through all the noise and everything and the box breaking, the television reporters didn't realize what was really happening. They said, 'Oh, that's a loud noise.' 'Yes, strange things happen at these low temperatures.' But the box actually broke on television.

"In addition, the last F–111 to be produced had taken off on a test flight from Fort Worth and had disappeared without a trace. Some people in intelligence thought it was in Cuba, but it was determined later that it had crashed. At the time, however, no one knew where it was and we couldn't find it. As if those two problems weren't enough, we had discovered that we were somewhere between $300 million and $500 million in the hole for work that had already been done, and we were in serious trouble.

"As I was nearing the end of the briefing, Dr. Seamans was shaking his fist at me; General Ryan was muttering, 'We're going to take a bath,' and chewing on his cigarette; and General Brown was just sitting there, stony faced. At the end of it, Ryan stomped out, telling Brown, 'I want to see you in my office.' Grant Hansen came up and said, 'You know, you've had this program less than a week and you've got it all screwed up.' It was a wonderful beginning.

"Then we started restructuring the program. There were many meetings with General Ryan, Dr. Seamans, and General Brown. I saw General Brown a great deal during this period. He gave me a lot of guidance, and I got to know him quite well. It was a fascinating time despite the serious difficulty we were in. We were trying to restructure the contract and get rid of all the debts and really make it all work out.

"One day we were discussing the preliminaries for the secretarial program review, and I was at the point of explaining that we had 'tapered off' on clearing up the contractual paper and completing the contract. I told Brown that I was unable to clear any more up at that time. He said, 'Why?' I replied, 'Well, I really don't have enough money; so we're just kind of holding things.' I then flipped the buzzer to go on to the next chart, and General Brown said, 'Wait a minute.'

"We were in the big conference room, so the chart came back up. The people who ran those charts were really tuned to the commander, not to anybody else. I kept trying to get that chart off, but it wasn't going anywhere.

" 'Let me tell you something,' he said. 'You ought to be in jail.' I said, 'Yes sir,' and flipped the thing and the chart went off. He said, 'Put that chart back up. You know, if I handled my personal finances the way you're running that program, I would expect to go to prison. What you're doing is just like kiting checks; you owe a bill, and you're not letting them definitize it because you don't have enough money. That's illegal. You know you ought to be in prison; do you understand that?' And I said, 'Yes sir.' And he said, 'Okay, go ahead and brief.'

"So we went ahead with the briefing and afterward people said, 'We're sorry the boss is so mad at you, but you have to understand that's a very sore subject.' Well, he couldn't have been *too* mad, because he didn't fire me, but he was absolutely correct. If you committed the government to something for which money had not been appropriated and existing funds were inadequate, you were acting illegally. I had not done it, and he knew that, but somebody had. He then proceeded to help get me some money. But he had made his point.

"Every time a new problem arose," continued Mathis, "he would appoint a group to look at it. He was a great believer in staff performing their functions and taking care of details. 'If you're going to hire good people, use them,' he would say."[16]

"There was a major inspector general inspection," recalled O'Connor, "on one of the big programs. People crawled over the program for two or three months. The head of the team had as one of his findings something quite uncomplimentary to Russell, the program manager. But George Brown defused the thing before it ever got started because he knew 'Moose,' the head of the inspection team. He said, 'Moose, how many former program managers do you have, or have you ever had, on your inspection team?' He hadn't had any. That was all Brown needed to ask. He said, 'Well, okay, let's go ahead with the briefing.' It inserted a little humility into the inspector's report."[17]

One other approach that Brown took was to reexamine everything AFSC was doing. He decided to get his best people to reexamine the programs, with the creation of Project ACE. He told them, "If it needs fixing, we're going to fix it." [18]

"I worked directly for General Brown as the executive secretary of Project ACE," recalled Jim Stansberry. "He started this project to help him decide what could be done differently in systems acquisition to reduce our costs. He appointed Maj. Gen. Hank Cushman to head up the project, with twelve other officers. One of the first things he told me to do was to come up with a good title for it. I racked my brain and got suggestions from the staff and turned in three titles a day for two weeks. General Brown never derided my choices, some of which were pretty poor, especially toward the end when I was running out of steam.

"Finally, one night I was explaining the problem to my wife and she said, 'Well, why don't you call it "Ace"? That's a good Air Force name. That'll give some pizzazz to it.' I said, 'Wait a minute. I just thought of what it can stand for: Acquisition Cost Evaluation.' The next morning, I sent it in to General Brown with a note which said, 'I have flunked the course, but Audrey thinks we ought to call it Project ACE—Acquisition Cost Evaluation.' And a note came back marked 'Yes.' So Project ACE was born.

"During the course of Project ACE, General Brown got two hundred people together out in Albuquerque to kick off a culmination of many months of study by various panels. Thirteen generals from Systems Command were sitting in that room, together with many other people. I had prepared a speech for General Brown that addressed the overall spirit of what we were trying to do and tied it into what I thought were some of my better ideas. I was proud that he decided to deliver it. When he addressed the crowd, he began by saying, 'Jim Stansberry has written a speech, and I like it, and I want to read it to you.' Then, with each successive idea outlined in the speech, he would interject, 'Jim says this,' or 'Jim says that.' I thought, 'What a terrific man he is to be giving me credit for something that was simply my duty to prepare for him.' So I am biased when it comes to George Brown; he earned my intense loyalty early on and kept it throughout my association with him.

"We hoped Project ACE would ultimately reduce costs and improve the way we did business and thus result in a better deal for the government. We were not looking for solutions. We believed that defining the problem was the main objective, feeling that if we drove ahead, the solutions would, in time, identify themselves. That approach turned out to be the right one.

"We had terrific talent in that program, and I must give him credit for that too. In the beginning he told his commanders that he wanted some of their best people assigned to it. As a result, we had people like Col. Bob Mathis, Col. Jim Abramson, and Brig. Gen. Kenny Chapman, a group which in later years would read like a 'Who's Who' of Systems Command. Many things now practiced can be traced to the influence of those fellows. As in all big institutions, nothing happens overnight, but many good things did as a result of ACE.

"I think we captured the spirit of innovation, not being afraid to make changes. I attribute this to the atmosphere created by Brown's unique leadership. He wasn't afraid to try out new ideas. A lot of people need a lot of data before they'll even take the first step into unfamiliar territory. I remember hearing Brown say, 'What we're doing now doesn't look like it's produced all that perfect a result; but maybe *anything* we try will produce some improvement. So let's not be afraid to try things.'

"That epitomizes the spirit that swept through our group. Many great ideas came out of it. For example, Bob Mathis's panel took a deep look into reliability and succeeded in fashioning something ultimately known as the Reliability Improvement Warranty—our first effort to get warranty provisions written into our contracts. A year or so later the new ARC-164 radio came along with strong warrantylike provisions, and it was a far more reliable radio than those then in the hands of the troops. It was a multi-aircraft UHF radio manufactured by Magnavox. We had radios in use at that time with a reliability mean time between failures of only fifty hours. As startling as it may seem, the new ARC-164 had a mean time between failures in excess of twelve thousand hours.

"We started ACE early in 1972," Stansberry went on. "The studies leading to our final conference took perhaps three months. We got together out in Albuquerque for two weeks. We all reported to him on what we thought should be changed. The most important thing to me was the refreshing candor and courage transmitted to a bunch of younger officers by the commander saying, in effect, 'Don't be satisfied; get in there, change things and make them better. Don't worry too much about the rule book and the bureaucracy, because all those things can be changed if you achieve something worthwhile.' I give General Brown full credit for extracting from the group what these days they call good group dynamics or interaction.

"My next assignment was to get it all into a final report that the thirteen generals would agree on. That was the hardest job I've ever had in my life. He gave me a team and an airplane, and we went to all of our command bases and briefed thousands of our people on what was in the report. We tried to engender in them some of the same spirit of innovation that he had fostered in us. And then we took our report up on the line, ultimately briefing the Assistant Secretary of Defense. After that, the Army and Navy decided to do something similar, and their reports were also of great value. I credit George Brown for kicking off the idea of a thorough and searching analysis of how to conduct our procurement business."[19]

"In the midst of it all, there arose a problem at Edwards Air Force Base. George wasn't going to kill anyone for making a mistake," recalled General Hendricks, "so a certain confidence and aggressiveness set in, which seemed to work everywhere except in one command. They had a series of bad accidents at Edwards Air Force Base, a bad situation. He said to us, 'I think I'll go out; that base commander must feel worse than anybody in the world.' When he got back, he said, 'It was a wasted trip. I went to hold the fellow's hand and make him feel better, and I'll be damned if he didn't bore me to death with a constant and inane chatter the whole time I was there. It was meaningless, completely irrelevant; I didn't get a word in edgewise—so how in hell can you help somebody like that?' Then, focusing directly on us, Brown said, 'Look, men, you may be experimental test pilots, but that doesn't give you license to commit suicide and tear up the equipment.' That's the only time I can recall General Brown ever sounding a sour note."[20]

Lt. Gen. Howard Lane discussed the Edwards crisis: "In 1972, I received orders to report to Edwards Air Force Base, California. This had been a catastrophic year at Edwards in terms of aircraft accidents, some fifteen test airplanes being lost in a year. Since Edwards was under Systems Command, the problem was a deep concern to George Brown. I rushed to the United States from my previous assignment in Germany with instructions to report to General Brown. He didn't offer any specific directions or guidelines on how I was to proceed. He said, 'Go take a look at the organization and their procedures, the way they operate, the controls they have. Do what you think is necessary; keep me informed, and I will support you.' Throughout the next year and a half, serious personnel, organizational, and procedural problems had to be dealt with, and many changes had to be made in the way things were done. Not once during that time were any of my recommendations, proposals, or changes overruled by General Brown. He supported my actions completely, and I could not have worked for a more straightforward individual. I was occasionally questioned or even cautioned, but I was never seriously challenged. In the year after I assumed command of Edwards, we had but one accident, and that was due to materiel failure.

"He occasionally flew out to see me to give visible endorsement of his support. There was always time during his visits when the two of us could talk privately and informally. I always found these occasions to be very helpful. He understood human nature and how to encourage people to do their best, the basis of his strength as a leader."[21]

General Cook commented on an aspect of Brown's approach to staff coordination: "George had an excellent perception of command. As head of Systems Command, he felt that he worked for the Chief of Staff but not for the myriad of Air Staff officers under the Chief. They all cooperated with him, and he knew how to handle them, but he reported only to the Chief. He did not regard himself as accountable to the three-star generals who served as deputy chiefs of staff, who had many problems in programming and finance. We had our own people in comparable staff positions, and he engendered useful working relationships between them and the Air Staff. But he got involved at the subordinate levels when it became absolutely necessary. His concept was utter simplicity in command and staff relationships."[22]

Perhaps one of Brown's strongest assets as a leader during this period was his attention to personnel problems and their long-term effects on the Air Force as a whole. This was discussed by Lt. Gen. Kenneth Tallman, later Deputy Chief of Staff for Personnel: "After he became commander of Systems Command, General Brown visited the Military Personnel Center at Randolph twice during my tenure there, discussing personnel matters with me on both those occasions. He took great interest in the future procurement of scientists and engineers for the Air Force. He went about this in both short- and long-range terms. He knew that as long as we maintained a high annual procurement of officers during the Vietnam War, his short-range picture was going to remain tolerably good. But he was looking beyond that and could perceive a reduction in numbers, and in fact, some reduction had already started. He could see that in the years ahead this continuing reduction was going to have a negative impact on the research and development capability of the Air Force. He was concerned that we continue to seek qualified college graduates for scientific and engineering positions."[23]

Tallman's observations sum up Brown's perception of the need for far-sighted personnel planning: "He had a far-flung command and was then a relative newcomer, but he placed great emphasis on supporting the needs of his commanders for highly qualified people. His primary thrust was always the downstream future of AFSC in terms of qualified engineers and scientists. But he also had a sincere interest in the future of the entire Air Force. That was reflected in everything he did. One of the first things he did on assuming a new command was to find out the role it played in the total Air Force picture. He was a completely unselfish individual, one who placed his own command interests behind those of the Air Force as a whole."[24]

Gen. Spike Momyer, Commander-in-Chief of Tactical Air Command, summed up Brown's success at AFSC by saying, "When I took over TAC, we got started on the fighter modernization program with the introduction of the F–15 and with the translation of the research and development of the A–10 into a production aircraft. We got the AWACS justification finally established on the basis of tactical need rather than the air-defense need, based on our experience in Vietnam. We had started the modernization of the C–130 fleet with the AMST. All of the programs were started when I was working with Brown on the movement of all these programs. We've seen the fruition of the F–15 and the A–10, and the assimilation of AWACS into the operational Air Force. The AMST we built to prototypes but elected not to go into production on that. All of those programs had to be worked very closely with AFSC, and George's leadership is evident in the fact that we brought those programs on board and today they constitute the hard-core capability of the Air Force."[25]

"George did an outstanding job as the commander of AFSC," said Momyer. "All my dealings with him were oriented toward getting programs moving that had operational requirements. We worked very well together, with George supporting operational requirements that I was trying to defend. He was effective in working with major commanders, always a difficult position because operational commanders are pressing for shorter term needs, whereas people in research and development are pressing for longer term requirements. George did a good job of working with SAC, TAC, and with overseas commanders."[26]

NOTES

1. Personal interview with Gen. George S. Brown, September 14, 1977.
2. Ibid.
3. Personal interview with Gen. John D. Ryan, USAF (Ret.), August 9, 1979.
4. Personal interview with John L. McLucas, February 21, 1980.
5. Letter from Maj. Gen. Gerald K. Hendricks, USAF, February 14, 1980.
6. *History of the Air Force Systems Command,* FY 1971/72, vol. I, p. 62.
7. *History of the Air Force Systems Command,* FY 1971/72 (1 July 1970–30 June 1972), vol. I, Office of History, Headquarters Air Force Systems Command, USAF, p. 17.
8. Hendricks correspondence.
9. Personal interview with Lt. Gen. Edward O'Connor, July 22, 1980.
10. Personal interview with Maj. Gen. Jerry Cook, April 12, 1980.
11. Hendricks correspondence.
12. Personal interview with Maj. Gen. James W. Stansberry, USAF, April 8, 1980.
13. O'Connor interview.
14. Hendricks correspondence.
15. Stansberry interview.

16. Personal interview with Gen. Robert C. Mathis, USAF, April 8, 1980.
17. O'Connor interview.
18. Ibid.
19. Stansberry interview.
20. Cook interview.
21. Personal interview with Lt. Gen. Howard M. Lane, USAF, May 16, 1980.
22. Cook interview.
23. Personal interview with Lt. Gen. Kenneth A. Tallman, USAF, June 18, 1980.
24. Ibid.
25. Personal interview with Gen. William Momyer, USAF (Ret.), September 9, 1981.
26. Ibid.

CHAPTER 19

WASHINGTON, D.C.:
AUGUST 1973–JUNE 1974

Gen. John Ryan, immediately after he was nominated for Air Force Chief of Staff, informed George Brown that he was his choice to succeed him as Chief. Although this was four years before Brown was selected, George was being groomed long before this.

There were other people who had a role, but a key player in Brown's development was Gen. Horace Wade. "As DCS Personnel," reflected Wade, "one of my jobs was to look ahead to see that officers got broadened. We had a number of officers to select from when we got ready to select a three- or four-star general as Chief of Staff. I had worked for Chief of Staff Gen. J. P. McConnell and got to know him well. We had put our finger on George Brown as Chief of Staff early in his career."[1]

On March 5, 1973, at a meeting with the service secretaries and chiefs, Secretary of Defense Elliot Richardson announced that he wanted "considerable lead time on the selection of senior general officers, preferably six months."

Since Gen. John Ryan was scheduled for retirement on July 31, 1973, Air Force Secretary Frank Seamans proceeded immediately to act on Mr. Richardson's directive. He submitted a memorandum to Secretary Richardson that narrowed the candidates to three: Generals George Brown, David Jones, and John Meyer. But he recommended George Brown as his personal choice.

"My recommendation for the position," wrote Secretary Seamans in comparing the final three candidates, "is General George S. Brown. The Chief of Staff, USAF, concurs. Each officer has distinguished himself in command and staff positions of great importance, and each has a fine combat record. General Brown's experience is, in my opinion, broader in each of these regards, however. He served in World War II and in Korea and commanded the Seventh Air Force in South Vietnam at the four-star level for twenty-six months. He has served as Executive Officer to the Chief of Staff, USAF. He served as Military Assistant to Secretary McNamara from 1959 to 1963 while a brigadier general and major general. He served the Chairman of the Joint Chiefs of Staff, General Wheeler, as a lieutenant general from 1966 to 1968, and General Wheeler noted that 'His potential for further outstanding service qualifies him for the highest offices of trust and responsibility in the Military Services of his country.' General Brown currently commands Air Force Systems Command in which capacity he has unique experience with the research and development of new weapons systems. I have attached career briefs on Generals Brown, Jones, and Meyer for your review. I have also enclosed General Brown's nomination to the President."

On April 20, 1973, Secretary Richardson sent his recommendation for the appointment of George Brown to President Richard Nixon:

> On April 10, 1973, I forwarded to you my nomination of General George S. Brown as the next Chief of Staff of the United States Air Force. At breakfast on April 11, Dr. Kissinger suggested that it might be helpful to you if I provided some additional information describing my reasons for nominating George Brown.
>
> My recommendation of General Brown follows a careful screening of the top officers in the Air Force. There are many who have all the qualities in varying degree that are needed in a Service Chief, but there are none who can match the across-the-board qualifications of General Brown. He is a man who can be counted on, not only as a battle-tested fighting man, but also as one who is capable of managing a large, expensive, complicated organization. He can also inspire men of all ages, he knows his way around Washington, is respected by Congress, admired by members of your own staff, and of unquestionable loyalty to his country and to his superiors.
>
> As we shift from a wartime to a peacetime Air Force, I believe we must look for very special qualifications in our top mili-

tary leadership. I see our problems requiring greater emphasis on management and efficiency as we face determined challenges to cut our defense budget. We need men who are expert not only in combat but in the wise, effective allocation of scarce resources. General Brown, in my estimation, has these needed qualifications to a greater degree than any other Air Force General now on active duty.

If your time permits, I believe it would be helpful if you interviewed General Brown before submitting his nomination to the Senate. I will make the necessary arrangements for such a visit if you wish.

In addition, I would be happy, if you wish, to meet with you to discuss the other candidates I considered, or any that you might have in mind, for this top Air Force job.

Before Brown was to replace General Ryan on July 31, 1973, a new Secretary of Defense, James R. Schlesinger, took office. I asked him what role he had in the selection of George Brown as Chief of Staff. "I was Director of the Central Intelligence Agency and had just been designated Secretary of Defense. I was informed of George's selection prior to the official confirmation, and I wanted to see him firsthand. Basically, the Chiefs at that time were chosen by the Secretary of Defense. George met with me for several hours.

"I found that he was reflective, and I knew he was one of the finest officers in the Air Force, indeed in all the services. I knew he had been effective as a commander. He had a reputation for loyalty and consideration for his people, but in moments when the need arose he could and did crack down on them. I decided he was clearly the man for the job."[2]

Secretary Schlesinger communicated his thoughts to the President after that meeting with Brown. He stated:

Memorandum for the President

Subject: Nomination for Chief of Staff of the Air Force

I am aware that Secretary Richardson has forwarded to you the nomination of General George S. Brown to become Chief of Staff of the Air Force upon General Ryan's retirement on July 31.

I share Secretary Richardson's high regard for General Brown. In my considered view, his experience in critical management areas and the quality of his service in positions of great responsibility to the country place him first among Air Force generals as the nominee for appointment as Chief of Staff.

If you wish, I would be happy to meet with you to discuss this nomination.

The Under Secretary of the Air Force, John McLucas, who became Secretary at the same time Brown was sworn in as Chief, commented, "I had a lot of confidence in George. Bob Seamans and I had talked about him a lot as the logical man to replace General Ryan. He was assuming his mantle as Chief with my complete concurrence. He radiated the right kind of image, a man who had been there, had held all the right commands so the Air Force people would respect him as a man who had worked up through the system. He had done well in these various jobs, had a good view on the relative role of the various ranks in the services. He knew the role of the enlisted man, as well as that of the middle managers, and the things that motivated people. I thought that he was a great choice. Fortunately, he knew a lot more about weapons systems procurement than I thought most Chiefs had known."[3]

President Nixon sent the nomination to the Senate, and on July 14, 1973, Frances R. Valio, Secretary of the Senate, sent out a document:

SENATE OF THE UNITED STATES

In Executive Session

July 14, 1973

Resolved, That the Senate advise and consent to the following nomination:

General George S. Brown, 579-52-7651FR (Major General, Regular Air Force), United States Air Force, to be appointed as Chief of Staff, United States Air Force, for a period of four years beginning August 1, 1973, under provisions of Section 8034, Title 10, of the United States Code.

Section 8034, Title 10, of the United States Code, spelled out the responsibilities of the Chief of Staff.

8034.   Chief of Staff:appointment:duties

(a) The Chief of Staff shall be appointed for a period of four years by the President, by and with the advice and consent of the Senate, from the general officers of the Air Force. He serves during the pleasure of the President. In time of War or national emergency declared by the Congress after December 31, 1968, he may be reappointed for a term of not more than four years. . . .

(c) Except as otherwise prescribed by law and subject to section 8012(c) and (d) of this title, the Chief of Staff performs his duties under the direction of the Secretary of the Air Force, and is directly responsible to the Secretary for the efficiency of the Air Force, its preparedness for military operations, and plans therefore.

(d) The Chief of Staff shall—

(1) preside over the Air Staff;

(2) send the plans and recommendations of the Air Staff to the Secretary, and advise him with regard thereto;

(3) after approval of the plans or recommendations of the Air Staff by the Secretary, act as the agent of the Secretary in carrying them into effect;

(4) exercise supervision over such of the members and organizations of the Air Force as the Secretary of the Air Force determines. Such supervision shall be exercised in a manner consistent with the full operational command vested in unified or specified combatant commanders under section 124 of this title;

(5) perform the duties prescribed for him by sections 141 and 171 of this title and other provisions of law; and

(6) perform such other military duties, not otherwise assigned by law, as are assigned to him by the President.

One of the statutory requirements directed that General Brown was to "preside over the Air Staff." Generals Henry H. Arnold, Carl A. Spaatz, Hoyt S. Vandenberg, Nathan F. Twining, Thomas D. White, Curtis E. LeMay, J. P. McConnell, and John D. Ryan, all of the previous Chiefs, had served tours as Vice Chief before becoming Chief. General Brown, however, had no such "apprenticeship," although he served as colonel outside the Chief's office as exec for two years. Yet he had considerable exposure to the responsibilities of this high position while serving four years as military assistant to the Secretary of Defense.

I asked the Vice Chief of Staff under General Ryan, Gen. Horace Wade, who remained in that position for a brief transition period under Brown, "How did he tackle the job as Chief?"

"The first day that George was in the office," Wade recalled, "it was as though he had been there a year. He knew the Air Staff backwards and forwards because as commander of Systems Command he had been dealing with them for a long time. He knew everybody, what was going on in the Pentagon, in the JCS area, in the SecDef's area; he had his pipeline all over. George walked into the office and was at home. His pictures went up on the wall, his plaques and the other things he had. It was as if it had always been his office."[4]

Part of the daily routine of the Chief was to meet each morning with his deputy chiefs of staff for Personnel, Operations and Plans, Programs, Research and Development, and Logistics and the Comptroller. This staff meeting was to keep him apprised of various developments. It was also useful in bringing the staff up to date on questions cutting across all areas of staff interest.

If he had a special message to give the staff, he might do it at the outset of the meeting. If not, he'd call upon the members of the staff in order. Ryan went around the room in a geographic fashion, working up one side of the long table, and then to the set of seats behind the table, around the seats on the wall, and then back to the other side of the table. Everyone sat at the same place each time.

Brown didn't like having such a large group at the staff meetings. "He didn't want everything surfaced every day as it was in the past," said Lt. Gen. Joseph G. Wilson, Deputy Chief of Staff for Operations. "He thought too many trivial things were brought out when each person had to say something. Brown decided that only the vice chief and the seven deputy chiefs of staff would attend the meetings. In going to seven, he cut out the nonsense and got down to business and important things. With the numbers cut down it also became more informal. We covered the problems of the previous day and what was going on that day. The meeting was reduced in length to about half an hour rather than one and a half to two hours."[5]

"He made it a lot more personal," reflected Deputy for Research and Development Gen. William Evans. "His feeling was 'You're not here to get an education so much as you're here to give me information that I need to run the Air Force. At the same time, you're the people that I have to talk and give instructions to and react to your inputs.' He didn't want to downgrade the Chaplain, or downgrade the Surgeon General, but he felt that they could use their time more beneficially by not sitting around listening to me telling about the inner workings of the AWACS development program. That was not that kind of meeting."[6]

Some who were cut out didn't like it, however. "I objected to it," commented Maj. Gen. Harold Vague, Judge Advocate General, "because I only got updated once a week rather than daily. I voiced my complaint through the assistant vice chief and was told, 'The Chief wants it. We'll try it out.' "[7]

I asked Maj. Gen. "Pete" Lewis, who represented the Reserve forces and was another staff member eliminated, his reaction to this decision. "I felt like a second-class citizen," he said, "because with my position I reported straight to the Chief. I represented a viable force, just like the Air Guard. We were both left out of the meetings. If we'd never been invited, it wouldn't make any difference. But since we'd already been invited, one of the great thrills of being in that position was to participate; that made it hard. Intelligence, Studies and Analysis, the Surgeon, the Guard, and Reserves had all been left out; indeed, all the special staff."[8]

Gen. Richard Ellis, who succeeded Wade as Vice Chief, remarked that Brown and the staff would often discuss something and need further input, "but because of the reduction of the staff present at the meeting, the Chief would look around and say, 'Who is responsible for this?' and the man responsible wouldn't be there."[9]

Major General Lukeman, in charge of Studies and Analysis, reflected, "Because General Brown was being deprived of the useful flow of information, he reversed his decision. It was characteristic of him that he didn't do it behind anybody's back—he hit it head on. He said, 'Men, I was wrong. The old system worked pretty well, and we're going to get together again.' That's the kind of man he was. From then on to the end of the time he was Chief of Staff of the Air Force we continued to have big, long staff meetings."[10]

General Ryan as Chief demanded much more detail than Brown. His morning briefings, for example, were complete in every phase of the Southeast Asian War in the area of close air support. Detailed charts were presented to General Ryan, the Secretary, and the Chairman every morning. "When George Brown had his first staff meeting," recalled Lt. Gen. Joseph Wilson, "I continued giving the same sort of briefing. We got halfway through the briefing and Brown just said, 'That's enough! I've fought a number of wars in my life. I've just spent a year and a half to two years in Southeast Asia as Seventh Air Force commander. I don't need all this detail. That's your job as DO, Deputy for Operations. If you have a problem, let me know.' He turned you loose to do your job and did not want details. He was quick to see problems."[11]

"Brown told me," commented William Evans, "that he didn't want to jam up his mental computer with a lot of details. He made a great point to me one day when I gave him some heavy details by saying, 'Bill, I don't want these details. I know what the issues are. You remember the details and I'll remember you and where to find you, and I'll call you if I need the background.' "[12]

Brown's exec, Col. Bradley K. Hosmer, commented, "The hallmarks to me of his year as Chief were his affinity for the fundamental issues—not the

detail—of defense policy, and his insistence on written clarity in the correspondence and directives issued from his office. I do not mean that General
Brown was cavalier about details. He was as comfortable with details as
anyone. However, he began and ended each review of an issue with the fundamentals."[13]

At times he became impatient with unnecessary details. Shortly after he
became Chief of Staff, the Inspector General completed inspection of the
Air Force Reserve. Pete Lewis reflected: "General Brown had been there
only three weeks. He was at the head of the table with the DCSs and many
of the special staff. The IG's briefing started out formally with many charts.
He got four or five minutes into the briefing and made some caustic remarks. Brown threw his pencil on the table. It bounced about five feet and
almost hit the ceiling. He said, 'That's enough of that. I don't want to hear
any more. I've been in the field all my life. I've had IGs inspect me, and all
they talked about are the nit-picking items like toilet paper in the latrines,
supplies in secretaries' desks, things that don't amount to anything.' He
went on for about five minutes. Everybody was very red in the face. He put
on a real show. We were all surprised to see a four-star general completely
explode, but I was elated because this was the second time within a short
period that we had been inspected as a component."[14] Brown told the Inspector General, "When you have a real problem, talk with the man you're
investigating. Work with him on a solution. Keep it on a higher plane and
stop all this nit-picking."[15]

There were other occasions when he displayed sparks of temper. For
example, he heard that an Air Force brigadier general was downgrading the
A-10. Brown at that time was trying to work closely with the Army on the
Air Force use of the A-10 for ground support. "He knew," said Dick Ellis,
"that if the Army thought the Air Force was not serious about the coordination and usefulness of the A-10, he would be in trouble with Army Chief
of Staff Creighton Abrams. I remember his telling me, 'Get that brigadier
up here and I'll have a good piece of him.' But this brigadier, when he came
in to see the Chief, was the smartest guy in the room. He had done his homework and knew the details of his position. After the explanation was given
of what had actually happened, George cooled off. After he left, George
said to me, 'That kid makes sense, doesn't he?' "[16]

An individual who worked closely with Brown, Lt. Gen. William Smith,
pointed out one of his major strengths. "He had an amazing ability to work
with his staff. People within the military can be divided into two kinds: first,
the individual who relies on his staff and who becomes a prisoner of the
staff; second, those who are 'antistaff,' the commander who objects to anything the staff does. Brown did not fit into either category. He relied on his

staff and really insisted that they tell him what they thought. But he didn't expect agreement and sometimes would say things that he knew were wrong to get people to disagree with him. He wanted a free expression of ideas, making it clear to the staff that he relied upon their judgment. At the same time, he could see weaknesses in a position and was able to choose his own course of action. But then he would explain why he had made the decision he did, never leaving his people resentful. I guess that comes from two things. One is letting your people express themselves, having faith in their judgment; the other, at the same time being a critical judge yourself in passing judgment."[17]

"General Brown wanted a different relationship with the staff than General Ryan," said Col. Glenn Jones, his executive officer. "He told me, 'Somebody here has to have the ideas. The staff is waiting for me to surface them so they can get to work. But I'm waiting for them to have the ideas. I'm looking for the bright young majors to surface through their deputy chiefs of staff. They will make the Air Force better because they have been closer to the action more recently than I have. I think the staff has been doing just the opposite. I think they've been staffing the Chief's good ideas.' It was a gradual transition. It was not painful for anyone because it was so well done. He made that speech several times to his three-star staff. I'm sure they then fell back in the driver's seat and began to surface those things that make for a better Air Force. It makes majors and colonels feel very important to see their ideas become policy."[18]

"One mark of General Brown's first months in office," commented Col. Bradley Hosmer, who was serving as executive officer to the Chief when Brown arrived, "was related to his affinity for the fundamentals; he needed to take initiatives where the fundamentals of what we were doing needed new direction. However, the pace of the Air Staff did not leave him much time. This point opens a small wound of my own because I feel responsible for a schedule that did not give him the time he needed. When Brown came in, I was not quick enough to sense that we owed him some settling-in time. Instead, I allowed the system to impose the same pace of business on Brown that it had on the outgoing Chief of Staff with four years of experience in the job. I did not have the wit to anticipate how inappropriate that was nor to change it quickly enough. I began to get signals from General Brown that he needed more time to think and take initiatives of his own. It eventually worked itself out.

"I suspect rather than try to change the Air Staff in the opening months, he simply outsmarted us. He spent a lot of time traveling and also took what time he could to play tennis. Trips and tennis matches often produced fresh approaches to current issues."[19]

Many decisions made in staff meetings had an effect on the public, and
Brown was keenly aware of the need for good public relations. As the Assistant Vice Chief of Staff, Lt. A. J. Russell, pointed out, "George insisted
that the generals talk more, that they get out, make speeches, make themselves available to the squadron officers' school, or talk to chambers of
commerce. He wanted more stress on publicity. He felt that the Air Force
had a good case and should be better understood. He believed that an informed public would come to the best solution for the country. The best
way to inform the public is to get the wing commander off the base and present the case. And when he would come to Washington, Brown wanted him
to go over to the Hill and meet his congressman or senator."[20]

At one of his first press conferences, Brown set the stage for his approach by saying, "The Air Force has been too close-mouthed. We ought to
admit our mistakes. . . . I think we've got to assume that whatever we do or
fail to do and whatever we say or write is going to find its way into the public
record. We're going to talk and talk properly so that what we say will stand
the light of public scrutiny. My reason is that the American people need to
understand. Integrity is most important. We must avoid extravagance in all
things. Appearance of right is almost as important as doing right."

One way in which Brown displayed integrity was his avoiding favoritism
in relations with his staff. When he became Chief, the Deputy Chief of
Staff, Programs, was Lt. Gen. George Boylan, who had served with him
during World War II. Also, one of the key people on the Air Staff was Lt.
Gen. Duward L. "Pete" Crow, George's West Point classmate. "George
was very much aware," reflected Boylan, "that the senior people in the Air
Staff knew that George and I had a special relationship. They also knew
that George and Pete Crow had been classmates, so a potential problem was
present. Old friend, classmate, Chief—people might stand back and say,
'Let's see how much leverage they've got,' meaning Pete and me. Well,
George made it clear immediately that there wasn't any special holy water
on George Sylvester Boylan and none on Pete. We were to do our jobs and
that's the only reason we were there."[21]

"I remember when Pete Crow became Assistant Vice Chief of Staff and
Joe DeLucca became Comptroller," said Gen. Howard Fish. "I became
Director of Budget, so would sit in on the staff meetings whenever the
Comptroller wasn't available. At one meeting we were discussing budgetary
matters. I was holding forth on what I thought we ought to do. Pete was
offering advice at least a nuance different from mine. George turned and
and said, 'Pete, you ran the budget for years; now you let Howard run it for
a while.' He knew that we couldn't have two budget officers although Pete
had been in the job for almost fifteen years. Pete took it in good grace and

laughed. This was the sort of thing that endeared me to Brown; he was saying he would support me. I'm sure it didn't mean much to him when he said it. It was spontaneous, but it meant a lot."[22]

General Boylan pointed out another such instance: "George made the relationship between himself and his deputy chiefs of staff clear at one of our first staff meetings. The Air Defense Commander stated his position on an issue. Then my people went against him. After my presentation George told me that I had to have better reasons than I had at that table before he was going to support me over his commander. The entire staff was relieved to see George establish that relationship. I found it fair. I never had expected George to show favoritism with me."[23]

"I was commander of NORAD," reflected Gen. Lucius Clay. "To me, Brown was the only senior officer in the Pentagon interested in air defense. Without his effort, air defense would have gone down the drain long before then. He had a firm belief that it ought to be an inherent function of the Air Force to retain some form of an air defense environment over the misgivings of many military and civilian leaders. He was able to prevail and keep together some elements of a command and control, interceptor, and warning system under one commander.

"There was a group of people always looking for dollars, always looking for how we could reduce overhead and other less essential things. I must admit there was an element of truth present in that we couldn't really postulate a significant acceptable threat. There was a threat, but not to the degree perhaps that some military felt was justifiable. And Mr. Schlesinger with his statement, 'We don't defend against missiles, why should we worry about airplanes?' spelled the death knell even though such things as the Backfire were coming along.

"But the point was that Brown was able to prevail in the sense that he was going to hold a thin line and perhaps some day move into some form of space defense. He and I felt that it was proper and appropriate to keep at least a thin line of direct interceptor control for the unknown.

"Ultimately it was decided that NORAD would deactivate, that they would reduce all the forces either by eliminating them or putting them into the Air National Guard with no active duty forces at all. George, however, said, 'I'll accept the Guard buildup; that makes sense to me, but I'm going to maintain some element of a regular force in the air defense business to provide standardization, supervision, and guidance on tactical doctrine and techniques.' "[24]

Although Brown's major concern was the military defense of our country, he also had a feel for personnel problems. One of these was the erosion of benefits for military personnel. He believed that the military had to do a lot more for its people. "Brown, however," said Lt. Gen. William Smith, "sensed that the military was going to have to do something to change the current law regarding retirement benefits. He was one of the first Chiefs to come out and say so. This was hard for him to do, but he realized that some changes would have to be made in the retirement setup."[25]

Brown had a special way of challenging something that was wrong, but doing it with kindness. "I was always impressed with the way that he ran his staff meetings," commented Chief of Chaplains Maj. Gen. Henry Meade. "He never tried to trap anyone, never used trick questions. If, in the discussion of an issue, one of his conferees at the table wasn't really up to snuff, he never tried to shortcut him. He made him comfortable, saying, 'Charlie, check that information and give me a jingle and update me on it.' "[26]

Brown was also sensitive to individual differences in the personalities of his staff. "One day," recalled Gen. John Roberts, Deputy Chief of Staff for Personnel, "he was going over a certain project with me. At that time I was working for General Dixon, Deputy Chief of Staff for Personnel. Dixon was getting command of Tactical Air Command, and he had already informed me that I was going to be his replacement. At the end of our conference, Brown said to me, 'John, I want you to take General Dixon's job when he goes to TAC. I'm not giving you this job to run it like Dixon. You are to run it like John Roberts.' That was an interesting comment because Brown thought a great deal of Dixon. This was a good point to make to someone who's just taking over a job, to say, in essence, it's your job, run it the way you want. Don't try to run it like somebody else."[27]

"Brown respected the Air Force as an institution," reflected William Smith, "and he also had a great respect for his contemporaries. General Brown believed in collective judgment on many matters, particularly about people and their selection for certain positions. When there was a senior position that needed to be filled, he would talk to his friends and say, 'What do you think about this individual for that job?' He tested the thing out to make sure that he had the support of the Air Force before he selected some person. He knew how to mine the system to get the best people out of it, and knew he could rely upon the system to help find and select them. He was interested, of course, in the more senior positions, the various commanders, but also in the younger people coming along. He wanted to make sure that the right people were representing the Air Force and that they had the support of the Air Force."[28]

Although he respected the Air Force as an institution, Brown was not afraid of change if he thought it was for the better. For example, the idea of an independent defense counsel organization had been under consideration for many years. Until Brown's time, a defense counsel appointed on a court-martial had always been someone in the same command as the person who appointed the court. The JAG had thus taken heat for years with critics saying, "How can a lawyer do a good job for a client when his interests are adverse to the commander's? The commander is trying to put him in jail, and here you give him a defense counsel whose effectiveness reports are written by that same commander."

"We came up with the idea," said General Vague, "of taking a group of people from under the commander and making them directly responsible to the Judge Advocate General. Their job, even though they might be physically located on the same base, would have no command relationship to that commander; they would simply do the defense work for people needing such representation. This concept wasn't popular with many commanders because they didn't want people on their bases not under their command. However, I got my ducks in order and said to General Brown, 'We want to try this out for a year. Then we want to appoint a board with both commanders and lawyers on it and evaluate the system to see how it's working.' Brown was absolutely in favor of it. The new system did work and has become a permanent thing in the Air Force."[29]

Brown could get to the heart of a matter by cutting through superfluous details. Duward Crow said of him, "George had a facility for reducing things to very simple terms. One phrase that he used often in our discussions of complex problems was 'I would hate to try to explain that to my mother. Now let's go over it again.' "[30]

Brown's exec, Bradley Hosmer, made the same observation: "One of Brown's concerns was to clarify the written word. He would not be party to a message, letter, or speech which was ambiguous or clumsy, or contained jargon. His desire for elegance in the written word brought him into conflict with the standard Air Force product. In order to adapt Air Force language to meet his standards, we rewrote a great deal of material. Of course, we always took care to check with the originator and the deputy chief of staff involved to make sure that the substance had not been altered. Gradually, the clarity of written material seemed to improve, but rewriting for clarity continued to be a major part of our daily chores.

"One episode may illustrate how pointed this issue could become. A staff paper arrived on my desk one day for General Brown's signature. Its style was government bureaucratic and was clearly going to need editing. We had office notepaper without signature blocks on it, and on such a slip of paper I wrote, 'This reads like a regulation,' and initialed it B (for Brad). I then put it on the stack that was to go across the hall for editing by our special assistants. Unfortunately, that paper was shuffled into a different stack and was returned to the DCS through whom it had come. As I learned later, he assumed the note came from B (for General Brown). Twenty-four hours later, back on my desk appeared a beautifully written version of the original paper. The first I knew that it had gone astray was when I complimented our special assistants on that job and they did not know what I was talking about. It seems I had inadvertently led that DCS to believe that the Chief had personally returned his staff paper. Although it was an accident, the material coming from that office improved remarkably."[31]

Was Brown more effective with Congress than others? "I think he was," answered Lt. Gen. William W. Snavely, one of his Deputy Chiefs of Staff. "For one thing, I think that he felt comfortable in that environment, whereas other Chiefs might have felt more comfortable in an operational environment. While General Brown had a considerable amount of operational experience, it was interspersed with systems management and more interface with Congress. He worked closely with our budget people, with those who had close contacts with the congressional committees.[32]

"These contacts were helpful to him as Chief. I remember telling George one day, 'We're having trouble with Senator so-and-so.' He picked up the telephone to talk with the senator, but he made a point to let him do the talking. He spoke to him on the basis of 'I've heard there's a problem. Would you tell me what it is?' Then he proceeded to work the thing out."[33]

One of Brown's most important contacts with Congress was the budget. His budget officer, Howard Fish, commented, "General Brown refused to go to a budget hearing with several staff officers to help answer questions. He told me, 'If I go there with a lot of people, they'll expect detailed answers. I prefer to go by myself with one aide to find the way through the books, not with an entourage. If I don't know the answer, I'll say so and we'll provide it for the record.' Pete Crow had been around those committees for many years and strongly advised against it. However, Brown would not be dissuaded."[34]

An incident that demonstrated Brown's loyalty to his subordinates was recalled by his chief lawyer, Harold Vague. "Several lawsuits received wide publicity concerning a captain we refused to designate as a judge advocate. Brown called me and said, 'What about this thing, how did you handle this, because I'm getting questions from the press and Congress. Have you thought this through? Would it be better if you'd go ahead and designate him a judge advocate and get rid of this flap?' I told him, 'No, I don't think so. I feel that the captain is too immature to be legal advisor to any commander.' He said, 'OK, that's good. I back you.' "[35]

Brown's position on weapons and with defense contractors was made clear in a speech before a convention of contractors: "However little we may like the term," he said, "or the way it has been used over the past few years, we are part of a military-industrial complex. In the free enterprise economy of our democratic society, and with the technological sophistication of modern weaponry, I know of no other reasonable way to develop and produce the weapon systems that the security of the nation demands. The system works. Major war has been deterred, and smaller conflicts have been kept from going global. In no small part, these achievements have been possible because, up to now, the United States has had superior weapons in sufficient numbers to prevent and to limit war. We are at a point in our history where that kind of effectiveness will no longer be possible, unless it is matched by an equal measure of tough, economy-minded efficiency.

"All of us must recognize certain basic truths. First, defense costs have been climbing steadily. Second, even if defense spending could be maintained at a fixed level in current dollar terms, there is an erosion of real purchasing power. This has necessitated reduction in force size, which makes it imperative to offset numerical inferiority with qualitatively superior weapon systems. But the cost of these systems has also been climbing so rapidly that we face such alternatives as reduced quality, lesser numbers, or just not going forward with some programs that are needed.

"Cost consciousness, cost avoidance, and cost reduction will have to be our way of life. Not that we haven't made some good progress. In the Air Force we're seeing genuine results in such programs as the F-15, AWACS, SRAM, Minuteman III, and others. They're doing what they're supposed to do on, or ahead of, schedule, and they're staying inside the cost envelope. That kind of progress comes from putting strong program managers in charge, and from competitive prototyping, innovative contracting techniques, and better methods of making cost estimates.

"Yet all these things address perhaps one-half of the problem. They do a good job of controlling direct cost, but they do not have much impact on indirect costs or overhead. Of the $7 billion expended in the Air Force Systems Command in fiscal year 1972, roughly $3.5 billion went for overhead. So the control and reduction of overhead is going to be the subject of intensive attention, concern, and action.

"As with everything we enter into jointly—you the contractors and we in Defense—a major part of the responsibility resides with you. American industry has always demonstrated that it can keep costs within tight bounds. The time has come when the same discipline must be exerted in government work other than fixed-price contracting. The military services are joining the consumer movement. We know what's involved in managing large enterprises. Overhead per se is a part of doing business, but what I'm really concerned with are those cases where indirect costs exceed the bounds of legitimacy and necessity, be it from carelessness or downright abuse."[36]

Brown laid bare the constant battle between the budget and the contractors. General Boylan, who was present when this speech was given, made the comment, "I applauded Brown, but the industrial contractors were shocked. I overheard several saying, 'What the hell is wrong with that man? Doesn't he know we're the people who get it all done?' To me, George was telling them what should have been said a long time ago, 'You'd better shape up! The Air Force under my leadership is no longer going to accept the time delay override cost policy of the past.' "[37]

"George was a very cautious man in his role as Chief of Staff," reflected Secretary of Defense James R. Schlesinger. "He was, for example, very, very cautious in moving toward the F-16, which was a lightweight fighter concept. He really tore the idea of the F-16 apart, preferring to stay with the F-15. I was pushing for the development of the F-16. Remember, if you go back to that period, we were facing constraint in budgets. There was a good deal of suspicion when I moved into the office about the attitudes of the Secretary of Defense, particularly on the part of the military budget makers."

There was a great deal of criticism of the Air Force over the cost of new weapons. Brown handled it well, however, in trying to educate the American people as well as the White House and Congress. He pointed out a factor critics failed to mention, that weapons systems cost more in part because they now do a lot more. He gave an example in an interview with *U.S. News and World Report*, February 25, 1974 (p. 64): "For example, the P-47 in World War II cost us just under $100,000 a copy," said General Brown, "and we produced many thousands. The F-4, of which we've produced over 4,440, is costing little better than $2.5 million each. The F-4 carries the bomb load of the B-17 in World War II. In addition, the F-4 has 'blind capability'—that is, an inertial system and a good sight and all the rest that allows it to fight when visibility is poor.

"The airplanes that we paid $100,000 or $200,000 for in World War II didn't have any automation in them. You had an automatic pilot, but you had to sit there and finger it all the time. Now many things are automated. You've got radar and very sophisticated communications and electronic gear, all of which is very, very expensive.

"Today's planes perform a lot better. Airmen don't want to fly higher and faster just to fly higher and faster; they want to fly higher and faster to have an advantage over that other fellow."

Although one of Brown's major concerns was weapons production, he never lost interest in people and had a particular concern for their morale and spiritual welfare. "His attitude toward religion," said Chief of Chaplains Maj. Gen. Roy Terry, "made life easier for us. I asked him to appear at our chaplains' conference at Lowry Air Force Base during my last year. He was there and gave a tremendously fine address at the banquet on what his faith meant to him.

"There were also several occasions at staff meetings when he called for a short prayer, like for the release of the Vietnam POWs. At the Worldwide Commanders' Conference, we were called upon for a prayer for every occasion. I was also on the agenda at this commanders' conference to speak on the spiritual elements of leadership."[38]

One of Brown's tasks was the selection of officers for positions of responsibility. His approach shows the qualities of candor, thoroughness, and fair-mindedness that marked his career. During his tenure as Chief of Staff, the position of chief master sergeant of the Air Force became vacant. After intensive interviews, the field was narrowed to three people, who were sent to Washington for interviews with the Deputy Chief of Staff for Personnel and the Chief of Staff.

"During the initial interview with General Brown," reflected Chief Master Sergeant Thomas Barnes, who was ultimately selected for the job, "we three finalists met with him as a group and discussed some very broad things. This gave him the opportunity to see what our mutual thinking was. We discussed general Air Force programs, as well as the retention picture and professional aspirations of senior noncommissioned officers. I think some tasks transferred to senior noncommissioned officers came as a result of these discussions.

"During the individual interviews with General Brown, his interest in many of the new aspects of the force began to take shape. I think we all learned a great deal about his penchant for candor. He was direct in his approach to those things that he thought were necessary to achieve a meaningful Air Force, especially career attraction for people. This was not a matter of offers of money or offers of comfortable living conditions. Rather, it had to do with increasing the authority given to senior NCOs, and giving this increase the complete backing of the Chief's office."

Sergeant Barnes ultimately was selected. I asked him, "Why did General Brown select you for the position?" He responded, "I think a number of harmonies occurred during my second individual interview with him. We found we were able to communicate very directly. I didn't necessarily agree with everything he had to say, but he wasn't looking for a yes-man. I think his own basic nature needed an offset to him, and it probably had great bearing on my selection. He didn't express shock at being disagreed with, but instead found it an interesting point of departure.

"We also talked about how I would communicate those things that I wanted to come to his attention. He was a delegator. He wanted an able person who would take burdens off him. When problems surfaced, he wanted to have a recommended solution."[39]

Sergeant Barnes' selection was made to a distinguished audience at the 1973 September Air Force Association convention. Unfortunately, there were some present who insisted on reading a kind of reverse racial discrimination into Brown's choice of Barnes, who is black.

"George Brown called me," said Gen. William McBride, who was commander of Air Training Command at the time of Barnes' selection, "some thirty days after he became Chief. He was looking for a new chief master sergeant of the Air Force, and I had nominated Tom Barnes. He said, 'Why the hell did you recommend Barnes?' I said, 'Because I think he's the best man that I know to be Chief.' I thought he was trying to intimidate me. He said, 'Are you really sure we want a black for this job?' I said, 'It hasn't anything to do with that.' He said, 'You know, I know you're right. The only reason I'm asking you is to be sure that you hadn't put him in because he was a black. I want to make a good decision, so I'm going to rely on you. If you tell me he'll be a good choice, that's good enough for me.' He started off as though he was giving me hell because I recommended Barnes, whereas his being a black didn't bother him at all. He was feeling me out, testing me on Tom Barnes."[40]

Brown's judgment ultimately was proved correct. The chief master sergeant's tour was normally limited to two years, but Sergeant Barnes was given two unprecedented one-year extensions; thus he served a total of four years.

One of the most serious crises during Brown's tour as Chief was the Arab-Israeli War of 1973. "On the first day of the war, he attended an early meeting in the National Military Command Center and came out with a blur," recalled Maj. Gen. George F. Keegan. "He immediately held a meeting with the Air Staff, all the staff present, and he said to me, 'George, what's the war about? What's going to happen?' "

> I'll never forget the meeting. I said, "This is the best-prepared war in Arab history. They're going to have a massive impact against Israel and unless Israel gets help immediately she's going to lose the war. The Air Force will be blamed and scapegoated for having failed to deliver supplies in time." I explained that it

would be an extremely intense, high-rate-of-consumption war, in which the Israelis would be out of their major consumables such as rockets, bombs, and ammunition in about seven days. Henry Kissinger's blockade of the supplies that we were supposed to have been delivering all along had to be lifted immediately, and the Air Force had to move them to the aerial ports of embarkation. So that morning, Brown decided to supply weapons to Israel without coordinating with the SecDef. He told him later. George made the decision to allocate immediately two F-4 fighter squadrons for immediate delivery to the Israelis and to move a hundred thousand tons of ammunition to the aerial ports of embarkation. He tied down the whole military airlift capability of the United States doing just that without anyone's approval. That was one of the most courageous decisions of that incredible period of history. Then, like the good officer he was, he told the Secretary of Defense what he had done in an aggressive, challenging way, in effect daring him to undo these decisions. Unless Brown had acted, the supplies never would have reached Israel.

"He then left to take a long-scheduled leave, saying, 'If I am needed, here's how you get hold of me.' That was provided for, and things moved like clockwork. His decisions were carried out to the letter, exactly as he had predicted the requirements would come. Kissinger lifted his ban very late, and the Air Force began to move."[41]

Whenever he went on leave, Brown delegated his authority to capable members of his staff. In this case, it was to Vice Chief Horace Wade, who recalled: "George told me, 'Horace, when I'm gone you're running the Air Force. You make the decisions. Don't hesitate. I have all the faith and confidence in the world in you. You don't have to get on the phone and clear anything with me.' "[42]

However, a problem came up as the war developed that needed attention. "I had a little trouble getting to George," said General Wade. "I finally got through to the lodge and asked them to have George call me. When he did, I talked to him and told him what was going on. I recall his saying, 'If you need me, let me know and I'll come back.' We were so far down the line at that time, however, that it wasn't necessary for him to return early. Some people thought he should have run right back to Washington. I think it's a great credit to him that he said, 'Look, I've got good people back there. If the leadership is running it well, it should run well when I'm gone.'

"This was the pattern of George Brown's leadership. He had faith in the man to whom he turned the job over. He let him run it rather than to come right back. It's a great compliment that he had that much confidence in me. Also, it showed the type of confidence he had in himself—that he didn't have to be always running something. That's something special about a commander and a leader."[43]

Brown was an outstanding speaker. "General Brown's greatest single leverage as Chief was his supremacy as a thirty-second debater," recalled his exec, Colonel Hosmer. "The power of a good thirty-second debate, or elevator speech, was best explained to me by Gen. J. C. Meyer, Vice Chief under General Ryan. He claimed that an elevator speech was the final way to settle an issue as you picked up the Secretary of Defense on the third floor and got off on the second floor for a meeting with the JCS. Meyer said he had seen major issues settled by the comments made during that elevator ride. He was always looking for the shortest possible version of an Air Force position—one that could be given on the elevator. General Brown made superb elevator speeches."[44]

Although Brown did not like to get bogged down in details, he was sensitive to small things that might affect others. One such thing was a sign over the Chief's office that read, "The mission of the Air Force is to fly and fight and don't you forget it."

"That sign was in a strategic place," recalled Horace Wade. "It was put there by Gen. J. P. McConnell to impress civilians more than the military. We had problems with civilians in the building being upset and carrying on about the war in Southeast Asia. However, it presented problems with the nonrated officers. They were not flying and were not fighters, so maybe they were thinking that we didn't believe they had a mission in the Air Force."[45]

The sign did not escape the attention of the senior enlisted representative, Chief Master Sergeant Barnes. "Soon after I arrived I noticed that sign in the hallway over the Chief of Staff's door. General Brown took it down shortly thereafter. That marked the beginning of change toward consideration for other people in the Air Force. The sign implied that people not associated with flying and fighting were not equal. When it was taken down, it was the beginning of a change in the attitude toward the role played by the nonrated person."[46]

Brown also was concerned over the fact that rated navigators in the Air Force were by law prohibited from commanding a flying unit. This prohibition had been in existence for some time, but the Navy was successful in removing it in February 1970. The British and Canadian Air Forces had long before eliminated this discrimination.

In the spring of 1971, Headquarters, USAF, inquired of its field commanders whether they believed the law should be changed to permit navigators to command flying units. Those commanders who favored the selection of navigators for command did so on the rationale that commanders should pick the best man for the job on a case-by-case basis. Those who opposed navigators in command positions argued that the effectiveness of the Air Force mission would suffer because the nonpilot would be a "do-as-I-say,-not-as-I-do" commander. In addition, the opposition argued there were already insufficient opportunities for pilots to command and that one had to have the experience of a pilot to make flight and operational decisions. The discussion went on, but no change was made in the law.[47]

The issue surfaced again early in Brown's tenure as Chief at a conference of his Air Force commanders in December 1973. He brought it up and the overall consensus was in opposition to changing the law, but Brown continued to give it thought and to seek the views of others.

Maj. Gen. Robert Lukeman, a navigator, was on General Brown's staff heading the Studies and Analysis group. "I made a presentation at a staff meeting on January 14, 1974," said Lukeman, "which made a great impact when he brought the subject up. At that time there was rumbling from the Congress on this issue. Navigators throughout the Air Force had been writing congressmen, complaining about the lack of career opportunity. It was not intended to be an item of discussion at that staff meeting, but when it came up Howie Fish, himself a navigator, said, 'Why the hell don't we give them command opportunities? Why don't you give us command opportunity? It doesn't make a damned bit of difference whether the law says you should or shouldn't.'

"Normally, I was the only navigator voice at the staff meeting, but since Howie had spoken, I said, 'Well, as senior navigator in the Air Force, I believe I owe it to you, Chief, and to the navigators to make a couple of observations on this subject,' and I made a speech. I think Brown was impressed with what I said about the disparity between the opportunities that I had had on the way up when things were far less fettered than they became with all the nonsense that was put in regulations subsequent to that, and the restrictions that then existed on people in my same circumstances."[48]

Brown's aide and pilot, Glenn Jones, recalls another incident that undoubtedly affected the general's thinking on this issue: "I remember being at Griffiss Air Force Base when General Brown was talking to a SAC bomb wing. He went to visit the alert site and visit with the crews in the briefing room. He came in and sat in front of the group, answering questions as they thought of them. There was one angry navigator who stood up and said, 'Sir, why is it that you would entrust me with this job of getting my airplane to a target in wartime and yet you would not entrust me with command?' Brown tried for a brief moment to defend that policy, which was law, but couldn't in good conscience. He said, 'You know, you raise a very basic question. It may have made sense at some time in the past, but I'm not sure it does anymore. I promise you I will raise that issue when I get back.' "[49]

It was probably a combination of Fish, Lukeman, and the young officer's comment at Griffiss Air Force Base, for the next day General Brown sent a handwritten note to the Vice Chief of Staff, Gen. Richard Ellis:

1/15/74

VC

Dick—per our conversation I would like to take initiative to remove prohibitive legislation from books and broaden career field along Lukeman lines.

B

"Brown himself worked on the issue within the Air Force with his Vice Chief and Deputy Chief of Staff for Personnel," remarked Glenn Jones. "Also he went to Barry Goldwater and said, 'I no longer support this policy within the Air Force, or this law. I plan to take it on and need your support.' Senator Goldwater gave him his support on the Hill."

This started the removal of the law that had been on the books since 1926. After Brown made the decision, things moved quickly. The legislative process in Congress was lengthy, but the President signed it into law on December 18, 1974, thus ending forty-eight years of discrimination for navigators and, through General Brown's leadership, creating new opportunities for a deserving group of officers.

Gen. Lucius Clay discussed with me the relationship between Brown and his commanders. Clay stated that Brown told him when he became Chief, "I'm not going to run your commands. That's what you're hired to do. I'm going to set the policies. I expect you to carry out my policies loyally, faithfully, and effectively, but I'm not going to run your command. I'll let you know if I'm not happy with what you're doing."

"This is the way I think things should be run," said Clay. "I had the freedom to run my command with my own ideas of what command is all about. Everybody has a little different approach; yet the job gets done. Sometimes I think now we get too interested in having everybody shave on the same side of the face every morning and forget that other people just like to do it their own way."[50]

The bottom line with George Brown was that if he had confidence in you he left you alone to do your job. "I hadn't thought about it in that way until I tried to put down some specifics on my relationship with him," commented Bill McBride, former Vice Chief of Staff of the United States Air Force. "I never remember George giving me guidance by saying, 'This is what I want you to do, or this is what I expect my major commanders to do.' I never remember hearing him say that in commanders' conferences. But, indirectly, and on very specific subjects, he came through loud and clear on a few items.

"In the year that I was commander of Training Command," continued McBride, "George made only one visit to San Antonio. He came down to speak and stayed with us at Randolph. I fixed up an itinerary of things I wanted to brief him on, a half dozen items. George said, 'Hell, I don't want to do all that stuff. I want to sit and talk with you for a while. There's one subject on there that I'll sit still for a briefing on, but I don't want to look at the rest of that stuff. That's your job. Unless you want me to do something about it, I'm really not interested.'

"I didn't know it at the time and had difficulty interpreting his apparent lack of interest in Air Training Command. I didn't know whether he was aloof or set apart or whether he just didn't care about Air Training Command. I didn't fully realize his method of operating until I got to know him better when I went into the Vice Chief's job and he was Chairman and I saw him frequently. For the first time, I found George was a man who, if you weren't doing your job, heckled the hell out of you. There was no doubt where you stood with him. If I were to list one weakness of George Brown (and this really isn't a weakness), it was his being totally honest. There was no way that he could ever tell a lie. If he rehearsed a script with a lie in it for a hundred years, he would goof it up and tell the truth when he finally presented it. He couldn't lie. That was George Brown's makeup. I think he looked at some commanders carefully, was uneasy with them. I really do think he was satisfied with Air Training Command at that particular time."[51]

Brown could leave his commanders alone to do their jobs because of good judgment in selecting them, in knowing where he could place confidence, and in being able to get the best out of them. "George Brown liked to have faith in his staff," commented Lt. Gen. Joseph Wilson. "If he found a staff member wasn't supporting him, he got rid of him. If the relationship wasn't what he wanted, he found somebody else."[52]

Despite his time-consuming duties as Chief of Staff, Brown nonetheless maintained his interest and proficiency as a pilot. His own pilot, Glenn Jones, recalled, "I flew with him in the T–39. He was an avid flier and always flew takeoffs and landings. He enjoyed flying as an avocation, a sort of therapy to him. He could be overloaded with thoughts from the office, but when he took off his coat and sat down in the cockpit, the cares went off with the coat. He was also great with the instructor pilots. They were majors and lieutenant colonels usually, career pilots who had flown throughout their entire service; consequently, their areas of interest, and certainly career growths, were so far different you would think they would have nothing to talk about with General Brown. It was quite the opposite, however. He would talk about whatever the interest of the pilot was. He could make them feel at ease in a matter of moments. These trips taught me a lot about his disarming personality; he could get a man at ease and talking very quickly.''

Brown remained as unpretentious as Chief of Staff as he had been earlier in his career. For example, the Air Force wanted to produce a movie on him as part of its ''Air Force Now'' series. He didn't want to do that, however, and, when the request was made, said, ''I'm not interested in being a movie star.''

''I then did something rare,'' said Glenn Jones. ''I went back in with their request in hand and said, 'Sir, I can put together a visit to Andrews Air Force Base, with your doing all the things you normally do, including a tennis game, and never slow you down for a minute. You will never have to be on stage, never have to do anything that you don't do every time you go to a base. It won't impede your day in the least.' He said, 'I'll bet you can't.' It thus became a challenge to me to capture his day, a day in the life of the Chief.

''Indeed, he did not alter what he had agreed to do simply for the sake of the film. Everything in the film was what he did that day, including the tennis game, his lunch with the airmen, and the thing he enjoyed most, visiting the troops at the Speckled Trout, the outfit that does the testing on the KC–135, which he used to fly. He visited with them, having them show him a new piece of equipment on the airplane. Then he visited a National Guard unit. This was the winter of '73, when the fuel crisis had just come down on us. He asked them how this affected them. They said, 'So far we may come out 30 percent in flying time.' He said, 'I want you to tell me the first time your safety is endangered.' They assured him they would. He did the things that he did at every base. It drove the camera crew crazy because they would have to skip about every other thing he did to be at the next place. However, he wouldn't change his routine for them. We worked it out that the things they wanted to capture were at every other stop. He would be at one place and they would be racing trying to get to one place removed. It was frustrating, but turned out to be a delightful film. It was realistic and captured exactly what he did.''[53]

Another incident further illustrates Brown's humility despite his position as Chief of Staff; his reaction was the same as occurred earlier in Vietnam. "He told me one time," recalled his aide, Glenn Jones, " 'I never want honors at plane side. I don't want people coming out in uniform to form a rank and file for me at plane side.' So I was careful to pass that dictum along. One commander at a western base, however, had an honor guard he was proud of. Consequently, when we arrived at this base, there was the honor guard lined up. Brown saw them and yelled back to me, 'Glenn, did you tell them I don't want honor guards?' I said, 'Yes, sir, I did.' He got out and the commander was very happy to meet him, but he was immediately faced with a very irate four-star who said, 'Who ordered these men to be out here this time of day? It's after hours.' The commander said, 'I did.' Brown said, 'Well, it's a waste of their time and my anger.' It might have been different if it had been during regular duty hours rather than in the evening, but Brown was concerned that these men were not at home with their families." [54]

Brown's career in the Air Force was filled with acts of thoughtfulness and consideration for others, an important factor in his success. "My wife, Zita," reflected Bradley Hosmer, "particularly remembers an event that occurred during General Ryan's change of command and retirement party at Andrews. These were followed by a large informal gathering at the Officers' Club attended by many friends and well-wishers. In the middle of the gathering, General Brown came up and introduced himself to Zita, and in the most charming and forthcoming manner expressed his appreciation, in advance, for the support and understanding she would be called on to provide—by virtue of my working schedule in the coming months. After that conversation, I think she would cheerfully have sent me off to the bottom of the ocean on a research project or anything else because the man obviously had his whole fiber caught up in leading the Air Force and he inoculated those around him with the same enthusiasm." [55]

One of the highlights of Brown's career was his success in working with the United States Army. "I don't believe we should overlook recognizing his improving our relationship with the Army," pointed out General McBride. "Nobody has made a greater contribution to bringing the Army and the Air Force closer together than George Brown. I know Abrams would agree with that. It was a two-way street, not just one man. George really improved that relationship. He expected it of all of us.

"I'll give you a precise example involving an in-service training review. The Department of Defense was making a strong effort to cut down costs on technical training. One of their objectives was to eliminate duplicate schools, like those for cooks and bakers. They asked, 'Why do the Army, Air Force, and Navy have to have individual cooks' schools? Why can't we have a centrally located school with a small staff and do it professionally? Everybody cooks food the same way.' I remember George telling me, 'Be careful in this interservice training. I want you to do what's right for the Air Force. If you want combined schools, I will back your decisions.' There were people in the Air Force who took an extreme view, saying, 'Look, we have the best training establishment, the best school, the best facilities. We've worked on them for thirty years. Why should we compromise what we've done to combine and weaken our school and education system?' I was getting this kind of opinion from the personnel people: 'Hold the line; don't give up a thing unless we win something.' I had no pressure from him to push the Air Force position. He said, 'Do what's right and whatever decision you make, I'll back you 100 percent.' Ultimately, we combined half a dozen different schools. I think George would have been critical of me if he had found I didn't agree to combine something that made sense. If we could help the other services, we were to do it.''[56]

Another example of his concern for a good working relationship with the other services occurred at a commanders' conference where a briefing was presented that revealed a weak analysis by Army experts on the capability of their forces against the airfields in Communist bloc nations in the Eastern European area. The Air Force proceeded to do its own analysis which, when presented, would have been embarrassing for the Army. The officer responsible for the study, Maj. Gen. Robert Lukeman, recalled, "General Brown got the impression that this was something we had done behind the Army's back and that we were going to zap them. When we got through showing the weaknesses of the Army's study, he spoke up indignantly to everyone in the group, especially to me, and said, 'If you discovered that they made serious mistakes in their approach to the problem, and that their approach didn't hold water, why the hell didn't you go tell them?' He barely gave me a chance to answer. The important thing about his comment was his demonstration that he was an aboveboard guy. He was not parochial, did not try to conceal something from people in other services.''[57]

What kind of marks does Brown get in his short tenure as Chief of Staff? I asked this question of many of his major commanders and deputy chiefs of staff. Bill McBride, who held two major commands, responded: "One of his policies was maintaining a high quality of personnel in the Air Force. He said to me, 'I don't understand all this category I, II, III, IV business, and the recruiting system, and I'm not going to get a chance to go into it in detail. The only thing I want you to do is if you make any change in the people coming into the Air Force, I want you to raise the standards. Make them higher instead of lower. I will accept recruiting fewer people if you will assure me those that we're getting are higher quality.' ''[58]

Gen. Lucius Clay had this to say: "First of all, there was nobody at command level who didn't consider Brown as the man to be Chief of Staff. So there was unanimity in that we all had nothing but the greatest admiration for him. George was a unique man in that he had the ability to make a decision, decentralize the execution, and then walk off and say, 'Do your job.' He always had coherent programs, clearly outlined as he saw them in terms of budgets and political programs, getting programs through the Congress, what the administration was trying to do, and what the areas of concern were where the goals were not reflective of what we thought was the best way for the Air Force to go. I had a feeling that Brown really knew what the Chief of Staff's job was all about. He was the spokesman for air power, but he was not going to be the detail man who was going to sit down and check every left shoe every morning. He clearly stated what the goals were, why they had to be that way, and what he expected of each of his commands in order to move in that direction. This was always done in a friendly way, yet there was no question about who was running the show."[59]

Gen. Jack J. Catton of the Logistics Command said, "I'd give George very high marks as Chief and I was sorry to see him go. He was forthright, bold without being careless, thoroughly dependable. You could depend upon George to do the right thing regardless of environment. He would be heard and be positive in going on about it. He was an excellent commander with a good rapport with the people in the Air Force."[60]

Maj. Gen. Robert Lukeman said: "It never failed when he discussed some major issue of controversy with Secretary Schlesinger or the OSD staff with respect to Air Force objectives or force requirements, he came back having achieved understanding from them. He was tremendously effective in making Schlesinger understand the basis for Air Force views on a matter."[61]

A summary of the responses from various key subordinates produces this synthesis of his service as Chief: He was personally inspiring because integrity stood out. He always told it like it was, with no artifice; he laid it out on the table. He cared deeply about people as individuals, each DSC and ACS and their responsibilities, as well as each airman. He motivated people and provided inspiring leadership. He ensured that everybody on the Air Staff became involved in the major projects and objectives of the Air Force. Intercommunication between the many parts of the Air Force went to a very high peak under Brown. Staff members and commanders all became involved in one another's objectives with true understanding. He knew where the Air Force had been, where it should go and how it should get there. He accepted the responsibility of the job. He delegated much of the work to the staff, but if something went wrong, he took the blame and backed his people.

He had a close rapport with the Secretary of Defense and with his colleagues in the Joint Chiefs of Staff. When he had a session with the Secretary of Defense, he would come back, and within the bounds of propriety and executive privacy, would communicate the concerns of the Secretary to his senior staff so that they would know the environment in which they were working. He had a good rapport with Congress; they knew he would give them straight answers, and he came to them prepared.

Brown had hardly started his tour as Chief before he was considered for an even more important assignment. Gen. Horace Wade recalls a conversation with Secretary of the Air Force John McLucas. Wade said to him, " 'John, we've been grooming George Brown for a number of years, first to be Chief of Staff and next, Chairman. If the Air Force ever has a chance to have a Chairman it's George. You've got to start thinking about Brown's replacement.' He looked at me and said, 'Are you kidding? George just took over!' I said, 'That's right. But a new Chairman has to be appointed in the summer of 1974.' "[62]

Brown's tenure as Chief of Staff was brief. On May 14, 1974, after only eight-and-a-half months in that job, the President announced that he had been selected to succeed Adm. Thomas Moorer as Chairman of the Joint Chiefs of Staff. Not since September 30, 1960, had an Air Force officer held the position.

Although his new position was a great honor, it required him to give up the assignment he loved so much. "I was in George's office late one night," recalled Gen. Richard Ellis, then Brown's Vice Chief of Staff. "He told me, 'You know, I sort of wish I weren't leaving this job. I'm having a lot of fun. I enjoy the hell out of it. But, I guess when you have a chance to take the top job in your chosen profession, there's not much choice.' "[63] Like it or not, it was time for the Chairmanship.

NOTES

1. Personal interview with Gen. Horace Wade, USAF (Ret.), November 17, 1980.
2. Personal interview with James R. Schlesinger, 1981.
3. Personal interview with John L. McLucas, February 21, 1980.
4. Wade interview.
5. Personal interview with Lt. Gen. Joseph G. Wilson, USAF (Ret.), August 5, 1981.
6. Personal interview with Gen. William J. Evans, USAF (Ret.), 1981.
7. Personal interview with Maj. Gen. Harold R. Vague, USAF (Ret.), 1981.
8. Personal interview with Maj. Gen. Homer I. Lewis, USAF (Ret.), August 27, 1981.
9. Personal interview with Gen. Richard Ellis.
10. Personal interview with Maj. Gen. Robert P. Lukeman, USAF (Ret.), August 27, 1981.

11. Wilson interview.
12. Evans interview.
13. Letter from Col. Bradley K. Hosmer, USAF (Ret.), to EFP, August 3, 1979.
14. Lewis interview.
15. Personal interview with Col. Glenn Jones, USAF, November 14, 1980.
16. Ellis interview.
17. Personal interview with Lt. Gen. William Y. Smith, USAF, April 25, 1979.
18. Jones interview.
19. Hosmer correspondence.
20. Personal interview with Lt. Gen. A. J. Russell, USAF (Ret.), November 20, 1980.
21. Personal interview with Lt. Gen. George S. Boylan, Jr., USAF (Ret.), April 27, 1980.
22. Personal interview with Lt. Gen. Howard M. Fish, USAF (Ret.), March 8, 1980.
23. Boylan interview.
24. Personal interview with Gen. Lucius D. Clay, Jr., USAF (Ret.), September 19, 1981.
25. Smith interview.
26. Personal interview with Maj. Gen. Henry J. Meade, USAF (Ret.), April 1, 1981.
27. Personal interview with Gen. John W. Roberts, USAF (Ret.), March 6, 1980.
28. Smith interview.
29. Vague interview.
30. Crow interview.
31. Hosmer correspondence.
32. Personal interview with Lt. Gen. William W. Snavely, USAF (Ret.), March 3, 1981.
33. Ibid.
34. Fish interview.
35. Vague interview.
36. Evans interview.
37. Boylan interview.
38. Personal interview with Maj. Gen. Roy M. Terry, USAF (Ret.).
39. Personal interview with CMSgt. Thomas N. Barnes, USAF (Ret.), March 7, 1980.
40. Personal interview with Maj. Gen. William P. McBride, USAF (Ret.), May 4, 1979.
41. Keegan interview.
42. Wade interview.
43. Ibid.
44. Hosmer correspondence.
45. Wade interview.
46. Barnes interview.
47. Ibid.
48. Maj. Gen. Robert P. Lukeman, *Navigator,* Summer 1975, p. 18.
49. Jones interview.
50. Clay interview.
51. McBride interview.

52. Ibid.
53. Jones interview.
54. Ibid.
55. Hosmer correspondence.
56. McBride interview.
57. Lukeman interview.
58. McBride interview.
59. Clay interview.
60. Personal interview with Gen. Jack J. Catton, USAF (Ret.), September 18, 1981.
61. Lukeman interview.
62. Wade interview.
63. Ellis interview.

CHAPTER 20

CHAIRMAN, JOINT CHIEFS OF STAFF: JULY 1974–JUNE 1978

Lying ill with terminal leukemia in 1964, former Air Force Chief of Staff Gen. Thomas White called for protégé Robert Dixon to come see him. "He was on his deathbed," recalled Bob Dixon. "Knowing this, he told me, 'I want you, when George Brown becomes Chairman of the Joint Chiefs of Staff, to send him a wire and give him General White's congratulations.' " It was a prophecy that came true, a request Bob Dixon was happy to fulfill and did.[1]

There is a misconception that the original idea since the Chairman's position was created in 1949 was to rotate it among the services. At the time of Brown's appointment the position of Chairman had been in existence for twenty-five years. During that time the Army had held the job for fifteen years, the Navy for six, and the Air Force for only four. To many, the Air Force was long overdue to have one of its generals as Chairman, but Brown's selection did not occur because it was the Air Force's turn. He was the President's choice because he was the most qualified officer on active duty in all of the services although junior to the other Chiefs.

George Brown brought to the job of Chairman an exceptionally broad background in joint service matters. He had been military aide to the Secretary of Defense for four years; had headed JTF–2, a Joint Chief of Staff operation, for two years; and had been assistant to Chairman Earle G. Wheeler.

"In selecting General Brown as Chairman," stated a *New York Times* editorial of June 6, 1974, "Mr. Schlesinger was hoping not only to install a professional with an outlook similar to his, but also to invigorate the intellectual calibre of the Joint Chiefs, which by common Pentagon judgment has deteriorated over the last decade." The same newspaper aptly described General Brown's career as "a victory for the military professionals who work their way up the promotion ladder, stopping at all the right rungs on the way."[2]

Some of Brown's Air Force colleagues openly hoped President Nixon would nominate Army Chief of Staff Creighton Abrams to succeed Admiral Moorer as Chairman because they thought Brown was needed so badly as Air Force Chief of Staff. He certainly did not campaign for the job, but the Air Force realized that with his success in such broad areas of responsibility throughout his career he had to be a strong contender.

The responsibilities of the Chairman as spelled out in Title 10, Armed Forces, Section 142, are:

> (a) The Chairman of the Joint Chiefs of Staff shall be appointed by the President, by and with the advice and consent of the Senate, from the officers of the regular components of the armed forces. He serves at the pleasure of the President for a term of two years, and may be reappointed in the same manner for one additional term. However, in time of war declared by Congress there is no limit on the number of reappointments.

> (b) In addition to his other duties as a member of the Joint Chiefs of Staff, the Chairman shall, subject to the authority and direction of the President and the Secretary of Defense—

> (1) preside over the Joint Chiefs of Staff;

> (2) provide agenda for the meetings of the Joint Chiefs of Staff and assist them in carrying on their business as promptly as practicable; and

> (3) inform the Secretary of Defense, and, when the President or the Secretary of Defense considers it appropriate, the President, of those issues upon which the Joint Chiefs of Staff have not agreed.

> (c) While holding office, the Chairman outranks all other officers of the armed forces. However, he may not exercise military command over the Joint Chiefs of Staff or any of the armed forces.

One of the Chairman's most important responsibilities is the force structure of all U.S. military forces. What is his role in accomplishing this? "The development of overall force structure is achieved by a dialogue between the Joint Chiefs of Staff and the Secretary of Defense," Brown told me. "The product is submitted for approval ultimately by the Commander in Chief and the Congress. The cycle begins with the Joint Chiefs of Staff providing advice to the Secretary of Defense concerning military strategy based on the world situation and national security objectives as they are perceived from Presidential statements, National Security Council policy, expressions of congressional will, and prior decisions of the Secretary of Defense. This iterative process results in the Secretary of Defense issuing defense policy and planning guidance. Force planning then proceeds in the following manner:

1. The threat is examined and detailed threat estimates developed.

2. Against the threat, estimates are made of U.S. and allied forces needed to successfully defend against, and thus deter, an attack by a potential enemy by preventing him from being confident that he could achieve his objectives at acceptable cost.

3. The present and future forces and capabilities of our allies are assessed.

4. U.S. forces and capabilities are assessed.

5. Combined U.S.-allied capabilities are then compared with the threat and assessed as to adequacy.

6. U.S. force planning is adjusted and coordinated with our allies such that the combined capabilities are adequate to achieve mutual objectives against the threat at a prudent level of risk.

"The Joint Chiefs of Staff, the services, and the commanders of unified and specified commands all participate. This objective force is developed without specific dollar constraints, but the process insures that it is reasonably attainable from a fiscal standpoint. It provides a basis for appraising the risks involved in the adoption of any lesser force levels in that the objective force is considered that minimum essential to support the national military strategy with prudent risk.

"Applying this information, the Secretary of Defense issues further force, fiscal, and support planning and programming guidance. Upon receipt of this additional guidance, the JCS prepares for the Secretary a Joint Forces Memorandum which contains fiscally constrained force structure and levels, together with a reappraisal of the associated risks. The services then develop and submit for approval their manpower requirements. Thus, the strategy, fiscal and force planning goals, and the contribution of our allies, weighed against the threat, determine the mix and level of forces Congress is asked to provide in order to serve the nation's needs."[3]

One of Brown's first objectives as Chairman was to keep the American people informed of our defense needs. On February 5, 1975, in a speech to the Navy League, he commented:

> The military-industrial community of which we are a part has not done well in the past if we judge by the continual decline in military force and in our budget as a percentage of either total federal spending or gross national product. All of us must do a much better job of informing the public of our defense needs and that our national security requirements are vital when considering public expenditures and national priorities.[4]

A year and a half later, speaking to the Retired Officers Association in Philadelphia, Brown reiterated, "I believe our country's security is best achieved by telling the people where we stand . . . by speaking clearly and accurately of the challenges we face, by stating our needs openly and forthrightly, by admitting our shortcomings—and acting to correct them—as rapidly as we take credit for our achievements."[5]

There is a conflict in the limited funds available, even in a rich country such as the United States. Frequently, Brown used a quotation of Britain's Air Marshal Sir John Slessor that zeroed in on the inevitable clash and which presented Brown's point that "it is customary in democratic countries to deplore expenditures on armaments as conflicting with the requirements of the social services. There is a tendency to forget that the most important social service that a government can do for its people is to keep them alive and free."[6]

Brown was concerned about defense expenditures, especially when compared to those of the Soviet Union. In 1975, these expenditures fell to less than 6 percent of U.S. productive capacity, or to "the lowest point since the post-World War II demobilization." Conversely, the Soviets had "increased their real military expenditures by 3 to 5 percent each year."[7]

Inflation was also a constant problem to the Joint Chiefs. As Brown pointed out, "We feel the squeeze brought on by inflation, the cost of manpower, supplies, and equipment on the one side and the pressing needs for modernization and force readiness on the other." Brown gave his solution to these increased costs to "make every dollar buy a dollar's worth and every hour of our people's time a productive hour," further pointing out that the military was only 1 percent of our population and was at its lowest level in numbers since we had demobilized after World War II.[8]

In 1973, Secretary James Schlesinger decided that a study should be made to review thoroughly the superstructure of the Defense Department, its field organizations, and in particular, the major military command headquarters. This assignment was given to William Brehm, former Assistant Secretary in the office of the Secretary of Defense for Manpower and Reserve Affairs, who began it by talking with the individual Chiefs of Staff which brought him into close contact with Brown. "When I talked with General Brown," said Brehm, "I found that he was very positive about the whole idea of conducting this review, particularly after he became Chairman. When I would go out to field commands, for example, to Hawaii, Europe or Korea, Brown would always clear a path for me by getting in touch with the senior military people there. I always felt comfortable knowing that I had his support when visiting these places. This was important if I were to be effective. General Brown had the good judgment and vision to realize that the best way to maximize the success of this study was to see to it that it was supported."

There were some very significant changes that came about as a result of this study. For example, in Korea, three separate headquarters were merged into one, resulting in a substantial savings in personnel. But, as Brehm pointed out, "It wasn't just the people savings we were after. It also made life more interesting and more challenging for the people involved in the headquarters operation. They were spending less time running around coordinating papers and more time thinking about the substance of the papers."

Another result of this study was the change in the command situation in Hawaii. Gen. Creighton Abrams, Army Chief of Staff, was convinced that the headquarters in Hawaii was no longer needed. The Army wanted it phased out, saving at least 2,000 personnel spaces. When Abrams presented the Army's proposal, the Secretary of Defense would not agree to it unless the Chairman also accepted it. "General Brown did support it," said Brehm, "and this was important in making the change come about. He was positive and constructive. I think the word innovative is proper here. It applies because it took innovation on the military's part to make these things happen. It's not just a matter of closing a headquarters. One has to think about the functions to be retained."

A third area where changes were necessary was the Panama Canal Zone. At the time there were four headquarters there under a four-star general. Congressional critics had a field day with this situation, questioning the necessity for such extensive resources and accusing the military of trying to protect a four-star billet. "General Brown realized this and got involved personally," pointed out Brehm, "indeed, actively in the Canal Zone headquarters issues and helped us to formulate the revised headquarters arrangement and consolidate everything into one command under a three-star officer."

Having completed a review of the field commands, the study group turned inward and began to scrutinize the Pentagon organization itself. They ultimately concluded that there were too many people in the headquarters, and that there was too much functional redundancy. Leaders in the various services were encouraged to examine carefully their respective functions with an eye to consolidation wherever possible.

"Brown developed a tough plan, deciding to test every function within the organization of the Joint Chiefs," said Brehm. "Nothing escaped his review. He looked at every function, organization, and position, asking, 'Why are we doing this? Is this something the Joint Staff really needs to do? We've been doing this for fifteen years. Is it something we still need?' For example, the J-1, the manpower directorate within the Joint Staff, really wasn't necessary because the services basically took care of manpower, so there just wasn't much for the J-1 to do. So General Brown said, 'Let's phase it out.' He then went on and eliminated it."

Brown also eliminated the J-2, which had basically a communications function, by combining it with J-3 and with the Director of the Staff. In addition, he cut his staff by about 20 percent over a period of some eighteen months. Brehm concluded, "Part of George's effectiveness as a leader was his willingness to move out to do things. He was not reluctant, bureaucratically or otherwise, to accept something because that's the way it was always done. He did not think you should continue to do something just because of tradition. He was willing to ask the tough questions, and if he found a situation needed changing, he was willing to change it. I think that people look to a leadership position like the Chairman's for innovativeness and willingness to make change."[9]

Within a matter of days after Brown was sworn in as Chairman, he commented on the military posture of the United States vis-à-vis the Soviet Union. In a hearing before the Manpower and Personnel Subcommittee of the Senate Armed Forces Committee on August 13, 1974, he stated that the "strategic balance today remains in dynamic equilibrium. By some indicators the U.S.S.R. has a numerical edge which is offset by the United States' qualitative advantage. The U.S.S.R., however, has embarked upon a massive program of major strategic force improvements and deployments which, if not constrained by the negotiating process or balanced by major U.S. arms initiatives, will result in serious superiority over the United States in the years ahead.

"Our present strength is not so sufficient that we can be complacent. Our important interests can be threatened in the years ahead unless positive steps continue to improve the quality of our forces."[10]

During Brown's tenure, our national policy toward the Russians was known as "détente," a French word denoting relaxation of tension. Brown had definite ideas about the meaning of "détente," likening it to a word spelled similarly, "detent," which is defined as "having to do with weapons, such as the entire trigger mechanism of a pistol, also for uncocking a cocked pistol—that is, releasing the tension on the spring that moves the hammer. Détente could also be used to describe relaxing the tension of a taut bow-string." But, he warned, despite its definition of relaxing of tension, "in none of its meanings is there any suggestion that détente means friendship, trust, affection or assured peace."[11]

Brown fervently believed that military strength was essential for the implementation of the policy of détente. In a speech to the Comstock Club of Sacramento in 1974, he stated, "Our ability to negotiate within the spirit of détente must be based on a posture of strength and resolve. . . . The peace that we know today did not come as a gift. It has been earned by the courage and sacrifices of your Armed Forces." Later he declared, "If military strength is to undergird persuasion, reason and compromise, it must be of sufficient quantity and quality as to present a reasonable probability of its successful application if no reasonable alternative suggests itself."[12]

Soviet actions and military buildup made it increasingly clear that the U.S. had to be careful about détente. Brown stressed this point when he spoke at Duke University in 1974: "The recent emphasis on diplomacy, negotiations, and economic measures may tempt us to assume there is no longer a place for military power in the conduct of international affairs. But this would be a naive and wishful reading of history." He cited some of the successes in diplomacy in the Middle East in 1973, adding that "force either made possible a diplomatic solution, or was itself the final arbiter. In reality, persuasion and compromise lose some of their vitality if force, the ultimate sanction, is discounted."[13]

In a presentation to the Senate Appropriations Committee on February 2, 1976, Brown put his position in historical perspective: "At one time or another, it has been argued that with the advent of the crossbow, gunpowder, machine gun, airplane, submarine, and bomber, warfare had become so destructive that it could never occur again. And as you well know, wars continued with the adoption of those once unthinkable weapons and with the further development of new ones. In fact, it is my contention that all these arguments ignore a basic fact of international politics, one that has been proven repeatedly throughout history: national interests can be protected only by national strength."[14]

He continued to urge caution on détente throughout his tenure as Chairman. On May 17, 1975, he stated, "Americans . . . must be warned that it would be a dangerous delusion to cause a unilateral reduction in our military posture. From a position of military inferiority, the United States can neither successfully negotiate nor successfully deter."[15]

Frequently citing two U.S. presidents who said that as a nation we should "never fear to negotiate, but never negotiate out of fear," Brown added, "The weak can hope for peace, but without assurance. They simply must accept the future with little or no influence upon it."[16] To him, our search for peace began with America's strength. Our military was the foundation of that strength, and conciliation could only be a virtue in those who were thought to have a choice.

Brown became increasingly concerned about the future security of the United States. He felt that the military balance of power had been shifting away from the United States and the free world toward the Soviet Union, and that vital U.S. long-range interests might be jeopardized. He emphasized, "We sometimes forget that U.S. commercial, agricultural, and financial interests—those pursuits that make up the day-to-day activity of many Americans—could be drastically changed if this country could not protect its overseas interests and have free access to international markets."[17]

Realizing that the U.S. forces were lower in manpower and materiel than prior to the Vietnam War, and aware of the tremendous increase in Soviet military power, Brown warned his countrymen, "It may be the decision of the American people and the Congress that we no longer want to be a military power second to none. . . . If we are to disarm as a nation and accept second-class status, we should do so consciously rather than allowing the erosion of purchasing power for the Department of Defense to drive us . . . in that direction. . . . I maintain that the first claim on American resources should be our national security and the preservation of an international structure in which to sustain our way of life and in which we can prosper— not only next year, but into the future."[18]

While Brown held a firm belief in the necessity for U.S. military strength, he could nonetheless recognize the value of arms control as a means toward peace: "Our national security can be enhanced by both arms controls and arms programs—complementing, rather than conflicting with, each other. But as a nation, we must be prepared to maintain the military balance if arms controls should fail."[19] He felt that American military power had paved the way for such negotiations "aimed at reducing the chances of miscalculation and reducing the risk of nuclear war," but added that "we, of course, must take risks for peace, but these risks must be prudent. Arms control is a means, not an objective. The objective is peace."[20]

Brown's position regarding arms control was sensitive because he had to act as an intermediary between the President and the Joint Chiefs. Adm. James Holloway, CNO, put the situation in perspective when he stated: "The Chiefs were being relatively hard-nosed about the SALT II negotiations for two reasons. One, we wanted an equitable treaty, and two, we didn't want provisions in the treaty that would put pressures and requirements on our military that would really diminish our capabilities in other areas. George, I remember on one occasion, called a meeting of the JCS for about four o'clock in the afternoon. He was coming back from the White House, and he said, 'We've had a long hard session. The President is being pushed hard to adopt this plan, and the feeling is that we will probably get agreement from the other side. I had to tell the President that the Chiefs were not supportive of it. You know, guys, this is real rough because I'm the bad guy to everybody sitting around the table, and you guys have given me a hard position. I want you to know the pressure I'm under over there.' Then he laughed and said, 'But don't change a thing.'

"What he was really telling us was that we had to vote our consciences and that even though it was tough, even though he was bucking the President, the Secretary of State, the national security advisor, and the SALT advisor, George was hanging in there. And he was saying, 'Mr. President, it's your judgment, but I'll have to be honest with you and tell you that if you make this decision, the Chiefs are going to support you, but you'll be going against their advice. And, if we get before the Senate and somebody asks how we advised you, we're going to have to tell the truth.' George laid it out in the clearest of terms, but he was under great pressure. He could have come back and said, 'You guys are wrong. I'm going to give a little bit.' But he didn't because, number one, he believed in the Chiefs, and two, he had the guts to play it absolutely straight with both sides, with the President and with the Chiefs."[21]

I asked Secretary of Defense Harold Brown to comment on Brown's leadership and to cite any specific incidents. He replied, "His loyalty and character were outstanding. In 1977, we were putting the SALT positions together, and some of the things being proposed were deep cuts which were substantial departures from what had gone before. There were significant changes and modifications in the direction the negotiations were taking, things like additional limitations on warheads and their numbers, for example. They were changes that were advantageous, in my judgment, to the United States. But they did involve a need to rethink the problem because they would have involved limitations on us as well as the Soviets that had not previously been contemplated. George was able to get the Chiefs to agree to an open-minded approach on this. I won't say he talked them around. In fact, before this got very far, he got sick, so he really wasn't able to carry this through. But I found that he was able to get the Chiefs to take a more open-minded view than they had been willing to take in previous years."[22]

One of the reasons for Brown's strong stance regarding U.S. military power was his awareness that public understanding and support of our national security policy are essential to its ultimate success. After the withdrawal of U.S. forces from Vietnam, there was a great deal of doubt whether U.S. citizens would be willing to give their military the moral and financial support it needed. In a dinner address on May 17, 1975, Brown pointed up the need for a reaffirmation of American strength and purpose: "In the wake of the Southeast Asia tragedy, much is being written and said at home and abroad about U.S. dependability as an ally and the credibility of our foreign commitments. In my opinion, we have got to face this issue head-on and reestablish our national credibility with our allies, with our adversaries, and, especially, with ourselves. It gives one pause to see public opinion polls which show that a majority of Americans would not intervene militarily to protect any foreign country except Canada, which is hardly one of the most threatened nations in the world. I believe that we must begin by restoring our national self-confidence, and to do this we must build up our economic and military strength. And I further believe that we can accomplish both these strength-building tasks by devoting the necessary share of our gross national product to national security."[23]

While Brown's position as Chairman gave him increased responsibility in matters of national security, his role was different from that as Chief of Staff about "people" matters. "The detailed responsibility for acquiring and training our authorized forces resides, of course, in each of the services," he commented in a speech soon after he became Chairman. "I have no direct responsibility for the assignment, adequacy, and retention of the men and women of the services. I do, however, have an abiding interest in the people of the armed forces. The most efficient and most modern weapon is without meaning unless it is manned by proficient professionals willing to put nation above self. Thus, the personnel problems confronting the military services today relate not only to adequate numbers but most importantly, to quality, a factor which cannot be ignored in a time of complex tasks and highly sophisticated equipment.

"The Congress has acted positively to assist our armed forces to achieve an all-volunteer force by raising the level of compensation, as well as authorizing incentives for enlistment. The services, in turn, are making progress in improving the quality of life of the young men and women in service. The success or failure of our national defense investment depends, in the last analysis, upon our success in attracting outstanding young men and women who will seek a full military career and accept the sacrifices of a life of service to their country."[24]

Brown continued to be aware of problems affecting the personnel of all the services, being concerned about intangibles for them. "A critical element of military power, more important than individual weapons systems and force deployments," he stated, "is people. Unjustified criticism of the military establishment is, in my opinion, detrimental to the best interests of our country. Those uniformed people who serve the nation in peacetime and stand ready to make the sacrifices inherent in war require an occasional word that is other than critical. We accept and appreciate constructive criticism; abuses must be exposed and corrected. However, we will not attract to military service the kind of individual needed in the all-volunteer force if the image of career service people is that of inept second-class citizens."[25]

He thought that the military was in danger of losing some of the outlook that service to one's country was a calling and not just a job: "Another area I'm concerned about is the attitude that some people are taking toward our men and women in uniform. More and more I sense that these servicemen and women are being viewed as employees—like any other employees.

"My concern is that this view of our soldiers, sailors, marines, and airmen will provide a basis for breaking faith with them. The idea of informal contract is being eroded as people overlook the service aspects of military life and the special liabilities of our people in uniform; in their place are concepts of employment and contract. All of you know the special costs of military life: frequent dislocations, separation from families, inconveniences that affect the entire family, the considerable personal risk—and, of course, the possibility of death.

"When these freely given contributions are considered, it is obvious that there's much more to military service than employment, and much more to our military benefit programs than contract fulfillment. There must be a recognition of the special nature of military service.

"You see this change of attitude in the current review of the retirement program. Concern for retirement benefits among retirees, as far as I can ascertain, is not based on any abstract philosophical or contractual argument. It is based on faith—faith that went with the commitments made years ago that in exchange for years of hard, and often dangerous, service—replete with dislocations and inconveniences of service life—servicemen and women would be able to enjoy a decent retirement, sustained by a respectable income and supported by many of the services provided to active-duty members.

"I don't know what the outcome on retirement benefits will be. I am concerned by the trend, however. If we try to substitute a contract attitude for this fundamental faith, then we have weakened the whole basis of military service."[26]

THE DUKE UNIVERSITY SPEECH

On November 13, 1974, an article appeared on the front page of the *Washington Post* with the headline, "Head of Joint Chiefs Criticizes Jewish Influence in the U.S." This story sparked a controversy that almost ended Brown's career less than five months after his appointment as Chairman of the Joint Chiefs of Staff. The article, written by Michael Getler, a *Washington Post* staff writer, opened with: "Gen. George S. Brown, the Chairman of the Joint Chiefs of Staff, has publicly suggested that Israel has too much influence in the U.S. Congress and that, he said, Jews 'own, you know, the banks in this country, the newspapers.' " The article went on to say that he suggested that if a severe new oil embargo caused not merely inconvenience but suffering among people in this country, Americans might "get tough-minded enough to set down the Jewish influence in this country and break that lobby."[27]

Brown's explanation to Congress of the incident was: "I appeared at the Duke University Law School at their invitation, to speak to the students and the faculty on, I believe it was, the tenth of October 1974. It was a small, informal gathering, and in the question and answer period, a question arose about the problem of Israel and the United States' possible involvement, which I did not go into in depth because I felt it would be inappropriate. And a question followed, because I obviously wasn't completely forthcoming in the first question—with intent. And I tried to answer a very seriously involved question, and I did it so poorly, with the result that I apparently offended some members of the Jewish race."[28]

The actual statement made at Duke was: "Now, in answer to the question of would we use force in the Middle East, I don't know. I hope not. We have no plans to. It is conceivable, I guess, in fact kind of almost as bad as the 'Seven Days in May' thing, but you conjure up a situation where there is another oil embargo and people in this country are not only inconvenienced and uncomfortable, but suffer, and they get tough-minded enough to set down the Jewish influence in this country and break that lobby.

"It's so strong," he continued at Duke, "you wouldn't believe now. We have Israelis coming to us for equipment. We say, 'We can't possibly get the Congress to support a program like that.' They say, 'Don't worry about the Congress. We'll take care of the Congress.'

"Now this is somebody from another country, but they can do it. They own, you know, the banks in this country, the newspapers. You just look where the Jewish money is in this country."[29]

A reporter was present, studying at Duke University on sabbatical. A student recorded Brown's speech, together with the question and answer period (although not for attribution) and mentioned it to the reporter. Then Michael Getler of the *Washington Post* informed Brown that they had the story and were going to run it, and asked him if he had anything to say. Brown responded that he could not deny making the statements, but that it did not mean that he had any anti-Semitic views. If anything, it meant that he was not concerned about the faith of an individual or his beliefs. He felt he probably should have been more aware of the problem of his words, but not to indicate that he had any feelings against the Jewish people at all.

The November 13 article in the *Washington Post* stated clearly that as Air Force Chief of Staff, Brown had instigated the American arms airlift to Israel in 1973 that was widely credited with helping to stave off military disaster for the Israelis. That reminder, however, did not prevent the wave of criticism that followed.

"I called the commander of the Jewish War Veterans," said Brown before a congressional committee, "when I heard he was going to hold a press conference at noon that day. . . . I phoned Judge Rivner . . . in Philadelphia and identified myself and told him that I had sent him a cable apologizing because I felt it was a group with whom I could relate. After all, I had fought in three wars with members of his organization.

"And he said he appreciated my calling and thanked me very much. But, he said, 'I want you to know that this won't change our position.' And I said, 'I didn't know you had a position.' He said, 'Yes, we have wired the President and have asked him for your hide.' I said, 'On the strength of a newspaper story, you did that?' "[30]

The national coordinator of Jewish War Veterans, Seymour Weisman, called General Brown's comments "an open invitation to the Arabs to renew the oil embargo and blame it on the Jews." Mr. Weisman also said that if Mr. Ford did not fire General Brown, his group would seek action by Congress.[31]

In addition to the Jewish War Veterans wanting General Brown out of office, the Anti-Defamation League of B'nai B'rith made the charge that General Brown's comments "are not only false, but contemptible, and have an illiterate odor of prejudice and malice."[32] Rabbi Arthur Hertzberg, president of the American Jewish Congress, sent a telegram to President Ford saying that General Brown's remarks demonstrated "a degree of ignorance and susceptibility to classic anti-Semitic propaganda that cast grave doubt on his ability to serve in his present critically important position."[33]

A November 14 editorial in the *Washington Post* commented:

> Within the Pentagon, Brown has been held in high regard and there was hope that this episode would blow over and that the general could stay on as the nation's highest ranking military officer.
>
> But within the administration and in some quarters of Congress, questions about Brown's future have been raised focusing not only on his comments but on whether his voicing them in public reflects on his abilities as Chairman of the Joint Chiefs.
>
> In general, administration sources believed Brown's future is "tenuous," dependent on how events unfold. There was concern that his comments could complicate U.S. Middle East policy by raising false conceptions among Arab Leaders. There was also some concern about the effect on Jewish members of the armed forces.
>
> Within the Pentagon, where officials both publicly and privately said there had never been a hint of anti-Semitism in Brown's previous comments or actions, there was a sense of bewilderment at what had happened.
>
> Brown's comments at Duke about Jewish influence, in general, were directed at the strength of the Israeli lobby in getting its way in the U.S. Congress, a point which has been made in milder language by some U.S. legislators.
>
> But Brown made an additional statement that the Jews, "own, you know, the banks in this country, the newspapers. You just look at where the Jewish money is in this country." It was that comment, widely viewed as an ethnic slur, which senior officials in and out of the Pentagon and White House said yesterday sent shock waves through the Ford administration.[34]

Brown immediately apologized for the unfortunate interpretation of his comments. "I deeply regret my remarks at Duke University. . . . They were both unfortunate and ill-considered and certainly do not represent my convictions.

"In particular, the remarks might mistakenly lead to the wholly erroneous inference that American citizen groups do not enjoy in this nation the privilege of expressing their views forcefully. What are called pressures lie at the very heart of democracy. We in Defense know that; we experience pressure from contractors, pressures from those opposed to defense expenditures, pressures from foreign governments.

"Moreover, my comments could be read to suggest the American Jewish community and Israel are somehow the same. Americans of Jewish background have an understandable interest in the future of Israel parallel to similar sentiments among other Americans, all of whom at one time or another trace their descent to other lands.

"I do in fact appreciate the great support and deep interest in the nature of our security problems in our defenses that the American Jewish community has steadily demonstrated, and I want to reemphasize that my unfounded and all too casual remarks on that particular occasion are wholly unrepresentative of my continuing respect and appreciation for the role played by Jewish citizens, which I have reiterated to the Jewish War Veterans."[35]

This apology, declared the *Washington Post,* "stopped short of a direct retraction." Indeed, Pentagon spokesman William Beecher was quoted as saying, "I will leave it up to your own judgment whether it represents a retraction."[36]

Nor did the apology ward off further criticism. On November 14, the *Washington Post* published an article under the headline "Ford Scores General on Jewish Remarks." The article stated that Ron Nessen, the White House press secretary, had commented that "the President considers General Brown's remarks ill-advised and poorly handled" and that they "in no way represent the views of any senior officer of his administration, military or civilian." Nessen then went on to inform the reporters that the President felt very strongly about this matter and had communicated his reaction to Brown's superior, Secretary of Defense Schlesinger. Asked by the press if the President had rebuked General Brown, Nessen responded, "I wouldn't discourage you from saying that."[37]

Secretary Schlesinger stated to reporters that Brown's comments were "unfortunate and regrettable," but he still retained confidence in him. "I intervened with the President to some extent," the Secretary said to me. "We had to turn public opinion around and calm down the Jewish community. Some were demanding he be fired. I listened to the complaints, explaining the disadvantages if George were to leave the service."[38]

President Ford summoned General Brown to the White House and, according to *U.S. News and World Report* (November 20, 1974), "personally rebuked him." However, the President at a later press conference said, "I have no intention of asking General Brown to resign. . . . He has been an excellent Chairman of the Joint Chiefs of Staff. He made a mistake. He has recognized it. He is going to continue as Chairman. . . ."

A *Post* editorial of November 14 said of the apology and the statements from President Ford and Secretary of Defense James R. Schlesinger, "What is missing from the general's superiors is some sign of awareness of the impropriety of *any* public statements by the Chairman of the Joint Chiefs about the conduct of this country's Mideast policy."[39]

In response to various Jewish groups demanding General Brown's resignation, a Pentagon spokesman said that Defense Secretary James R. Schlesinger "continues to have confidence" in General Brown and "realizes this was a very unfortunate misrepresentation of the general's opinions." The Jewish War Veterans said that if President Ford did not dismiss General Brown, it would work through Congress to obtain his dismissal.[40]

In a speech given by Brown on November 25, 1974, in Sacramento, California, to the Comstock Club, Brown said:

> And, now, one final thought. I could not address a group of distinguished Americans without some reference to the recent controversy I unwittingly stirred up by my statement at Duke University, which, over a month later, has understandably produced public controversy.
>
> In response to a question from a student on a very complex and difficult subject, I provided an unthinking shorthand answer. In an all too casual fashion, I used inaccurate words, poorly chosen at random, without knowledge of their emotional impact. I meant no affront. On every possible occasion, I have expressed my concern at having unintentionally offended my fellow Americans, not merely Americans of Jewish faith.
>
> More than anything else, I am both awed and appalled by the divisiveness this incident has caused. I understand the upset and dismay that have been expressed. I have received some letters of support of a type I totally reject as alien to America and alien to me. Polarization of our society is contrary to our traditions and clearly not in the best interests of the nation.
>
> There are two lessons that I have learned: First, I have learned a good deal about the corporate structure of banks and newspapers, and in addition, I have learned how little I previously knew about that subject. Second, I have learned that the strategic direction of the armed forces in the defense of America is my forte and is a full-time job. With this in mind, I intend to avoid even the appearance of dealing with anything else.[41]

But the controversy continued. Senator William Proxmire of Wisconsin and Congresswomen Bella Abzug and Elizabeth Holtzman, both of New York, issued statements charging General Brown with anti-Semitic statements and demanding his dismissal. Senator Thomas J. McIntyre of New

Hampshire demanded full-scale hearings into Brown's comments and also demanded his resignation, stating that he "has lost his claim to public trust" because of his remarks about Jews.[42]

There was great concern that Brown had weakened his effectiveness because of these remarks and that he would thus be hampered in being a forceful spokesman on behalf of the military, particularly before a budget-minded Congress.

The Senate Armed Services Committee met behind closed doors on November 25, 1974, to discuss, among other things, Senator McIntyre's demand for General Brown's resignation. Joining McIntyre's request for an inquiry were Senators Henry Jackson of Washington, Howard Hughes of Iowa, and Stuart Symington of Missouri.

Senator McIntyre told reporters, "The general's statement was more than just a stab at the Jewish lobby. . . . Does he feel our policy in the Mid-east is incorrect? Does he feel the number one military man should be commenting on it and making such stupid remarks as he made? It's a matter of civilian control of the military."[43]

Senator Stennis opposed McIntyre's position, saying that "General Brown made a mistake, he overspoke himself, he got out of bounds. . . . but he has been reprimanded by the President, he has apologized. . . . I think he's a very fine military officer. . . . If he was arrogant, unyielding, uncompromising, that would be a different matter, but he has recognized his error and shown contrition."[44]

Eventually, the committee refused, by an 11 to 4 vote, to open an official inquiry into the alleged anti-Semitic remarks by General Brown, closing the incident.

There were other responses, however, which were less emotional. Nationally syndicated columnists Rowland Evans and Robert Novak stated in a commentary appearing in the November 18 *Washington Post*, "Behind the outrageously over-blown slurs on American Jews by General George Brown is his sober, well-justified concern at the Pentagon over the dream of ever more costly military aid to Israel at a time of growing Congressional resistance to defense spending.

"Accordingly, the General's blunt warning at Duke University last month that Israel's influence in Congress is 'so strong you wouldn't believe it,' had a solid foundation. Leaving aside his gratuitous, untrue and grossly offensive crack about American Jews owning 'the banks in this country, the newspapers,' Brown's warning about Israel's control of the Congress is reflected in the vast transfer of scarce military supplies to Israel."

The article went on to comment that the United States spent $2.2 billion to assist in the October '73 war, and that the Israelis were supplied with late model M–60 tanks that were airlifted out of United States military depots in West Germany and flown to the Mideast battlefield. There were numerous other military supplies also transferred.

"There are other examples of the dangerous draw-down of American military capabilities," continued Evans and Novak, "forced on the Pentagon by the October war. For instance, the Air Force today is short of the small percentage of the F–4 fighter aircraft—the mainstay of Israel's air force—that is equipped with extremely costly electronic countermeasures (ECM). A very high percentage of the small number of those aircraft the United States had went to Israel.

"But the biggest problem was the shortage in the number of M–60 tanks. In short, the emotional preoccupation in Congress with defense of Israel short circuits Pentagon fears about U.S. influence throughout the vast Moslem world, particularly in the Arab oil states. It is a little-known fact that the Air Force pilots today are restricted to extremely short flight time to conserve fuel. Likewise, the Navy's 'streamlined days' for front-line warships have been drastically reduced."[45]

Further balanced insight was provided by columnist Joseph Alsop, who said in his syndicated column in November 1974:

> You can learn a lot about the times we live in from the latest flap about the alleged anti-Semitism of the Chairman of the Joint Chiefs of Staff, Gen. George S. Brown. . . .
>
> As to the charge of fundamental anti-Semitism, it is enough to note Gen. Brown's record in the Yom Kippur war. On that occasion, he and his intelligence advisers foresaw Israel's desperate need for resupply in many categories of arms at least six days before the order to resupply Israel was issued by the White House.
>
> By Gen. Brown's command, all that could be provided for Israel by the Air Force—which he then headed—was therefore assembled in readiness at the points of embarkation during the six days of grace. Preplanning for the airlift to Israel was also done. Without these steps, it may be doubted whether the resupply of Israel would have been sufficiently speedy in 1973.
>
> As to what Gen. Brown actually said at Duke University, there were some things that are plainly pretty hard to take. One such was the reference to "where the Jewish money is in this country." . . .
>
> Finally, there is Gen. Brown's forecast that serious American anti-Semitism may result from another Mid-East war accom-

panied by an oil embargo imposed because of U.S. aid to Israel —and there is no advocate more convinced than this reporter who has heard the same gloomy forecast from Israeli and Jewish-American friends. If the problem arises, as may well happen, it will merely be another of those problems that every decent American has to gird himself to fight and to solve from time to time.

In short, Gen. Brown mainly said in semi-private what informed and thinking Israelis and Jewish-Americans have long been saying among themselves in real privacy. Instead of denouncing Gen. Brown for anti-Semitism, it would therefore be wiser to remedy the real cause of the trouble that so worries Gen. Brown.

The real cause is the current lunacy of the leftwing Democrats and the liberal-intellectuals. Despite the Israelis, this lunacy has now left us with a defense program little richer than the weakened fake-defense program of the late Secretary Louis A. Johnson, which in turn produced the Korean War.[46]

Perhaps one of the best perspectives was provided by Israeli Prime Minister Yitzhak Rabin, who said on December 6, 1974, that Gen. George S. Brown, as U.S. Air Force Chief of Staff, "probably helped Israel during the last war more than anyone else did." Rabin, speaking to high school students in Tel Aviv, expressed fear that General Brown's remarks might result in "too much talk about the Jewish lobby," and cautioned that exaggerating the effectiveness of the Jewish pressure could boomerang against Israel. To Rabin, the United States supported Israel because the interests of the two countries coincided, not because of Jewish influence.[47]

On November 18, 1974, fourteen American Jewish leaders met privately with Defense Secretary Schlesinger. After this meeting, the Jewish group decided not to press for the resignation of General Brown as Chairman of the Joint Chiefs of Staff at that time. They all agreed that the discussions be "off the record," and after it was over, neither Secretary Schlesinger, nor anyone on his staff, nor any of the Jewish leaders who attended the meeting would make any comment to reporters other than to say that the meeting was "helpful and worthwhile."

Gen. Ross Milton, a friend of George Brown since childhood days, offers his personal comments on George Brown's difficulties in the aftermath of the Duke incident: "We had a long talk about this in his office. He told me the full circumstances of what happened. I thought it was curious the way the *Washington Post* sat on the story until a time when it suited them to break it. I have to give a lot of credit to Schlesinger for holding things together for George. It came early in his tenure as Chairman, and left him probably more bothered than anything else that ever happened in his career—the fact that he came in for such an attack. The funny thing was that the military thought he said just what should have been said. He had the support of all of us.

"We knew that George was not anti-Semitic. He was just stating the facts—that the influence of the Israeli lobby was a powerful factor in a lot of things this country did. I think that what was bothering George at the time was that we had already pulled down our readiness very consciously to build up the Israelis. The thing that sticks out in my mind is that he really did give Schlesinger quite a bit of credit."[48]

Lt. Gen. William Smith, Brown's assistant while Chairman, said, "One of Brown's weaknesses was that since he was so straightforward and honest, he assumed other people would be the same. When someone asked him a question, he would tell what he thought. He would expect that, unless he knew it was on the record when he would have to be more careful, other people would respect the fact that his comments were off the record. When you take his comments at Duke University and put them into context, what he was saying was not nearly as bad as it sounded when taken out of context. George certainly was not anti-Semitic, nor was he malicious. But he groped when he answered questions and sometimes expressed things very graphically, with a quite truthful element. He had such faith in people that if something like that were said, he would expect people to say, 'No, no. That's not really what he meant.' He just had so much faith in other people."[49]

A former classmate of Brown at the National War College wrote as follows to me: "I also wrote to George Brown to lend him support when he was accused of being an anti-Semite. I believe it was known that I was Jewish, and I thought the note might be helpful. I did not believe he was an ideologue of any kind and could not be an anti-Semite even if he had some erroneous notions that he'd never checked out. Again, I got a friendly, first-name reply that made it clear success had not gone to his head."[50]

Secretary Schlesinger summed up this stage of the incident: "George was candid, straightforward. When he went public, he did the same thing. I told him he was going to have to issue a statement. He said, 'I have given offense. As a gentleman therefore I must make amends.' "[51]

As Brown's two-year term was coming to an end, there was speculation that he wouldn't be renominated for a second two-year term because of the Duke incident. Senator Robert Taft, at the confirmation hearing for a second term as Chairman, referring back to the Duke speech, asked of General Brown, "You stated that in two of the matters you were wrong (meaning Jewish interest in U.S. newspapers and banks). What was the third matter you were referring to?" Brown responded, "The third matter that I felt—and it was a matter of opinion—that the Jewish community in the United States had an undue influence on the Congress of the United States."

Then Taft asked, "Do you still feel that is true?" Brown responded, "In all candor, I do." He then went on to explain, "But I feel that that is not unusual. There are other special interest groups that have influence or seek to achieve influence on the Congress of the United States. But I will hasten to add that I don't think this necessarily works to the disadvantage of the United States in all cases."

As the interrogation continued, Senator McIntyre asked, "Why do you think they have an undue influence?" Brown responded, "Well, Senator, let me say that . . . [it] caused me, because of my concern and the obvious interest it stimulated in the committee, to go back and look up the definition of the word 'undue,' because I am not a lawyer. . . .

"The Chairman mentioned to me yesterday that 'undue' had this dishonest or nonright, improper connotation. I think probably a more accurate word for what my reaction to this whole thing should be is 'unusual.' And the unusual came . . . more from the Israeli side really. I have never had an officer of a uniform of another country talk to me as the Israeli officer talked to me about how they would handle the Congress, and I must say that this made a tremendous impression upon me.

"And I think that the word 'unusual' is more accurate of my description of what I was trying to acknowledge, in all candor . . . with the connotation and the definition you have laid out so clearly."

Senator Nunn asked Brown, "Do you think, then, the influence is undue?" He responded, "No, I never implied, and I wouldn't now, that there is anything sinister, or wrong, or illegal in any of their actions at all."[52]

Harold Brown, Secretary of Defense under President Carter, said of this issue, "I found when I came in as Secretary, we had to address whether George Brown would be kept on as Chairman. Vice President Mondale had said during his campaign that George Brown shouldn't be dogcatcher. Now, he was willing to take it back, and I took a rather firm position that it would be a mistake to let him go. I felt that George had made a bad blunder and told him so. But for a new administration to come in and change the Chairman on the basis of statements made months ago or political statements made by an incoming party would set a very bad precedent.

"I also told George that in my judgment the situation could be salvaged, and it was. We agreed that he would be more careful about future speeches, and he was. Of course, once you make a mistake like that you've got a lot of people out gunning for you, like the press. But one salutory effect was that

there are always military people who fail to comprehend the political consequences of their unguarded remarks, whether on domestic politics or on
international politics, and having gone through this himself, he became
quite sensitive to this risk in other senior military people, and so he was able
to pass the word to be very careful what they might say."

I asked Secretary Brown if General Brown's effectiveness was less in the
Carter administration because of the Duke speech. He replied, "I think
there was a certain suspicion at the beginning on the part of some of the
political people in the administration who didn't know him. This suspicion
didn't apply to me or to Secretary of State Cyrus Vance. We had known him
for sixteen years and thought highly of him. I was scientific advisor to Secretary McNamara and Vance was legal counsel when George was the Secretary's military assistant. So there was never any problem with us. As time
went by and the new people in the White House got to know George, the
problem eased there."[53]

Although some senators opposed Brown's second term, the Chairman
of the Senate Armed Forces Committee, Senator John Stennis, ended the
controversy by stating, "I never heard of anyone making a more complete,
total statement of regrets and apology to the President of the United States
than did General Brown, and the completeness and the sincerity of it was
just as total as was the statement itself. And I was sorry that this thing happened, and he was sorry, but I never saw a more complete recovery and
sincere apology. And I think it is fully understood. I know it is by me."[54]
The vote was taken, and Brown entered into another two-year term in our
nation's highest military position.

There were some, however, who could still see some humor in the incident in spite of the bitterness engendered by the whole matter. "I can recall," said Gen. James Knight, "that after President Jimmy Carter took
over, he came down to the Pentagon for a briefing with General Brown,
who was then Chairman. They were on their way to the situation room,
walking down the hall. General Brown said the President stopped and said
to him, putting his hand on General Brown's shoulder, 'I'll forgive you for
Duke if you'll forgive me for *Playboy.*' "[55]

A final perspective to this controversy and Brown's leadership throughout this incident was provided by Gen. Andrew Goodpaster, who commented, "You're vulnerable to that kind of thing at all times. You have to
face the question, 'Do I pull in my shell and pull that around me, or do I try
to do my job?' You do your job and take the risk that you're going to be
presented and, I think, misrepresented, as in these cases. If you talk in confidence and you talk speculatively and if somebody breaches the confidence,
you're vulnerable. You have to make a decision about playing it safe and

cozy, or speaking up and giving your views. The man that I admire is he who will step up and take the risks."[56]

CRISIS LEADERSHIP AS CHAIRMAN

In the Pentagon there are a number of passageways named after certain of our great military leaders. Perhaps the best known are the Marshall, Eisenhower, and Bradley corridors. Just off the Bradley corridor is one known as Chairman's Hall. Along this corridor are photographs of former Chairmen, and underneath each is a brief sketch of his contributions. Under George Brown's photograph is the comment:

> During his tenure as Chairman, General Brown strived for increased efficiency and combat readiness within the constrained United States military force structure under the unified and specified commands, and for improved crisis management and command/control of those forces.
>
> Crisis military operations included: The 1975 evacuation of United States and foreign nationals from Phnom Penh, Cambodia, and Saigon, South Vietnam, just prior to their fall to Communist forces; the 1975 recovery of the merchant ship S.S. *Mayaguez* from hostile Cambodian forces; the evacuation in 1976 of United States and foreign nationals from war-torn Beirut, Lebanon; and the increased military alert of United States Army officers. In 1975–76, the first major reorganization of the Joint Chiefs of Staff since 1958 took place.

Several of the events will be described because they offer examples of General Brown exercising "crisis" leadership.

THE CYPRUS PROBLEM

Brown's first crisis as Chairman involved the Turks and the Greeks who were warring over Cyprus. The United States had to evacuate all foreign nationals, primarily American and British. "This was my first association with George Brown as my boss in a crisis kind of situation," recalled Lt. Gen. Ray Sitton, a member of the staff of the Joint Chiefs of Staff. "I was very comfortable from the outset working for him. He was very solid; no panic, no excitement. He would sit down and carefully consider the situation and the facts involved, what your capabilities were as opposed to those of the other fellow, as well as his probable intentions. He then came up with his recommended course of action and presented that to the White House, the Secretary of Defense, or the Congress. Brown was a cool customer, one who always carried the ball for us based on our advice. We found we had a real obligation to make sure that we gave him the best available advice. He was a delegator of authority, so if you had the responsibility for getting a job done, you had the authority to do it."[57]

In addition to the evacuation of U.S. nationals from Cyprus, the JCS were concerned over the safeguarding of nuclear weapons deployed to that area, although under the guard of U.S. troops. "At that time, while I was Acting Chairman," recalled Adm. James Holloway, "George was off on a trip, and it was my first exposure to this sort of crisis. The Secretary and I talked about the situation and he said, 'Well, let me try to get hold of George. I know he'd like to get back.' So I got in touch with him, but George said, 'No, I'm not coming back; you are Acting Chairman. That's the way the system is set up and that's the way it will be. I have full confidence in you and the other Chiefs to do the job. If I didn't, I wouldn't go away in the first place. I think it undermines the system for me to have to run back often to play this role.' This was how George played the game, producing two results: It gave me enormous respect for George and reinforced the bonds of loyalty that were already there. It also made us grow into the role where we could do the job better in performing in a purple suit fashion as members of the JCS."[58]

"As the evacuation progressed," said General Sitton, "Brown returned and was in the National Military Command Center. If there was a lull or critical things that had to be taken care of, he would disappear, but soon he'd be back, an on-the-scene kind of supervisor. By no means does this imply that General Brown came in and sat down and said, 'I'm the boss, I will run the show.' He came in as the senior decision maker and accepted inputs from whoever made the decisions and did not get in the way of us operators."[59]

THE *MAYAGUEZ*

One of Brown's greatest crises was the American merchant ship *Mayaguez* incident. On May 12, 1975, at 6:00 A.M., a Cambodian torpedo boat fired on the *Mayaguez*. Seven armed men forced the captain, Charles T. Miller, to the Kas Trang Islands. Miller, however, was able to radio an SOS.

President Gerald Ford was extremely upset by this action. In the first few hours, he tried to get the crew returned through diplomatic channels, dealing direct with the Cambodians in Peking as well as the Communist Chinese. However, he got no immediate response. He then shifted to military operations.

The next day, American reconnaissance planes flying over the *Mayaguez* were fired upon. On the third day, United States aircraft sank three Cambodian gunboats believed ready to move the *Mayaguez* crew to the mainland.

It was considered too risky to wait another twenty-four to forty-eight hours in the absence of any communication from either the Cambodian or Chinese government. Ford was worried that the crew might be moved to the mainland and become hostages, like the crew of the USS *Pueblo*.

That same day, three hundred marines landed on Trang Island, followed by strikes on the Cambodian mainland that destroyed an oil depot at Sihanoukville. The casualties numbered five dead, three marines and two airmen; sixteen were missing; forty-nine, wounded.

It worked. The Cambodians surrendered the crew and the ship. The President's leadership was applauded by both political parties and the public, who saw it as a reassertion of American will after Vietnam. Many believed that our country's international stature was restored by this demonstration of strength.

What role did George Brown have in the *Mayaguez* incident? "When it broke, Brown was fishing in Canada," recalled Ray Sitton. "When he left, there were two guys who usually brought up problems, John Pauly and myself. John was his special assistant and I was his J-3 Operations. The problems we handled were usually of a crisis nature. General Brown said to us, a little on the light side, 'I'm going out on a stream where there's no way to get to me by telephone. I'm not going to have a radio present, and I don't want you guys to bother me. I'm going to relax and catch some fish.'

"The *Mayaguez* situation broke and started to get sticky," continued Sitton. "Between Pauly and me, we thought that in spite of our instructions from the boss, all kinds of eventualities could occur. We were about to put the Marines on somebody else's sovereign territory. If we didn't find the crew, we wouldn't know how far we could go on the mainland, so we wanted the Chairman himself making these decisions. So we sent a chopper out, found him, and brought him back."[60]

Admiral Holloway was in Boston giving a speech when the *Mayaguez* incident broke. Under Secretary of Defense Clements called him and told him to return to Washington immediately. "I got back to the White House, and there was a feeling of dissatisfaction with the way things were unfolding from the JCS," said Admiral Holloway. "They asked for my views, and to be perfectly frank, it tended to be a maritime operation. I had the answer. A carrier was under way; I knew when it would get there, what the frigate could do, what the carrier could do, and so forth. So it evolved that I was the person giving advice to the President from that point at four o'clock that afternoon on through until the decision was made that we would take decisive action."[61]

Brown arrived during the second day and said to Pauly and Sitton, "I thought I told you guys not to bother me." They replied, "We considered that, but we thought you would want to come back, and we wanted you." He grinned and agreed that, of course, they had made the right decision. They briefed him on the situation, and he then proceeded to the command center. He was soon updated on plans made in response to the President's decision to rescue the crew. "George simply took what had been done, the advice that had been given," said Holloway, "and said, 'That sounds good to me. I'm not going to jiggle this thing. We're going to move on.' "[62]

After the Marines' operations against Trang Island and the air attacks on Cambodian installations on the mainland, further pressure was put on the Cambodians. They voluntarily surrendered the crew to American forces, which caused our rescue operations to be called off immediately.

THE EVACUATION OF UNITED STATES
NATIONALS FROM LEBANON

By the spring of 1976, civil war had been going on in Lebanon for fourteen months. A number of issues had led to the Lebanese civil war, primarily the status of the Palestinian guerrillas there and the grievances of Lebanon's Moslem majority against the dominant Christian minority. The war between Christian rightists and Moslem leftists turned increasingly violent and unpredictable, and reached a crisis stage for the United States on June 16, 1976. On that date Francis Meloy, the newly appointed American ambassador to Lebanon, was assassinated along with his economic counselor and embassy driver.

On June 18, the United States Embassy, repeating a presidential directive, ordered all fourteen hundred American citizens to leave the country.

Ray Sitton recalled, "The State Department gave us an estimate of how many people needed to be evacuated. We considered many courses of action, finally deciding to take them out by sea. So we formed a task force and decided on an open motorboat handled by a boatswain and six sailors. The little whale boat went in and brought them out, with the first trip taking about 360 people.

"Brown played his traditional role in this decision. This was a far less frightening thing than the *Mayaguez* operation. Our only concern was the safety of the people we were picking up. We and State decided that it would be wrong to put marines ashore."[63]

THE AX KILLINGS BY NORTH KOREA

On August 18, 1976, North Korean soldiers, wielding axes and metal pipes, assaulted some American and South Korean soldiers in the demilitarized zone between North and South Korea. Two American officers were killed, and four enlisted men wounded, along with five South Korean soldiers. The attack occurred while American and South Korean soldiers were trimming branches from a tree at the Panmunjom truce site near an Allied checkpoint at the south end of the "Bridge of No Return."

The tree trimming was a routine function, done to remove limbs hindering the view of the forwardmost observation posts. Along this demilitarized zone is a series of relatively unprotected checkpoints where American and South Korean soldiers stand guard. They are located in sight of each other, so it is important that one always be able to see the other. On this occasion some North Koreans approached the tree-trimming party, demanding they stop the trimming, which they refused. Shortly thereafter a truckful of North Korean soldiers drove up and proceeded to rush the Americans and South Koreans with axes, metal pipes, rocks, and axe handles.

The Americans in the group were armed with .45 caliber pistols, but did not fire them. There were standing instructions that if an incident occurred, United Nations forces were to evacuate immediately and then assess the situation. The evacuation was accomplished within six minutes. "We wanted to avoid escalating any incidents" was the explanation given by an American official.[64]

The area where the incident occurred was still officially designated as a combat zone by the United States and was the only site in Asia where American and Communist forces directly confronted each other. Since the truce of July 27, 1953, there had been a number of incidents in the demilitarized zone in which forty-nine Americans had died, along with over a thousand North and South Korean soldiers. Usually the pattern in the incidents was that they occurred without warning and ended quickly with little or no time for reaction. With this incident there appeared to be elements of premeditation.

"A flash message went to the National Military Command Center (NMCC) telling us that it had occurred," recalled Ray Sitton. "Gen. Richard Stilwell was then Commander of United States Forces in Korea. He called me on a secure line and asked, 'What do we now do? I know you have all the details and I can't add anything that I haven't already reported. The important thing now is what do we do about it. I think we have no alternative. We have to cut those damn trees down, emphasize this thing. I realize what the consequences could be. At worst, we could start another Korean war, but if it works, we could establish something with those people who understand only strength. They abhor a weakling, just have no use for you. But, they admire strength and understand nothing else. If our assessment is correct, they are not going to do anything, because they will accept this as a display of will and a display of strength. That is the message we want to transmit.' ''[65]

Admiral Holloway said of the incident, ''The issue was how are we going to cut down the tree in front of the North Koreans without starting another war. Getting rid of the tree was not the objective, but letting them see you cut it down was. Stilwell and I agreed that we were going to chop the tree down, and not covertly. First we would tell them we would do it at seven o'clock in the morning and invite them to watch us. We would move troops up and then chop down the tree.

''The other view from certain people in Washington was that that was terribly dangerous, risking a firefight which could escalate into war. My view was that if we didn't cut down the tree, our prestige would go to zero, that they would continue to do things to erode our authority, rights, and prestige, and the next showdown would be much more grave. Some civilian advisors were saying, 'Let's sneak out there during the night and cut the tree down, and then we've got the tree out of the way.' ''[66]

I asked Ray Sitton where Brown had fit in. Sitton replied that Brown heard about the plan direct from Stilwell and from him. He also received a lot of conflicting reports from the fainthearts and decided to go along with Dick Stilwell.

''Ultimately,'' Sitton said, ''Brown presented the plan to the Secretary of Defense and the White House, where it was approved. Brown was the kind of person who could make a difficult decision, even under heavy pressure. The difficulty didn't in any way slow down or deter his doing what had to be done. I can't emphasize that too much. Not everybody has that attribute. There are many people who can make a decision only when forced to do so. They ask for other plans or more facts. But Brown stepped up to the plate and swung about as readily as any senior person I've ever worked for. He had the ability to assess and evaluate other people. When you presented something to him, he had an innate cultivated capability to analyze you. From working with you previously, he knew what your batting average was and how much he could depend on you.

''Brown always depended on his staff, as well as advisors from other agencies. He had a knack of putting it all together and seeing the total picture, assessing, as I said, capabilities, likelihoods, and probabilities, and then weighing them.

"When the actual operation commenced, the Chiefs were convened in the NMCC, monitoring the entire operation and the possible consequences."[67] Over one hundred American and South Korean soldiers were sent into the Korean demilitarized zone on August 21, 1976, to cut down the forty-foot tree. To reach the site the group tore down two road blocks put in the way by the North Koreans. The operation took approximately forty-five minutes, and as they worked helicopter gunships and F–4 Phantom jet fighters flew in the area of the demilitarized zone, while farther south three B–52 bombers could be seen flying in the area.

The North Koreans made no attempt to interfere, but they did say this show of force moved the situation "closer to the brink of war."

In addition, on August 19, 1976, the United States announced steps to increase the readiness of her forces in the Korean peninsula, but no overt signs were given of increased military activity. As a precaution the Pentagon announced it was sending two additional jet fighter-bomber squadrons to Korea. The forty-one thousand United States troops were placed on an elevated combat-ready status.

The actions taken by the United States got results. After the tree was cut down, North Korean President Kim Il Sung, on August 22, 1976, stated that the incident in which the two Americans were killed was "regrettable" and that both sides should take steps to insure that such accidents did not recur. Our State Department responded that Kim's brief statement was unacceptable because North Korea had not admitted responsibility for the deaths of the two Americans and that the increased military readiness would continue.

Within four hours after the tree cutting, there was a meeting of the Korean Armistice Commission. The senior North Korean military officer said, "It is regrettable that the recent incident occurred," and closed his remarks by saying, "I hope that you convey this message to your side's Commander in Chief at the quickest possible time."[68]

THE RYAN LURIE INTERVIEW

On April 12, 1976, George Brown was interviewed by Ryan Lurie, a cartoonist for *Newsweek* magazine. The interview was not published until October 18, 1976, when it appeared in the *Washington Post* under the headline, "Gen. Brown Is in Hot Water Again for Remarks on 3 U.S. Allies." The article began, "Brown told Israeli cartoonist Ryan Lurie during an interview that Israel was a 'burden' to the United States, that Britain's military capability is 'pathetic' and that Iran is bent on restoring the Persian empire." The story alleged that "once again the Ford administration rushed to his rescue. With two weeks remaining before the Presidential election, the administration was at pains to help Brown explain what he really meant in an interview that may give insult to three of United States' closest allies— Great Britain, Israel, and Iran."[69]

This time, however, there was no reprimand from President Ford. "Presidential Press Secretary Ron Nessen insisted that nothing more would be done about Brown. 'The proper place to handle it was . . . at the Pentagon,' he told reporters yesterday, turning aside questions about Brown's future." Mr. Nessen went on to say that as far as the President was concerned the matter was closed and it was now up to the Pentagon, meaning the Secretary of Defense.

One reporter, Fred Emery, in the same issue on October 18, said, "With the White House frantic over the supposed damage to President Ford's campaign, General Brown was brought out to make apologies this afternoon at the press conference in the Pentagon."

Defense Secretary Donald Rumsfeld and General Brown appeared together at a Pentagon press conference to discuss Brown's remarks. Secretary Rumsfeld said that President Ford had "made it clear" that he "did not agree with the general's poor choice of words," and Rumsfeld said he himself found Brown's phrase "obviously inelegant. . . . But," said Rumsfeld, "Brown was not being reprimanded, nor was he going to be fired." He also observed that "General Brown continues to serve his country with distinction."

Brown's comments at this press conference failed to defuse his remarks as a political issue, however, and as with the Duke affair, there was a clamor for his firing or resignation. The national commander of the Jewish War Veterans of the U.S.A., Robert Shor, called on President Ford to express his "lack of confidence" in Brown. "The Chairman of the Joint Chiefs of Staff should be a man whose judgment and discretion are beyond reproach," Shor said in a telegram to President Ford. "This is clearly not the case with General Brown."

Congresswoman Bella Abzug remarked that "President Ford's failure to act quickly and decisively against top administration officials guilty of racial and religious bigotry is an affront to the American people." She said she was concerned that Brown's remarks could have "serious adverse repercussions" on the United States' relations with Israel and on Israel's security. "How can the people of Israel be assured of America's unwavering support when our highest military official publicly complains that Israel is a 'burden'?" Mrs. Abzug commented.

Joseph Sternstein, president of the Zionist Organization of America, said Brown's comments were "a serious breach of discipline and a sign of interference by the military in American foreign policy." He urged Brown's "immediate dismissal."

Senator Charles Percy, a moderate, and Senator James Buckley, a conservative, agreed: "Brown must go." Buckley said Brown "should offer his resignation and the President should accept it immediately—if Brown feels compelled to make policy statements, let him make them as a civilian."

In analyzing each of the three controversies, one finds that the comment concerning Iran did not receive much attention. General Brown had stated:

> Now the other concern over there is Iran and there wasn't any question of why she's building such a tremendous military force. She couldn't with her population do anything that would provide protection from the Soviet Union, and there's a real threat. She's got adequate power to handle Afghanistan and Pakistan, so if they were a threat you can discount that. Iraq, she's a little better match for Iran, now. Gosh, the programs the Shah has coming, it just makes you wonder about whether he doesn't some day have visions of the Persian Empire.
>
> They don't call that the Persian Gulf for nothing. But, of course, our concern with the Middle East is her tremendous oil. Our dependence runs about 17–18 percent now, I guess, of our national consumption and you have all of Europe and Japan. It's just got to continue to flow or the world is going to change; it's not going to be the world we know.

In putting these comments in perspective, Brown said, "In my view, the Shah of Iran has done and is doing an immense amount for his country. . . . He correctly sees the need for Iran to be militarily strong, and thus, is strengthening his armed forces—under conditions that not only serve Iran's security interests, but also those of the free world. I have no reason to believe that he has any aspirations beyond continuing to ably lead his nation and contributing to the stability in that part of the world."

Regarding the comment about Great Britain, a *Post* article written by Lee Lescaze, quoting only an excerpt of the Brown comments, stated: "On Britain, Brown said, 'It's pathetic now, it just makes you want to cry. They're no longer a world power. All they've got are generals and admirals and bands. They do things in great style, grand style, God, they do it well—on the protocol side. But it makes you sick to see their forces.' "

In response to this statement, the article continued, "General Brown did not dispute today the accuracy of the quotations attributed to him, but he asked that they be placed in 'proper perspective.'

" 'Americans understand and sympathize with the current economic difficulties of the British people,' he said. 'We know of their gallantry. There are no braver people. I have the greatest admiration and respect for

Her Majesty's highly professional armed forces.' " Brown also said at the press conference that his remarks were made out of "compassion and understanding, not criticism and ridicule."

The best way to put this statement into proper perspective is to quote from a transcript made from a tape described as "imperfect," a portion of the Lurie interview of April 12, 1976. Lurie noted that in the 1930s when Italy and Germany were posing threats to world peace, the British government was afraid that some of its citizens would not fight to oppose them, that they were thus encouraged to commit aggression. He asked Brown's comments, and he stated:

> Of course, that's the one thing we haven't talked about and that is that it's the thing that we don't spend much time on—we don't spend as much time agonizing over that question as we do over programs for hardware and budgets, readiness of forces and the normal things we do, and that is the will of our good people. And, of course, we came out of a very long and traumatic experience in Vietnam. We're starting to come out of it; people will talk about these things, as I say, two or three years ago they wouldn't. And I am still enough of an optimist to think that once the American people are informed, they will make the right decisions on things that are really important. I think the Congress will, too. I think they will step up things that are most important. But we certainly didn't act that way in Angola and no one involved in Congress is prohibiting us from spending money to provide some balance to the Soviet initiative which we conceivably could have—what it would have done locally wasn't as important, I think, as what we would have done in the long range in terms of Soviet assessment of the United States. And not only Soviets, but everybody else.
>
> I had a discussion last week in London with the First Sea Lord, Ashmore is his name, and we were just talking at dinner about the problems of the world, the Mideast, and first and foremost the NATO community, and he said, you know, we hadn't touched the prime problem in the world. And I said, what's that? He said the big question mark about the United States. Has the United States really got the stomach for this? Are they going to see it through?
>
> I said, no, we hadn't. I wasn't going to discuss it with him; I would like to acknowledge it is one whale of a problem. And I could have been nasty and said, well, you all have experienced

that, how do you see it, or something, because they did just what
you said and then, Great Britain, it's a pathetic thing. It just
makes you want to cry. They are no longer a world power. All
they have got are generals and admirals and bands.

The reaction in the British press to these statements was mixed. Viscount
Allenby, a lieutenant colonel in the Second World War and a nephew of
World War II leader Field Marshal Allenby, thundered, "I have never heard
such rubbish in my life. I know about our armed forces—I have a son
serving at the moment—and I know they are manned by young and dedicated men. These remarks are absolute bunk. There is no foundation for
them at all."

Maj. Gen. Sir John Bates, who fought in Africa, the Middle East, Sicily,
Italy, and Greece in the Second World War, said his feelings were "unprint-
able." He went on to say, "I don't think they are fair comments at all. I
think people have been deeply offended by them." Sir John then went on to
launch his own counterattack against the American Army: "Anyone who is
seeking the truth has only to go to the NATO artillery attack ranges on
Luneburg Heath, as I did three months ago. If you compare the perfor-
mances of the various armies, although we are vastly outnumbered by the
Americans, the standard of the British is much higher.

"The only Christian explanation of these remarks is that they were made
at a time a few months ago when Parliament was debating a white paper on
defence cuts. This could have been a ham-fisted attempt to help those opposed to the cuts. I can't see how a man in his position could be so mal-
adroit as to make them otherwise."

Other military men in Great Britain saw only truth in General Brown's
comments. Major General Viscount Monckton, who won the Military Cross
while fighting in France and Belgium in World War II, considers the British
Army "probably the most efficient of its size in the world." However, he
took a more charitable view of Brown's remarks. It was true his armed
forces were at a "desperately low level," he added. "I am always sympa-
thetic to the truth. I think the messasge from across the Atlantic is that there
should be no further cuts. I was not offended by what was said."

Retired Gen. Pat Nan, who was the officer commanding the Aldershot
District until 1965, said: "The quality of the British Army is as high as it has
ever been. It is the quantity that has been cut, as it always is in peacetime, by
bloody politicians who depend on votes for their bloody salaries and who
care little or nothing about their country. Now print that and be damned!"

Brig. Peter Young, onetime lecturer in military history at the Camberley
Staff College, said, "I jolly well agree with all the General says about the

present-day state of the British Army. It is a damned disgrace the way our
forces have been cut and cut and cut. If he means the personnel are pathetic
then I'll take issue. The soldier today is as good as ever he was. The grand
old Duke of Wellington would not have blushed to command an army of
these chaps today.''

Feeling among the officers and men in and around Aldershot, the town
that calls itself "the home of the British Army," was strong, but no one was
willing to have his name tagged to a comment. One officer commented,
"This is a purely political subject. This is our life and work. There are too
many unemployed outside for some chap to face the sack for saying the
right thing in the wrong place."

But off-the-record comments included that "the American general is too
damn well right," "it should have been said before," and "these economies
in defense are emasculation of a great force."

The comment that received the greatest attention was the one on Israel.
The transcript, which again was inaudible in parts, stated:

> Q. Speaking about the Middle East from a purely military point
> of view, would you say that from the American global strategic
> interest, militarily, is Israel and its forces more a burden or a
> blessing from a pure military point of view, to the United States?

> A. Well, I think it's just got to be considered a burden. I had this
> same conversation with Javits right after I got in trouble down at
> Duke. We had breakfast and were talking and he said to me,
> can't you see the great strategic value of Israel to the United
> States and I said frankly no, which wasn't the point I was talking
> about at Duke at all, but my concern there is that they're a bur-
> den. Now if the trends were reversed, then I could see in the long
> term where that might be a tremendous asset, where they would
> gain power and could bring about stability in the area.[70]

In an editorial, the *Dallas Morning News* offered an interesting perspective on this question and on General Brown's response:

> The question was put to the head of the Joint Chiefs last
> spring in such a way that made it almost mandatory for Brown to
> reply as he did. . . . The interviewer Lurie stressed—by repeating
> it three times in one question—that he was referring to the strict-
> ly military aspect. Recall that at the time of the 1973 war, the
> United States had to take tanks, jets and other weapons from its

own war stocks and the equipment of active units in order to make good the combat losses of the Israel Defense Forces.

For more than three decades the American global strategy has been to regard the Soviet Union as the most dangerous threat to our survival. In carrying out the decision of the Nixon administration to replace Israeli losses at all costs, the United States military unquestionably weakened at least temporarily, its own defensive strength against the Soviet threat.

Any commander who declared that a drawdown on his stocks of weapons and equipment was a blessing would have to be considered an idiot, a liar or both. We constantly complain that our leaders gloss over, politick, or cover up painful truths and judgments. Yet Gen. Brown has given his opinion when asked by a reputable journalist and away we go, with insults, flying charges and demands, plus the usual cheap shots from the politicians.

Sen. Mondale, shooting from the lip, declared people like Brown "shouldn't be sewage commissioners."

Whatever else one may think of the general, it is clear he attempted to answer Lurie's question with an honest opinion rather than political hypocrisy. He's about the only one involved in this latest diversion who made that choice in that way.

Howard K. Smith, "ABC Evening News," made a commentary about Brown on his national evening news program:

A word of defense of General George S. Brown. As was abundantly reported yesterday, in an interview six months ago but curiously published only now on the eve of elections, General Brown said that Israel was, militarily speaking, a burden to the United States.

Well, that statement seems to me unexceptionable. He might, had he strayed from military analogies, have said that taxes are a burden and so is social security. So is welfare, so is medicare but they, like Israel, are necessary burdens willingly shouldered.

Remember Israel's last war when she needed tanks badly? We had no stocks, so we sent them from our active field forces in western Europe—our primary area of defense.

It was a strain, it was a burden, but it was done willingly and it will undoubtedly be done so in the future.

Somehow the fact has to penetrate that Israel is an independent nation-state subject to comment like all nation-states, comment that is not always complimentary, as we, the most criticized of nation-states, so well know.

It in no way implies anti-Semitism any more than our criticism of western Europe for not sharing a larger burden of defense of Europe implies hostility to their races or religions or nationalities.

Nothing General Brown said alters the fact that our support for Israel has been and is unflinching, will be so in the future, probably at the expense of other commitments, but always willingly and probably under command of General Brown.

UNIONIZATION OF THE MILITARY SERVICES

One large issue during Brown's tenure as Chairman was an attempt to unionize the military services. "Today, however, we hear sounds of a new and different voice: that of the unions," he commented in a speech given at Fort Rucker, Alabama, on August 18, 1977. "Some unions have shown considerable interest in developing military membership. It would not be a historic 'first'; several other nations have military unions.

"In my opinion—and in the corporate opinion of the Joint Chiefs of Staff—military unions are not in the best interests of our country or of our Armed Forces. Our people in uniform must be able to perceive that a union cannot provide fairer treatment or a better way of life than can the American people as a whole, through the Congress."[71]

The union issue was to receive international attention. An Associated Press article was published with a small headline: " 'In Dutch' with 'Dutch,' " and another with the headline "Back to Dive-bombing." Brown and Secretary of Defense Donald Rumsfeld were making a joint appearance before a Senate committee. Although the main topic was budget matters, the questions covered a broad spectrum. One senator wanted to know what Brown thought of unions for soldiers. His response was that one simply had to look at the unionized Dutch military services to get an idea of why he was opposed to military unions. Secretary Rumsfeld started jabbing an elbow into General Brown's ribs, suggesting that it would be a mistake to offend a valued NATO ally. "Ignoring the signal," said one news commentator, "Brown elaborated: 'Soldiers with shoulder-length hair and other unmilitary nastiness were the inevitable result.' Rumsfeld kept using the elbow. Brown kept right on talking until he had said it all." Another reporter quoted General Brown as having said, "The Dutch are the only ones who have unions and you ought to see them. It's frightening to inspect their Guard of Honor. They don't cut their hair or shine their boots."

Senator John Culver said, after Brown's statement, "Well, General, it's clear you're a soldier, not a diplomat."

Post writer Helen Dudar wrote of the incident that it was "an indiscretion," which apparently went unnoticed, but was rekindled after the Israeli interviewer had asked General Brown whether he considered Israel's army a "burden" or a "blessing."

"Once again," continued Helen Dudar, "the current flap raised the question of how a man so insensitive about domestic and international issues could have become the country's top professional warrior. 'Well, it was the Air Force's turn for the job,' was how one Brown critic put it."

THE PANAMA CANAL TREATY

One of the most critical decisions before the Joint Chiefs during Brown's tenure was consideration by the administration of a new Panama Canal Treaty, which would give ownership of the Canal to Panama. The security of the United States was tied closely to any treaty that provided for abandonment of sovereignty by the United States over the Panama Canal and the Canal Zone. Such a decision would have international consequences, particularly on United States influence in the Central America area.

From the time of the Monroe Doctrine, the United States has informed the world that her stability and security depended upon nonintervention of foreign powers in the Caribbean, with the United States dominant in the area. With the communist takeover in Cuba, this security position eroded, placing within ninety miles of Florida an unfriendly power. Hanson Baldwin, military analyst of the *New York Times,* summed it up when he wrote, "Our own mistakes and weaknesses have cost us dearly; the infiltrators are within the outer walls, and what should be our island-speckled ramparts are becoming the soft underbelly of North America. . . . It is this broad perspective—the future of the Caribbean–Gulf of Mexico area—that any basic change in the status of the Panama Canal must be judged, for any such change will profoundly affect our interest in the area and hence, ultimately, our political, psychological, economic, and military security. . . . The credibility of the United States has been severely impaired and our international solvency in doubt. Panama and the Canal, therefore, are both cause and symbol: The Canal is highly important in its own right, but far more so as a symbol of U.S. resolution and as one of the vital links in our vital interests in the Caribbean."

The U.S. Navy depends on the Canal because of its responsibility to provide security in two oceans. Passage through the Canal was critical for providing security in exchanging forces from one ocean to another.

Those who argued in favor of relinquishing sovereignty over the Panama Canal argued that we had unjustly taken this territory from Panama; that returning this territory would please the young independents; that we would attempt to placate third world countries upon whom we were increasingly dependent as a source of raw materials; and that the Latin American countries favored the transfer of the Canal.

On September 26, 1977, Brown testified concerning the Panama Canal at hearings held by the House Committee on International Relations. The essence of Brown's remarks was that the important need of the United States was the Canal's use, not its ownership. He felt, and spoke for the Joint Chiefs, that our armed forces had to have access to the Canal both in war and in peace, and that its security had to be continually assured. He saw that our capability to defend the Canal depended on cooperation between the United States and Panama, which the new treaty contained.

There was criticism in the media that the Chairman and the service chiefs were forced to endorse the Panama Canal Treaty or lose their jobs. In response to such allegations, General Brown said to the House Committee on International Affairs, "Mr. Chairman, the charge has been made by one or more columnists and several individuals around the country that the Joint Chiefs of Staff and I particularly support these treaties because the Commander in Chief has made a decision. As Secretary Brown [Secretary of Defense Harold Brown] has stated, the only appropriate way for us to fail to be supportive of a decision is to leave active duty and then take an adversary position.

"But there is another fact of life. The rules of the game quite clearly provide that we will testify before Congress and in response to interrogation will respond fully and factually to every question. This I have done for many years.

"I testified before this committee, if you will recall, on the issue of the proposed withdrawal of the U.S. ground combat forces in Korea, and the public record will show that the Joint Chiefs of Staff did not support that proposed action in January. We addressed a memorandum to the Secretary of Defense and in turn to the President, which stated that three provisions should be accounted for: (1) that we should withdraw our forces in such a manner that the military balance was retained or not disturbed; (2) that there should be a public pledge to the continued mutual security treaty with the Republic of Korea; and (3) that we remain a Pacific power. These were accepted, and at that point the Joint Chiefs of Staff supported the proposed program and have worked diligently to plan for that to occur over four or five years.

"Similarly, and it will come as no surprise, we did not share the judgment on the B-1. We thought the B-1 should go into production, and so recommended, but that judgment went against us.

"So it is not right to say that the Joint Chiefs of Staff are supportive of the President in all cases. The public record is quite clear in testimony before Congress, particularly on the Panama Canal Treaty issue. I have personally worked hard for four years to achieve these treaties. And we have had General Dolvin as a member of the negotiating delegation. We have worked out in detail, that is, the Joint Chiefs of Staff and the U.S. Commander of the Southern Command, the so-called waters and land issues, that is, what land and waters we could give up from the Canal Zone that were no longer required for defense or operation of the Canal.

"Similarly, I think I share with Secretary Brown a pride that it was in the Department of Defense that the formulation which found its way into the form of the Neutrality Treaty was given birth. As a matter of fact, it came from Secretary Brown in our conversation one day. From that it evolved into what we now find as the Neutrality Treaty, which was the hard essential thing to achieve, because we had asked in effect for Panama, and they have now agreed to do something forever, which they had said they would not do, that perpetuity was to be ended. And so it is just not right to say that the Joint Chiefs of Staff are with these treaties only because of the decision."

An active duty Army officer, Maj. Gen. John Singlaub, had openly criticized the administration's decision on withdrawing U.S. military forces from Korea and was chastised personally by the President. Senator John Glenn, at hearings on the Canal issue, questioned Brown at length. He reminded Brown that the Singlaub incident was still remembered by Congress and that four retired Chiefs of Naval Operations had taken exception to the treaty. Yet, he saw senior people on active duty like Brown in favor of the administration's position and wondered as to their motivation and their possible inability to speak out.

Brown answered: "Senator Glenn, I would also like to comment upon this. I would just like to make a comment on the Singlaub affair. I don't propose that it be reopened here, but I think it only fair to say since it has been mentioned, . . . you are absolutely right in how they understand it. But they really misunderstand it. They fail to recognize one fundamental thing that we cannot have in a military organization if we are to have a disciplined military force responsive to proper authority. This is, that once a decision is made, you support it or you get out and contest it. You don't stay on active duty and contest it. That is where I draw the line."

Another member of the Senate Committee raised the same point. Senator Clark asked, "Gentlemen, some of the most bitter critics of the treaty say that those of you in the Joint Chiefs of Staff and the higher ranks of the military command are supporting this treaty in fear of maintaining or enhancing your positions. They say that you are being intimidated. What is your response to these accusations?"

General Brown responded, "Senator, I just turned to Secretary Brown to ask if he would mind if I made an unsolicited statement at some point to get this on the record. I thank you for your question. The rules are quite clear and I think understood by all of us that nobody, no senior officer in uniform, will remain on active duty and publicly be critical of Presidential decisions. I, in my role as Chairman, and other members of the Joint Chiefs of Staff will articulate as forcefully and as logically as we can the view the Joint Chiefs of Staff hold on issues of national security, but if the judgment goes against us as it does in many cases, there is nothing in the law that says the President has to accept our advice, but we have to give it.

"We don't go public without leaving active duty first in doing so. However, the rules are also quite clear that in response to interrogation before a congressional committee that we answer fully and factually. The public record is quite clear where we have been in opposition to a Presidential decision."

A House Member asked the question a different way when Congresswoman Meyner said, "General Brown, I questioned the leaders of the veterans organizations when they testified last week, the American Legion, VFW, et cetera, about their claim that the military leadership of this country secretly opposes the Panama treaties. I pointed out that you and the rest of the Joint Chiefs of Staff favored the treaty, and one of them replied, and I quote, 'The military leaders are not going to do a "Singlaub"; they are going to keep their opinions to themselves. Off the record we have been told what their opinions really are.' End quote. Would you like to respond to that statement?"

General Brown: "Admittedly I have not talked with all of them, but all of the members of the Joint Chiefs, the senior planners in each of the military departments, the Vice Chiefs of Staff, all feel that these treaties should be ratified.

"Now, I got a little notoriety for having ordered the senior retired officers in the city to assemble while I twisted their collective arms. That was not so. I offered to the Chiefs of Staff, if they would invite their senior retired people, that General Dolvin and I would be happy to spend whatever time they wanted to explain the treaties. I made it clear that they would then have to do whatever their consciences dictated.

"Quite a number, the last of them being General Westmoreland, have voluntarily taken a stand endorsing ratification. In fact, General Westmoreland wrote the President a nice brief note to that effect. I talked to two of the CNOs who signed the letter to the President and they were not as adamant after the treaties were in hand as they had been before the treaties were available for them to study.

"But I know of no active duty officers who feel we should not ratify these treaties."

How effective was the leadership of General Brown as Chairman of the Joint Chiefs of Staff? Perhaps the best testimonial on Brown's leadership is from the Chiefs who served with him during his tenure as Chairman, men who achieved what few would question were the highest leadership positions in each of their services. Gen. Bernard Rogers, then Army Chief of Staff, said, "I think anybody who's been associated with him gives him high marks because of his knowledge, his capability to project, his ability to cut through what I call the underbrush and get to the heart of the matter, and his trying to waste the least amount of time finding solutions. He did this without any sacrifice of quality in decision making. It wasn't getting a decision for the sake of getting a decision. He knew the system, that if you sat and argued over language, verbiage, grammar, and punctuation, you would end up with a less useful product than if you just went ahead and said, 'OK, this is the way we're going to do it.' "[72]

Adm. James Holloway, Chief of Naval Operations, said, "Let me sum it up by saying that George Brown, in my book, was the sort of Chairman you'd get if you sent to central casting. He had everything: a superior combat record, personal heroism. He came from a military family and had a military bearing, commanding the respect both of the Chiefs and the civilians under whom he served. This is very important because George was included in the White House councils. They were glad to have him over there because they felt he added something. So often you find the records show that the military is deliberately excluded. But that was not the case with George Brown."[73]

One of the key reasons for Brown's success was his fair-mindedness. "I found George Brown very fair with all of us as far as what he believed was necessary," said General Rogers. "If he didn't think a particular weapons system or unit in the force structure was necessary, he'd say so, regardless of what service was involved. That was helpful and refreshing, the position a Chairman ought to take. The Chairman's the only one who can take that position without any qualms whatsoever because he owes no allegiance to any service."[74]

One of the key issues during Brown's tenure as Chairman was the effort of the Marine Corps to get six squadrons of fighter aircraft. There were great differences of opinion among the Chiefs on this issue. While none of them were specifically against it, neither did they want it adopted at the expense of anything that might affect their particular branch. Brown solved this problem, although the Marine Corps did not expect any support from him. At an Armed Forces Policy Council meeting he threw his personal support to the Marines' position and sold it to the Secretary of Defense.

Gen. Lewis Wilson was Commandant of the Marine Corps, and his position on the Joint Chiefs of Staff was more difficult than that of the other members. "When I came to the Washington arena, I had less experience than the other Chiefs," said General Wilson. "I didn't even know the language. The Commandant was not a full member of the Joint Chiefs, only a voting member when the issue involved the Marine Corps. I was feeling my way along, but George made me feel very comfortable in my role as the most junior member of the Joint Chiefs. He was always straightforward in our meetings and asked incisive questions. He would report back from his meetings with the National Security Council and the White House forthrightly, honestly, and carefully as to what went on."

When asked how Brown approached discussions of key issues in JCS meetings, General Wilson responded, "He expected all of us to do our homework so that when he led into an issue through briefings from our staff officers, we would then go into executive session. The service that had the most to gain or lose by it, by virtue of just the subject matter, would speak first, and then the others would comment. This in itself was a tribute to the way George led, where the initiative would come from the individual Chief and he didn't have to sit around and wait to be asked what he thought about it."[75]

I asked General Rogers how he would describe Brown's performance as a purple suiter. "I thought it was extremely good," said General Rogers, "and I think the same can be said for the time when I observed him as exec and military assistant to the Secretary of Defense. I think he epitomized the purple suit concept. He leaned over backwards to insure that he was not being oversupportive of his basic branch of the service.

"And George Brown didn't hold much truck for a lot of discussion on minor details among the Joint Chiefs. He would try to get a unanimous decision among the services, but if he found that he couldn't get it, he'd take the position that the paper should be split. He saw no sense in spending hour after hour compromising so that we got a paper that meant everything to all men and therefore satisfied all the Chiefs. Usually, if that happened, the decision was of little value. That's not the purpose of the Chiefs. He would ask: 'What is your position? Are you firm in that position? If so, we'll split the paper.' He didn't spend a lot of time trying to compromise. We didn't send many split papers up under George Brown, but with those that were split, at least the firm, solid position of each individual Chief was stated."[76]

Admiral Holloway was also positive in his assessment: "As far as his being a purple suiter, his ability to divest himself of service biases, it would be hard to find an experienced military officer better at that than he was. There are two ways a Chairman can go. One is to favor his own service; the other is overcompensation, where you lean over backwards out of a sense of fairness and try to emphasize other services. George did neither of those. When a crisis was developing, George wouldn't hesitate to ask the Chiefs for their input as to their service capability, and then, rather than try to make himself totally knowledgeable, to be the only one who would talk to the President, would bring one of the other Chiefs along. Now, I'm going to be very frank. Chiefs and senior people also have egos and hang-ups, maybe more so in some cases because when one becomes a prominent person in government, self-identification is very important. So it's understandable that when there is a Cabinet meeting or a National Security Council meeting, one would not bring his assistants along and be the person who answers all the questions. But George didn't let that happen. He always wanted the right man to come with him. George was good at putting whatever concerns of ego he might have had in his pocket and giving the Chiefs opportunities to display themselves."[77]

I asked the Air Force Chief of Staff if his service suffered by Brown bending over backwards to not show favoritism. "I didn't see that as a problem," replied Gen. David Jones. "I didn't feel any lack of support. I don't think he bent over backwards. There are some who will, because you might not pick up the torch and run with it hard, feel that you have bent over backwards to the other services. I would expect people would say the same things about me in an issue—that I didn't get out front and fight for an Air Force item, that somehow I was bending over backwards for the other services. It doesn't bother me. I'm sure it was the same with George. He did what he thought was right and didn't let concerns on either side bother him.

"I think George tried to be very even-handed. He had experience in the joint arena with Joint Task Force-2 and also worked for Mr. McNamara and General Wheeler. He had a reputation of being a very balanced person. I didn't see any parochialism in him, any bias in the sense of trying to work Air Force problems. He tried to be objective, judging an issue on its merit, and essentially what we as Chiefs tried to do is get agreement. That's the whole pressure in the joint system, to get agreement. Rather than expounding a position so much, you would try to get people to an agreement. His only interest was in doing what was best for our country."[78]

Brown's concern that all of the Chiefs be given the opportunity to participate in matters at the highest levels extended to the social realm as well. Admiral Holloway pointed out two instances of this: "When President Ford had White House dinner parties, he had a policy that the Chairman of the JCS would normally be included. And George, God bless him, said that really wasn't fair, that he was simply the Chairman, not necessarily the senior, and that it ought to be rotated. This is what happened. And then, when a visiting head of State comes to Washington, there's an arrival ceremony on the White House lawn. The usual people present are the President, the Vice President, the Secretary of State, and the Chief of Protocol and their wives, and the Chairman of the JCS—a very select group. George also got this honor rotated."[79]

This generosity and fair-mindedness, along with his ability to handle both crises and day-to-day matters, made George Brown an extremely effective Chairman of the Joint Chiefs. After interviewing the Chiefs of Staff under him, it became clear to me that he had their complete confidence. There was never any question that when he spoke outside the Pentagon he was speaking on behalf of the Chiefs. He was clearly the leader in the Tank. They had a great personal and professional respect for him.

When I asked Secretary Harold Brown for an incident that stood out, he commented, "There was early on a real problem of turf between the Defense Department and another government agency. The head of this agency approached the Chiefs and Chairman, stating, 'Why don't I deal directly with you? I will provide you with the information you need and cut the Secretary of Defense and his staff out of it.' George came to me asking how to keep this from happening. To him this was not the right way to do it. He wanted to deal with this in a way that served our interests and avoided splitting the JCS office from the rest of the Defense Department. The situation was worked out, but his loyalties were to the system and not in trying to go around it to build up his immediate position. He was very loyal to the chain of command and to the position of Secretary of Defense."[80]

Although Brown was loyal to the Secretary and followed the chain of command, he had a sense of what OSD civilians should do and what they shouldn't. "He kept us straight on that," commented one of the staff members. "He taught me an awful lot about force structure. I remember one time when we were going to move an aircraft carrier.

"Brown gave me a short lecture about how it was my responsibility to make sure that somebody on my staff who understood aircraft carriers well wrote messages like that. Or if it were Army companies, or if it were airplanes, he wanted me to consult real experts. He told me that nothing in Harold Brown's background qualified him to move U.S. forces anywhere, so he had to have expert advice and that was what I was to do. I thought this was a good lesson. He never questioned the Secretary's directive, just wanted to make sure that nobody in Harold Brown's outer office might write an unworkable directive.

"He clearly established immediately that an operational chain of command could not include anybody but Secretary Brown or Under Secretary Duncan. But, he said, even so, although technically the Secretary of Defense had the authority to pick up the phone and call CINCPAC and say, 'Move that aircraft carrier a hundred eighty degrees and start it toward Kenya,' that in fact he was not qualified to do that. The JCS were his operational staff and had to be used as such."[81]

All of Brown's work was obviously not just with the Chiefs of the services. He was an effective leader with his supporting staff. "He really used the staff," reflected Gen. Jerome O'Malley. "He would not stand for unresponsiveness in his functional staff. If he asked for something at ten o'clock, he wanted the answer in the early afternoon. We knew that. He never used an ad hoc group, even if he were in a hurry. He just made the functional staff work well. But, we worked as a team and loved him. I don't think I've ever seen anybody smile as often or as genuinely. He'd light up the whole damned table when he told a story."[82]

As was the case in his earlier assignments, Brown refused to become bogged down in detail. Soon after becoming Chairman, an action officer was briefing him, giving him a vast number of statistics in preparation for a National Security Council meeting. Finally Brown stopped him and said, "Colonel, why do I need to know that? Why do I have to know these numbers? I know your name and I'll remember it. If I need any of these details, I'll call you." As one officer put it, "He thought like a Chairman, not like an ops officer."

That was Brown's favorite question, "Why are you telling me that?" He was even that way with his superiors. Once he was having a session with Secretary Brown. It was about a nuclear warhead, and they were in an argument about it. Harold Brown, of course, knew more about nuclear warheads than just about anybody and he started into its details. Finally, George Brown said, "Look, Smith back there is a nuclear weapons expert. Why don't I call him up here and you and he can argue all you want, you as director of Livermore Lab and he as a nuclear weapons expert. When you're ready to talk to me as the Secretary of Defense to the Chairman, call me and I'll come on back."

In carrying out the immense responsibilities as Chairman, George Brown normally was relaxed; he could get angry, but he never lost his sense of humor. There was a time early in the Carter administration that there were information leaks all over Washington. It appeared that everything that was worked up on a Monday was published either Wednesday or Thursday. People were really getting uptight about it, including the Secretary. One day Brown came into a JCS meeting with the Secretary of Defense. Secretary Brown passed out six copies of a document to be discussed, one for each. He then explained the need for secrecy and George Brown didn't pick up his. The Secretary looked over at George and said, "Well, aren't you going to read it?" George said, "No, I think I'll wait until tomorrow and read it in Evans and Novak."

Similarly, Brown's sense of humor flashed one day while appearing before Congress. One congressman changed the train of thought from the main line of questioning and asked, "By the way, General Brown, you're a senior Air Force general. Carter has just decided to cancel the B-1. Why don't you resign from the Air Force?" General Brown, less than diplomatically, said, "I certainly could, but it would have about as much effect on this country as your resigning from the Congress."

Despite Brown's constant efforts to maintain himself in the best of health, about three months before the end of his tour as Chairman, he was stricken with a fast-moving cancer. This greatly curtailed his activities, so that at the end he was able to spend only a small amount of time at his duties.

His tour ended in June 1978 and he passed away on December 5, 1978. Although he was in pain most of this time, he maintained his cheerful demeanor, showing the strength and courage that typified his entire life. He seemed more concerned with the problems his illness was causing others than with his own condition.

NOTES

1. Personal interview with Gen. Robert J. Dixon, USAF (Ret.), June 10, 1980.
2. *New York Times,* June 6, 1974.
3. Gen. George S. Brown, Statement to Manpower and Personnel Subcommittee, Senate Armed Services Committee, August 13, 1974.
4. Gen. George S. Brown, Address to the Navy League of the United States, Washington, D.C., February 5, 1975.
5. Gen. George S. Brown, Address to the Retired Officers Association 1976 Convention, Philadelphia, Pennsylvania, September 17, 1976.
6. Sir John Slessor, quoted by Gen. George S. Brown, Address to the Navy League.

7. Gen. George S. Brown, Address to the Navy League.
8. Ibid.
9. Personal interview with William K. Brehm, former Assistant Secretary in the office of the Secretary of Defense for Manpower and Reserve Affairs, August 27, 1979.
10. Gen. George S. Brown, Statement to Manpower and Personnel Subcommittee.
11. Gen. George S. Brown, Address to Rotary Club of Chicago, Illinois, February 17, 1976.
12. Gen. George S. Brown, Address to Comstock Club of Sacramento, California, November 25, 1974.
13. Gen. George S. Brown, Address to Duke University School of Law, Durham, North Carolina, October 10, 1974.
14. Gen. George S. Brown, FY 1977 Department of Defense Authorization Request Before the Senate Appropriations Committee, February 2, 1976.
15. Gen. George S. Brown, Address to Awards Dinner, Order of Daedalians, San Antonio, Texas, May 17, 1975.
16. Gen. George S. Brown, Address to Duke University School of Law.
17. Gen. George S. Brown, Address to Chamber of Commerce, Clovis, New Mexico, October 17, 1975.
18. Gen. George S. Brown, Address to 76th National Convention of the Veterans of Foreign Wars of the United States, Los Angeles, California, August 21, 1975.
19. Gen. George S. Brown, Address to the Rotary Club of Chicago.
20. Gen. George S. Brown, Statement to House Armed Services Committee, February 18, 1975.
21. Personal interview with Adm. James L. Holloway, USN (Ret.), March 11, 1982.
22. Personal interview with Harold Brown, April 29, 1982.
23. Gen. George S. Brown, Address to the Order of Daedalians, San Antonio Texas, May 17, 1975.
24. Gen. George S. Brown, Statement to Manpower and Personnel Subcommittee.
25. Gen. George S. Brown, FY 1977 Department of Defense Authorization Request.
26. Gen. George S. Brown, Address to the Retired Officers Association 1976 Convention.
27. Michael Getler, *Washington Post,* November 13, 1974.
28. Gen. George S. Brown, Testimony before the Senate Armed Forces Committee for his nomination for a second term as Chairman of the Joint Chiefs of Staff, June 28, 1976.
29. Ibid.
30. Ibid.
31. *Washington Post,* November 13, 1974.
32. Ibid.
33. Ibid.
34. Ibid.
35. Gen. George S. Brown, Speech to the Comstock Club of Sacramento, November 25, 1974.
36. William Beecher, quoted in the *Washington Post,* November 14, 1974, and *New York Times,* November 15, 1974, p. 21.

37. Ron Nessen, quoted in the *Washington Post,* November 14, 1974.
38. Personal interview with James R. Schlesinger, April 1, 1981.
39. *Washington Post,* November 14, 1974.
40. *New York Times,* November 14, 1974, p. 1.
41. Gen. George S. Brown, Address to Comstock Club.
42. Senator Thomas J. McIntyre, Testimony of Gen. George S. Brown before Senate Armed Forces Committee, November 25, 1974.
43. Ibid.
44. Senator John C. Stennis, Ibid.
45. Rowland Evans and Robert Novak, "Behind the General's Outburst," *Washington Post,* November 18, 1974, Section A., p. 23.
46. Joseph Alsop, in his nationally syndicated column, November 20, 1974.
47. Ibid.
48. Personal interview with Gen. Theodore R. Milton, USAF (Ret.), June 28, 1979.
49. Personal interview with Lt. Gen. William Y. Smith, USAF (Ret.), April 25, 1979.
50. Letter from Milton Barall to EFP, May 16, 1979.
51. Schlesinger interview.
52. Gen. George S. Brown, Testimony before the Senate Armed Forces Committee for his nomination for a second term as Chairman.
53. Harold Brown interview.
54. Senator John C. Stennis.
55. Personal interview with Lt. Gen. James A. Knight, Jr., USAF (Ret.), August 7, 1979.
56. Personal interview with Gen. Andrew J. Goodpaster, USA (Ret.), July 22, 1980.
57. Personal interview with Lt. Gen. Ray B. Sitton, USAF (Ret.), September 9, 1981.
58. Holloway interview.
59. Sitton interview.
60. Ibid.
61. Holloway interview.
62. Ibid.
63. Sitton interview.
64. *New York Times,* August 20, 1976.
65. Sitton interview.
66. Holloway interview.
67. Sitton interview.
68. *New York Times,* August 26, 1976.
69. *Washington Post,* October 18, 1976.
70. Ryan Lurie interview.
71. Gen. George S. Brown, Address to Bogardus S. Cairns Chapter Association of the United States Army, Fort Rucker, Alabama, August 18, 1977.
72. Personal interview with Gen. Bernard W. Rogers, USA (Ret.), March 5, 1982.
73. Holloway interview.
74. Rogers interview.
75. Personal interview with Gen. Lewis H. Wilson, USMC (Ret.), February 12, 1981.
76. Rogers interview.

77. Holloway interview.
78. Personal interview with Gen. David C. Jones, USAF (Ret.), January 13, 1981.
79. Holloway interview.
80. Harold Brown interview.
81. Personal interview with Gen. Jerome F. O'Malley, USAF, August 10, 1981.
82. Ibid.

EPILOGUE

THE PATTERN

George Brown was one of the most outstanding leaders in Air Force history. He rose to the rank of full colonel in three years, going on to become Chief of Staff of the Air Force and Chairman of the Joint Chiefs of Staff. I asked those who served with him, under him, and over him through his military career, "Why was George S. Brown successful as a leader?" The purpose of this chapter is to pull together the answers to this question, to put into perspective the qualities that made him so successful. There is a pattern to successful leadership, and George Brown was the epitome of this pattern.

One officer commented, "I can't tell what a leader is, but I know one when I see one, and George Brown was a leader." Another reflected that Brown had that "intangible, natural ability to instill esprit in his subordinates." Others have said he had a magnetic personality, that people swore by him, but they couldn't say why. In short, people gravitated to him, but often couldn't state precisely what made them do so.

Although a concept of leadership is rather intangible, the reasons for Brown's success as a leader are clear. He had a thorough knowledge of his profession and he worked hard at it; he was an able decision maker; he didn't try to do everything himself but delegated to others; he was courageous in combat and, perhaps even more important, in noncombat situations; he was thoughtful and considerate of others; he was tough but was a warm human being, a man of humanity and humility; he was equitable with all those he worked with, loyal to his superiors, and capable of generating loyalty in subordinates; he possessed great character and integrity; and he dedicated his life to selfless service to God and country. All these qualities made him successful as a leader. Thus, though his leadership can't be defined, it can be described. That has been the purpose of this book, to give life and meaning to the qualities that made Brown successful.

Brown developed a momentum as a leader that surfaced very early in life and that never slowed or faltered. He loved the responsibility. He could make people do what he wanted them to do without force, inculcating in them a heightened dedication to duty and a sense of mission. He had a positive, "can-do" attitude as opposed to those who timidly thought, "I think I can do," and he was able to transfer that to those who looked to him for guidance.

Brown's leadership was rooted in an inner goodness. He was, simply stated, a great human being. He was a generous man and this generosity was evidenced in experiences with all people. He had a feel for people that can come only from caring deeply about them. He instinctively liked people, and people sensed this. He believed in and trusted them; those working around him sensed that. They wanted to give him their best, to not disappoint him.

He was as genuine to the enlisted man as he was to the highest ranking man he met. Indeed, one person commented, "He treated a sergeant like a general." But he didn't just look out for the "little guy"; he also looked out for his senior people.

Because of Brown's warm, gracious, personal manner, people felt comfortable with him. He put them at ease and made himself easy to approach. He was a sincerely friendly person, yet retained a certain reserve that permitted him to conduct official business in a way that neither embarrassed others nor compromised himself. He had a way of challenging without being demeaning. He could turn an uncomfortable situation into a comfortable one with just a few phrases getting everyone smiling. He was able to develop a team esprit in every assignment he had. It was routine with him, and people wanted to be on his team.

George Brown was handsome, with dancing eyes; he was impressive looking, looked the part of a leader, had charisma and presence. He was self-confident and self-assured, with a quiet authority about him. He also applied himself zealously and enthusiastically, and his enthusiasm was contagious. It was reflected in the attitudes of his people.

Was Brown a born leader or did he grow and develop into someone so outstanding? He emphasized the part that his training and life at West Point had in his development as a leader when he repeated a comment made in an article on the Military Academy: "The regimen that produces such men is far from natural. No weakling can stand it. The result of this life is likely to

be an untalkative and self-controlled young man, intensely self-respecting
and yet considerate toward others, but partial to action and results. West
Point produces the kind of intolerance of error that is the first law of a vic-
torious army.''

George Brown entered West Point with a maturity that would come to
the majority of his peers later, and to some not at all. It was a maturity that
enabled him to consider and weigh each aspect of a situation, whether on
the polo field, on the parade ground, or in regular day-to-day activities. As
a cadet he was admired and drew uniformly high praise. His peers recognized and admired his approach to his duties and to life.

Even before his years at West Point, Brown's Army background contributed to the molding of his code of ethics and his team approach. His
father, T. K. Brown, a West Point graduate and an old-time cavalryman,
was known as a gentleman. As a cadet, and throughout his career, George
Brown also came through as a gentleman in his dealings with others. A man
called a gentleman was set apart for imitation; it meant he was a man of
good taste and morals, that he was a person of quality, and of qualities that
made life more meaningful.

Being the son of a career cavalry officer, Brown knew what the military
service was like. He had firsthand exposure to the rigors and rewards of the
soldier's life and the organized discipline of the military community. More
important, he was raised in the military at a time when pride in service was
unmitigated, and the influence of the well-disciplined lifestyle of his father's
career upon him was great. His father was a leader, a hero, a role model in
this closed society. It was an environment of military family life, paternal
influence, inspiration, discipline, and competition that had a role in Brown's
leadership development.

George Brown gained through varied assignments a thorough knowledge of the Air Force. He was one of the best-prepared officers to ever
become Chief of Staff of the Air Force or Chairman of the Joint Chiefs. He
was a true professional, having experience and learning in practically every
aspect of the Air Force. He had an extensive operational experience as well
as long service in Washington.

It was no surprise to anyone knowledgeable about the Air Force when
Brown was selected to be Chief of Staff in June of 1973. He was everyone's
choice. Indeed, the Air Force only sent forward one name to the Secretary
of Defense and the President. But forward-thinking Air Force leaders knew
this was going to be a short tour for Brown because the Air Force had such
a superbly qualified person to become Chairman.

Brown didn't want the job as Chairman, and many Air Force subordinates did not want to lose him as Chief. But Brown as an individual and the Air Force as a service could not refuse the highest military position our country has to offer. Brown's entire career had prepared him for this opportunity.

PROFESSIONAL KNOWLEDGE

Certainly one of the most important factors in Brown's success as a leader was his knowledge of the military profession. If a commander does not know intimately the equipment his subordinates must use in their daily jobs, he will have great difficulty in communicating with them. Brown, as an aircraft commander in World War II, gave himself a practical course of instruction on all aspects of his B-24 to include its armament, mechanical features, and electronics. He learned all the duties of his crew and drilled these airmen until their functioning was as close to perfection as could be produced.

He demonstrated high pilot proficiency early in his career and insisted on increasing it as time went on in new assignments, whether in transport aircraft or interceptors. His flying ability was described in practically every interview I conducted during my search for information about him.

Adding to his personal professional attributes, Brown became an expert in modern defense strategy and tactics, weaponry, operations, budgetary matters, and research and development. He had an unusual background in joint operations which extended over his entire career, starting with his Korean War assignment, to Sandia Base, to the Pentagon to the highest level.

DECISION MAKING

How far one goes up the ladder as a leader in the military depends a great deal on one's ability as a decision maker. The more often the decisions are right, the better the judgment, the higher you go. General of the Army Dwight D. Eisenhower made the observation in a discussion with me, "When you come right down to it, leadership is, of course, being exerted all the time in the capacity of boosting morale, confidence, and all that, but leadership is most noticeable when tough decisions have finally to be made. . . . This is the kind of leadership that's often concealed from the public. . . . But making decisions is of the essence in leadership."

Brown was extremely competent as a decision maker. He could sort out issues and get rid of extraneous matter, focusing quickly on the key issue. But he didn't make overhasty decisions. He simply had the professional knowledge, confidence, and know-how to get to what the issues were and to decide what had to be done. Above average in intelligence, he was quick-witted and practical in his thinking, constantly demonstrating common sense and mental agility. He could handle both large and small crises and was able to take on broad responsibilities.

Brown could sit back calm and relaxed, smile and puzzle problems out, and reach a decision based on all available factors. When certain of his views, he did not become overbearing or tedious. Brown was always under control. He could usually persuade people that he was right, but they grew to be confident that he would always do the right thing. He was able to speak out to persuade; it was significant that he could do it without causing resentment.

Brown had great depth, a grasp of the broadest of military relationships. He never gave an opinion unless he knew what he was talking about. He followed the golden rule on decision making, never being afraid to dispute a position before decision time, but if the decision went against his advice, being able to support it with everything he had. He expected and received the same loyalty when he handed down his decisions.

Respecting the opinions of others, Brown tolerated no yes-men. Staff officers thus felt at ease and were not afraid to speak up. But he could always control free-ranging discussion and stay on target.

HUMILITY

Brown was a humble man, and certainly his humility was a vital part in his success as a leader. Pride never got in his way, nor was he too inflexible in his attitude to profit from the ideas and viewpoints of others, regardless of rank or position.

Because he was humble, George Brown realized he didn't have all the answers. He listened. He learned more that way and never left an assignment without thinking he still had more to learn. He believed he would and could continue to grow by listening to others, yet he had the intuition to know what was worth listening to. He could separate the important from the trivial.

With Brown, a subordinate had open season to lay ideas out without any penalties being exacted. In a discussion he could see both sides of an issue, would always keep an open mind. One of his favorite sayings to his people was "Bring me up to speed."

Brown excelled but did so in an unassuming way. Despite success and honors, he wore the trappings of rank gracefully. Rank and grade were not driving factors in Brown's personality. He never seemed to worry about being promoted or getting a career-enhancing assignment. He never evidenced any attitude of superiority or elitism with or to anyone. Nor did he ever display formality or stiffness. He was completely unpretentious. It was commonplace for him, as Chief of Staff, to walk the corridors of the Pentagon, stopping officers to talk with them, dropping into their offices to ask them about their jobs, seeking their advice on how the Air Force could do its job better.

While serving as Chief, Brown had occasion to speak at a Dining In of junior officers at Rome Air Development Command at Griffiss Air Force Base. He had a great affinity for the Systems Command officers because of his three years as commander of Systems Command. He enjoyed getting back to the group, and after his talk opened the door to questions and answers. A lieutenant stood up and said, "Sir, what was it like to be a twenty-five-year-old colonel?" The question completely stumped General Brown. He thought a moment, then said, "I never thought about it. I never thought of myself as being one and never think of myself as having been one. All I remember is having been a colonel in my life. By the time I had eighteen years as a colonel, I thought I had always been a colonel. I do remember being in New York City right after the war, feeling on top of the world, walking down the street toward the 21 Club with Skip on my arm. As we passed two sailors, one said to the other one, 'Wonder what that chick is doing with the old man?' So, either war had taken its toll or age was equated with rank, or maybe I looked as old as I felt."

There were not two George Browns. He was the same socially with close friends as he was at work. That was the secret of his enormous popularity. He didn't have a mask that he put on in the morning when he went to work. It is not easy to be the same personality in a crisis situation as you are in a social setting, but Brown was.

ENERGY

Brown worked hard at his profession. When he left Systems Command to become Chief, the master sergeants gave a dinner for him. As a going-away gift they presented him with a picture of the headquarters building taken at night, telling him he probably didn't know what it looked like during the day (obviously referring to the fact that he came to work before daylight and didn't leave until after dark). Brown had much energy and a great capacity for work.

Brown's career epitomized the spirit of America—that hard work and dedication can provide the opportunity to get to the top. When I asked Brown why he became Chief of Staff, he said, among other things, "I was lucky." This may be true in part, but actually the harder he worked, the luckier he got. Intelligence is, of course, necessary for success, but the capacity for and dedication to hard work is on the same level as intelligence. No one, no matter how gifted, can really become a super achiever without hard work.

Many times Brown made the comment, "People are inclined to believe you can have something without work." He, however, believed in working and he worked hard, knowing its importance. When working in Washington, he was usually in the office early and stayed there until all work was completed. He wasn't on call; he was there, and he expected others to be there as well. Brown expected those who worked for him to work hard, and they did. But he never asked anyone to do anything he would not do himself.

Brown knew how to pace himself and replenish his energies and thoughts by travel and exposure to new ideas. But he tried not to take work home with him at night or on weekends. He told his subordinates, "If you can't get it done during normal duty hours, you'd better take a look at how you're doing it because you're not doing something right."

Brown was described as one who applied himself "zealously" and "enthusiastically." His enthusiasm was contagious and was reflected in the attitudes of his personnel. Because of his hard work and his professionalism, his desire to give everything his best, he was, as General Wheeler described him, "one of those rare individuals to whom you can assign a job, regardless of its difficulty, and it will be done thoroughly, with dispatch, and with no loose ends." There is no better characterization of his personal work ethic than this.

Part of Brown's personal dedication to hard work was to give everything his best. He told his people, "Let's remember there are ways to do things right, even the smallest things. If you can do it well, do it that way, whatever it is." He also said, "As long as you don't cheat the taxpayers, as long as you remember what the real mission is, there is no reason to downgrade ourselves by carelessness or injudicious application of effort, no matter what. Try to do it well and try to do it at a high standard."

But there was a balance to Brown's hard work. He kept up an intense pace when the job demanded it, but he was not bound by habit. He was not a "workaholic." He was a man who responded to the situation. If he didn't have something to do, there was no need to hang around. If the mission required long hours, he worked long hours. If it didn't, he would get out and play golf, tennis, or squash, go swimming, or spend time with his family. Brown told an aide in Vietnam who went sleepless one night because of a critical problem, "You've got to learn not to let these things bother you.

You'll never survive in this business if you don't." Certainly with Brown the work stayed in the office.

DELEGATING

Brown told me that his most meaningful learning experience as exec to General White was White's emphasis on the point that to be successful as a leader you had to be able to distinguish the really vital from the less consequential—to be able to grasp the essentials and to refuse to be cluttered up with the nonessentials—then to delegate the rest to subordinates. These subordinates then do the work so the commander can perform the major tasks. Brown was superb at this, at separating the wheat from the chaff, the important from the unimportant. He had the ability to pick good people, to get the best out of everyone, to get more out of people than they ever thought they could produce. Every person is not a super performer, but the outstanding leader gets that something extra out of a person.

Something that inspires a person to give that something extra is to be given a job and then be left alone to do it. That was Brown's way—he put a competent man in charge of an operation and let him run it. He left him alone, then periodically went out to see how things were going, always insuring that the staff was helping that person. He placed trust in his subordinates and they respected this vote of faith and confidence and responded accordingly. They felt he was working with them, not against them. His philosophy was that you undercut a subordinate when you as a commander got into the detail. Yet as one officer put it, "You always felt a strong demand that you'd better get on with the job. . . . There was a sense of firmness about him . . . a determination in what he wanted you to do . . . that he had a mission and he wanted you to get on with it." He led primarily by example, but that did not mean he didn't force a little now and then. Yet he had a manner and a way of being forceful that endeared him to people.

In Vietnam, Brown told his operations people, "You are going to run the war—the air operations—the planning. If you have any differences with the higher command, I'll support you." He left his personnel officer to work on the assignment of people to his command, giving only the simple instruction, "Keep the good people coming." He told his wing commanders, "If you want me, call me; otherwise I'll see you at commander conferences." Brown never carried a "brick," a two-way radio, thus saying to his people, "I've got wing commanders. I've got assistants. There's a chain of command. If it doesn't work, we're in trouble." This is what delegation is all about.

When a decision was needed from Brown, a subordinate did not have to be concerned about getting one, and it was well thought out. "But on the other hand," reflected Bill Evans, "he would delegate. You felt you didn't have to go to him for every small decision." Brown did, however, have a cardinal rule with his subordinates, telling them: "Don't surprise me. If you have problems you can't handle, bring them to me and I'll help you solve them, but don't surprise me because that I can't stand."

This delegating to subordinates inspired them to give their best. They never wanted to disappoint Brown, to violate his trust in them. But he kept aware of what they were doing, for he always monitored what was going on, without getting bogged down in detail.

COURAGE

It takes a courageous person to delegate to subordinates. Within the military you take the responsibility for the mistakes of your subordinates. Brown had an excellent combat record in three wars, but the courage in delegating and other acts of courage outside the arena of war were even more meaningful than his actions in combat. It is a strange, but true, phenomenon that some men will die for their country but not have the courage to sacrifice a slot in the promotion ladder to defend a principle or an idea. This moral courage permeated everything Brown did but was highlighted by his willingness to speak up for whatever he thought was right. He truly had the courage of his convictions.

CONSIDERATION, HUMANITY

Brown was a considerate person, thoughtful of others. He was constantly looking for ways to benefit his men, both officers and enlisted. He always found time to listen to everyone, do generous acts for all people associated with him. He found time to listen to everyone's problems, making himself accessible to staff, commanders. and airmen.

Gen. Robin Olds remarked of Brown's leadership, "It was akin to a breath of fresh air and absolutely the *first time* that the man for whom I supposedly worked gave a damn for the circumstances, problems and needs of my unit." Brown really cared about his people. He showed a kindness, a gentleness, a real humanity. Brown gave a great deal of attention to detail when a person's welfare was at stake.

Brown was equitable in his dealings with others. He changed the breakfast hours for the enlisted men at Selfridge so the men living in the barracks could sleep in on Sunday mornings. Most commanders would never have been aware of this inequity, but Brown did because he was sensitive. He cared. He was told it would never work, but it did. After the program was implemented, he would often go and have breakfast at the enlisted mess with his wife and family before they went to chapel service. When a young airman's baby was sick and not getting proper treatment at the base hospital, Brown not only permitted a phone call to his home one evening, but he also went to the hospital with the airman to see that the matter was straightened out.

Brown wasn't perfect, of course. In Vietnam, for example, he sent out a message changing the organization in one of the wings without first hearing both sides. When the colonel affected requested to be heard, Brown listened to him and admitted, "I shouldn't have sent it until I had talked with you about it." He could admit being wrong.

At the ceremony recognizing the long-distance flight by General LeMay when one of the enlisted men was mistakenly left out, Brown caught the error and saw to it that it was corrected, even though it was embarrassing. Better the embarrassment than to have an enlisted man slighted.

When Brown was commander at Williams, the cliques that had existed previously disappeared immediately. Their very existence had been a symbol of inequity. He also began flying with the students and ended another inequity. He learned that the standard operating procedure was that a check ride for a possible washout was an automatic end and he became concerned. Brown found that the check ride was a formality and that a student was never returned to the program. He changed that immediately. Many talented pilots were being lost to the Air Force with an unnecessary waste of the taxpayers' investment.

Brown was commander at Williams Air Force Base when a pilot landed on a highway. Colonel Personette said, "Brown could easily have handled me in a very severe manner, could have chewed me out or embarrassed me. But he did not. He made his point, which I will remember, and the way he did so made me more eager than ever to do a better job."

At Selfridge, Brown gave the civilian employees the opportunity to play golf, but did it in such a way that it didn't interfere with the military use. Brown commented, "You cannot afford to ignore part of your command [meaning the civilians] and treat them like peasants." He treated everybody alike, officers, enlisted men, or civilians.

LOYALTY

One of the hallmarks of Brown's leadership was his ability to inspire loyalty in his subordinates. Those under him had a devoted attachment to him.

When I asked why they had this loyalty, it was unanimous that they were inspired by Brown's own loyalty to them as individuals and to the organization.

People also admired the loyalty Brown had toward his superiors. While working for controversial Secretary of Defense Robert McNamara, he remained loyal to him. As one close observer commented, "I think McNamara was made to understand very early in the game that George would serve him loyally, that he would not betray McNamara. . . . He would never leave anyone in any doubt that he was working for McNamara."

His concept of loyalty was summed up by Brown himself when he said, "When my loyalty to subordinates conflicts with loyalty to superiors, duty and discipline demand that I support my superiors. Undisciplined acts and attitudes do not lead to any effective military unit. . . . If I don't know how to follow, I don't know how to lead."

An action officer commented of Brown, as Chief of Staff, that he would do battle on any matter of importance, supporting "the little guy" who wrote the staff reports. Sometimes the advice he received was not correct, but he would stand up and defend his people to his superiors.

INTEGRITY

While he was a cadet at West Point, Brown lived under its strong honor code, and honor was an important part of his character. As he said in a speech at a West Point Founders' Day dinner:

> Some officers may sometimes lie or cheat a little, but a West Pointer is precisely as good as his word, without alibis or reservations. At West Point they have a cadet honor system 124 years old, which has but one rule: that no cadet may commit an intentional dishonesty. For any breach of that all-comprehensive code, no matter how trivial, a cadet is summarily purged without mercy. There are no exceptions.

He lived according to this tradition in every facet of his professional career and personal life. From this honor code he derived the strength of his essential honesty and moral integrity. Brown had real moral principles; he was forthright and honest. He tolerated no deviation from the truth from his subordinates and personally set an example for them by being a man of absolute integrity.

In dealing with his superiors Brown was fearless in saying what he thought. There was never anything shifty about him. He was neither politician nor compromiser, just straight down the line. He expressed his convictions in a vigorous and assured manner. As one officer put it, "He always dealt off the top of the deck. If you asked him a question, he'd come back and give you a good, straight, honest answer. He wouldn't give you an answer just to please you."

In Vietnam, after any aircraft accident, the wing commander involved was called in to explain how it had happened. As long as the reporting officer was honest and straightforward, he didn't incur Brown's wrath. It was to him an information session. As one officer explained it, "You were very comfortable with General Brown as long as you were straightforward. You could say to him, 'I screwed up that one,' and get ready to take your licks. But if you made excuses, you would be fired."

What role did integrity play in Brown's successful leadership? It compelled admiration and respect. It was part of his leading by example. One felt secure with him. It provided a consistency—one knew where one stood, what to expect. It resulted in his leadership being predictable.

Brown was an example of an officer who provided moral leadership. It must be remembered that a leader in the American military system is held responsible for the moral development of his subordinates. These standards of morality depend to a great extent on the pattern of morality set by their leader. Brown's was exemplary, a model to follow.

SELFLESSNESS

On June 12, 1944, a week after the D-day invasion, Gen. George C. Marshall, along with Gen. H. H. Arnold, commander of the Army Air Corps, and Adm. Ernest King, Chief of Naval Operations, made an inspection trip to Europe. With Gen. Dwight D. Eisenhower as their escort, the officers went over and up and down the beachheads in jeeps. They stopped at noon at a field lunch mess, and as they sat on ammunition boxes, General Marshall turned suddenly to General Eisenhower and said, "Eisenhower, you've chosen all these commanders or accepted the ones I suggested. What's the principal quality you look for?" Eisenhower told me, "Without thinking, I said, 'Selflessness.'" There were many sides to George S. Brown and all of them sparkled, but it was service to the country before self that stood out most.

What drove Brown to achieve such service to his country? It was selflessness, a quality that permeated every facet of his professional and family life. Why, for example, was Brown so successful with the controversial Secretary of Defense Robert McNamara? This success was highlighted by McNamara when he said of Brown, "I never saw him try to advance himself by taking a position that his service wanted him to take. I never saw him push himself forward. He never spoke to me about promotion. . . ." General Goodpaster made a similar comment. "There was a selflessness about him. He was not promoting or pushing George Brown, not trying to grab for power."

Brown's was a life of sacrifice, for himself and for his family. On the eve of his retirement he spoke to a group of ROTC students at a commissioning ceremony. There must be, he said, "a steadfast dedication and total commitment to the nation and all that it stands for. That dedication must be deep-felt and unwavering." He went on to say that it requires "a willingness to sacrifice. . . . the setting aside of personal desires, comfort, and security when the safety of the country is at stake."

At a speech on February 15, 1977, before the Los Angeles World Affairs Council, Brown observed that one who enters military service "gives up some personal freedoms of choice that civilians enjoy; they acknowledge that they can be called upon for long hours of work, additional duties, and significant hazards; that you put yourself and your family in an environment that may necessitate frequent uprooting; that you can be asked to give up your life, if necessary, for your country. All this," he said, "is part of the sacrifice of military service."

Brown was not driven by a desire for recognition or reward. He made the following comment regarding the rewards of service before a group of ROTC students, "You must find fulfillment in hard work, in giving and sacrifice—and be willing to serve in the absence of expressed appreciation." He further amplified this point in a speech when he said, "In America's goals of maintaining peace and preserving freedom lies our inspiration to serve. . . . As men of action we are inclined to show our appreciation more by deeds—by serving you to the best of our professional capacity—than by words."

A perspective on this sacrifice and service is provided by a quotation by General of the Army Dwight D. Eisenhower which was often cited by Brown: "Americans—indeed, all free men—remember that in the final choice a soldier's pack is not so heavy a burden as a prisoner's chains."

Brown lived the tenet of placing the nation above himself, above his family. And he never forgot his debt to West Point, saying at a speech on March 7, 1975, that graduates have to "live out our years as entrusted legatees, humbly assuming our individual share of a debt that can never be fully repaid."

I have had the opportunity to review the officer effectiveness reports of numerous Air Force Chiefs of Staff. The only officer whose reports included comments about his wife that I observed were George Brown's. His wife "Skip" had a sparkle and grace that played an important part in reinforcing and supporting his success, and no one appreciated her role more than he himself. On September 18, 1974, Brown was the recipient of the General of the Air Force Henry H. Arnold Award. He was not able to attend the awards ceremony, but his prepared remarks paid tribute to someone who was a large factor in his success:

> Since circumstances preclude my being with you tonight to receive in person the Air Force Association's highest award, the H. H. Arnold Award, I cannot think of anyone I would rather have representing me than my wife, Skip. What I have accomplished over these years has been with her faith, trust, and full support. In a sense, tonight she represents all of the fine wives who fulfill their own roles so graciously and competently that their men are free to go around receiving awards such as the ones you bestow this evening. It is only fair that we turn the tables and let the distaff side share this spotlight tonight. . . . Thank you again for the honor you bestow upon me this evening . . . and thanks also to Skip for this favor among so very many favors.

Brown, in a speech given on March 14, 1975, gave insight into the driving force and value of his military career when he said, "The quintessence of military professionalism is duty, honor, country. These are hard, exacting, and uncomfortable words which give no certified promise of a soft life, easy pleasure, and serene old age. These words may some day, on some strange field, commit . . . men to going forward to death. . . ."

Brown's contribution was unique and lasting. There is no better way to close this epilogue than with George Scratchley Brown's own words with which he closed out his career of thirty-seven years of selfless, distinguished service to God and country:

> As I leave active service, I am moved by the same deep feelings that have sustained me over the years:
>
> By love for this country which continues to be the world's best hope for freedom;
>
> By gratitude for the opportunities of service and responsibility;
>
> By pride in our people in uniform—those who have gone before and those who remain—who make sacrifices willingly, and who do their arduous and dangerous tasks so magnificently;

By faith in the American people who, when armed with the facts will make difficult choices and do what is right.

My life has been split between service to my country and to my family—perhaps at times to the detriment of the latter. However, both remain the objects of my devotion.

I am especially grateful to my family who have accepted the work, the inconveniences and demands of military life, especially to Skip who has done so much to make life richer not only for the Browns, but for all with whom we have served;

To good and faithful friends, who have lightened the burdens and shared the joys;

To courageous comrades who have shared the sacrifices.

They deserve a full measure of the rewards and appreciation with which you have honored me today.

Thank you all.

INDEX

299